Praise for *The Early American Rep*

"Selected with imagination and wisdom, these incisive and wide-ranging texts will provide a 'road map' for students of the first sixty years of American independence."—Daniel Walker Howe, author of *What hath God Wrought: The Transformation of America, 1815–1848* (winner, 2008 Pulitzer Prize for History)

"A nice blend of comprehensiveness and coherence, the selections are individually interesting, they relate well to each other, and provide a wide-ranging, imaginative, and disciplined conversation about the Early Republic."—Paul E. Johnson, Distinguished Professor Emeritus, University of South Carolina, author of *A Shopkeeper's Millennium and Sam Patch, The Famous Jumper;* and coauthor (with Sean Wilentz) of *The Kingdom of Matthias*

"This handy collection of speeches, documents, private letters, and pieces of literature, complete with context-setting prefaces, will be invaluable in any course covering major themes in the history of early national America."— *Joanne Freeman, Yale University*

"Expertly edited and chock-full of enlightening and telling primary documents, this reader conveys a beautifully textured sense of the past and attends to all of the key issues during the formative years of the United States."—*Mark M. Smith, Carolina Distinguished Professor of History, University of South Carolina*

"Finally, a primary sources reader that includes the full breadth of voices (both familiar and lesser known) that characterized the Early American Republic. Sean Adams's informative introduction ties these voices together well, making this book a helpful teaching tool for conveying the rich variety of social and political issues that the young nation faced."—*Steven Deyle, University of Houston*

"This book provides an exciting variety of primary sources and perspectives on the nation's first sixty years. Adams has drawn together voices from across the Early American Republic to illuminate the complexities of the era."—*Craig Friend, North Carolina State University*

"Students will marvel at the fifty-year struggle to forge a nation in the decades following the American Revolution."—*Seth Rockman, Brown University*

Uncovering the Past: Documentary Readers in American History
Series Editors: Steven F. Lawson and Nancy A. Hewitt

The books in this series introduce students in American history courses to two important dimensions of historical analysis. They enable students to engage actively in historical interpretation, and they further students' understanding of the interplay between social and political forces in historical developments.

Consisting of primary sources and an introductory essay, these readers are aimed at the major courses in the American history curriculum, as outlined further below. Each book in the series will be approximately 225–50 pages, including a 25–30 page introduction addressing key issues and questions about the subject under consideration, a discussion of sources and methodology, and a bibliography of suggested secondary readings.

Published

Paul G. E. Clemens
The Colonial Era: A Documentary Reader

Sean Patrick Adams
The Early American Republic: A Documentary Reader

Stanley Harrold
The Civil War and Reconstruction: A Documentary Reader

In preparation

Brian Ward
The 1960s: A Documentary Reader

Jeremi Suri
American Foreign Relations Since 1898: A Documentary Reader

Camilla Townsend
American Indian History: A Documentary Reader

Steven Mintz
Mexican American Voices: A Documentary Reader

Nancy Rosenbloom
Women in Modern America, 1880-Present: Documentary Reader

Steven Mintz
African American Voices: A Documentary Reader

Robert P. Ingalls and David K. Johnson
The United States Since 1945: A Documentary Reader

The Early American Republic

Republic

A Documentary Reader

Edited by
Sean Patrick Adams

WILEY-BLACKWELL

A John Wiley & Sons, Ltd., Publication

This edition first published 2009
Editorial material and organization © 2009 Blackwell Publishing Ltd

Blackwell Publishing was acquired by John Wiley & Sons in February 2007. Blackwell's publishing program has been merged with Wiley's global Scientific, Technical, and Medical business to form Wiley-Blackwell.

Registered Office
John Wiley & Sons Ltd, The Atrium, Southern Gate, Chichester, West Sussex, PO19 8SQ, United Kingdom

Editorial Offices
350 Main Street, Malden, MA 02148-5020, USA
9600 Garsington Road, Oxford, OX4 2DQ, UK
The Atrium, Southern Gate, Chichester, West Sussex, PO19 8SQ, UK

For details of our global editorial offices, for customer services, and for information about how to apply for permission to reuse the copyright material in this book please see our website at www.wiley.com/wiley-blackwell.

The right of Sean Patrick Adams to be identified as the author of the editorial material in this work has been asserted in accordance with the Copyright, Designs and Patents Act 1988.

Wiley also publishes its books in a variety of electronic formats. Some content that appears in print may not be available in electronic books.

Designations used by companies to distinguish their products are often claimed as trademarks. All brand names and product names used in this book are trade names, service marks, trademarks or registered trademarks of their respective owners. The publisher is not associated with any product or vendor mentioned in this book. This publication is designed to provide accurate and authoritative information in regard to the subject matter covered. It is sold on the understanding that the publisher is not engaged in rendering professional services. If professional advice or other expert assistance is required, the services of a competent professional should be sought.

Library of Congress Cataloging-in-Publication Data
The early American republic : a documentary reader / edited by Sean Patrick Adams.
      p. cm. — (Uncovering the past : documentary readers in American history)
   Includes bibliographical references and index.
   ISBN 978-1-4051-6097-1 (hardcover : alk. paper) — ISBN 978-1-4051-6098-8 (pbk. : alk. paper)
   1. United States—History—1783–1865—Sources. 2. United States—Politics and government—1783–1865—Sources. I. Adams, Sean P.
   E301.E13 2009
   973.3—dc22

                                                    2008018525

A catalogue record for this book is available from the British Library.

Set in 10/12.5pt Sabon by SPi Publisher Services, Pondicherry, India
Printed in Singapore by Fabulous Printers Pte Ltd

1   2009

Contents

Figures

Series Editors' Preface

Primary sources have become an essential component in the teaching of history to undergraduates. They engage students in the process of historical interpretation and analysis and help them understand that facts do not speak for themselves. Rather, students see how historians construct narratives that recreate the past. Most students assume that the pursuit of knowledge is a solitary endeavor; yet historians constantly interact with their peers, building upon previous research and arguing among themselves over the interpretation of documents and their larger meaning. The documentary readers in this series highlight the value of this collaborative creative process and encourage students to participate in it.

Each book in the series introduces students in American history courses to two important dimensions of historical analysis. They enable students to engage actively in historical interpretation, and they further students' understanding of the interplay among social, cultural, economic, and political forces in historical developments. In pursuit of these goals, the documents in each text embrace a broad range of sources, including such items as illustrations of material artifacts, letters and diaries, sermons, maps, photographs, song lyrics, selections from fiction and memoirs, legal statutes, court decisions, presidential orders, speeches, and political cartoons.

Each volume in the series is edited by a specialist in the field who is concerned with undergraduate teaching. The goal is not to offer a comprehensive selection of material but to provide items that reflect major themes and debates; that illustrate significant social, cultural, political, and economic dimensions of an era or subject; and that inform, intrigue, and inspire undergraduate students. The editor of each volume has written an introduction that discusses the central questions that have occupied historians in this field and the ways historians have used primary sources to answer them. In addition, each introductory essay contains an explanation of the kinds of materials available to investigate a particular subject, the methods by which scholars analyze them, and the considerations that go into interpreting them. Each source selection is introduced by a short head note that gives students the necessary information and a context for understanding the document. Also, each section of the volume includes questions to guide student reading and stimulate classroom discussion.

Sean Adams's *The Early American Republic* offers an array of documents dealing with the formation and expansion of the United States from the inauguration of President George Washington in 1789 through the end of the US war with Mexico in 1848. A period of rapid geographical, economic, and political development, these decades were marked by intense debates over the principles and policies that would define the American nation. Questions about race and slavery, war and conquest, taxes and voting rights, agriculture and industry, religion and commerce, progress and morality posed dilemmas for political and cultural leaders as well as ordinary women and men. These issues fueled partisan political contests, evangelical revivals, armed conflicts, and social movements. Technological innovations in transportation and communication ensured that competing opinions circulated more widely than ever before, allowing ordinary citizens to participate in the ongoing efforts to mold the American character. Adams provides a lucid introduction to the vast literature on this period and concise but rich head notes that locate specific documents in their larger context. This volume incorporates the views of northerners and southerners, city dwellers and frontiersmen, African-Americans and American Indians, long-time residents and short-term visitors, soldiers and civilians, women and men. The sources allow students to analyze the views of politicians, journalists, explorers, generals, chiefs, preachers, slaves, reformers, radicals, poets, painters, and satirists as they grappled with the transformations that shaped a young nation across six critical decades.

Steven F. Lawson and Nancy A. Hewitt, *Series Editors*

Acknowledgments

Although I like to think that the documents in this reader speak for themselves, a number of scholars and friends provided immeasurable help in allowing them to have a voice. First, I'd like to thank Peter Coveney of Wiley-Blackwell and Nancy Hewitt and Steven Lawson of Rutgers University for considering me for this important project and providing support and guidance throughout the process. Once the manuscript was ready, Deirdre Ilkson at Wiley-Blackwell proved a patient and helpful editor in ushering it through publication. Caroline Richards and Valery Rose lent their expertise in copyediting. As no scholar works alone, I need to acknowledge the help of Alwyn Barr, Juliana Barr, Craig Thompson Friend, Sam Haynes, Richard John, Seth Rockman, Jon Sensbach, and the anonymous readers for Blackwell Publishing for providing expert advice and criticism when it came to selecting and editing the documents. The librarians and archivists at the University of Florida, West Virginia University, the Library Company of Philadelphia, the Hagley Museum and Library, and the American Antiquarian Society all provided critical assistance to the project. Finally, I'd like to acknowledge two historians at Purdue University, Michael Morrison and John Larson, who instilled an interest in the Early American Republic at different points of my academic career. My only hope is that the students who read this volume will have a similar sense of the depth and significance of the Early American Republic that I garnered from Mike and John's expertise in this important field.

Text credits

The editor and publisher gratefully acknowledge the permission granted to reproduce the copyright material in this book:

1.1 Excerpt from W. W. Abbot, ed., *The Papers of George Washington. Presidential Series*, Vol. 2: *April–June 1789* (Charlottesville: University Press of Virginia, 1987), pp. 173–7. © 1987 by University of Virginia Press. Reprinted with permission from the University of Virginia Press.

2.4 Excerpt from Michael Merrill and Sean Wilentz, eds., *The Key of Liberty: The Life and Democratic Writings of William Manning, 'A Laborer,' 1747–1814* (Cambridge, Mass.: Harvard University Press, 1993), pp. 188–9. © 1993 by the President and Fellows of Harvard College. Reprinted with permission from Harvard University Press.

3.1 *The Papers of Thomas Jefferson*, Vol. 33: *17 February to 30 April 1801* (Princeton University Press, 2006), pp. 148–52.

4.1 From Gary Moulton, ed., *The Journals of the Lewis and Clark Expedition*, Vol. 11: *The Journals of Joseph Whitehouse, May 14, 1804–April 2, 1806* (Lincoln: University of Nebraska Press, 1997), pp. 279–80. © 1997 by the University of Nebraska Press. Reprinted with permission from the University of Nebraska Press.

5.1 Excerpt from J. C. A. Stagg et al., *The Papers of James Madison. Presidential Series, Vol. 4: 5 November 1811–9 July 1812 With a Supplement 5 March 1809–19 October 1811* (Charlottesville: University Press of Virginia, 1999), pp. 432–3, 436–7. © 2000 by University of Virginia Press. Reprinted with permission from the University of Virginia Press.

5.3 Excerpt from Gene A. Smith, ed., Arsène Lacarrière Latour, *Historical Memoir of the War in West Florida and Louisiana* (The Historic New Orleans Collection and University Press of Florida, 1999), pp. 107–11. Reprinted with permission from The Historic New Orleans Collection.

10.1 Excerpt from Frances Trollope, *Domestic Manners of the Americans* (New York: Vintage Books, 1949 [1832]), pp. 35–6, 38–41.

11.3 Excerpt from Zilpha Elaw, *Memoirs of the Life, Religious Experience, Ministerial Travels and Labors of Mrs. Zilpha Elaw*, in William L. Andrews, ed., *Sisters of the Spirit: Three Black Women's Autobiographies of the Nineteenth Century* (Bloomington: Indiana University Press, 1986), pp. 85–8, 90–1. © 1986 by Indiana University Press. Reprinted with permission from Indiana University Press.

13.1 "Address by Abraham D. Shadd, Peter Spencer, and William S. Thomas, 12 July 1831," Document 5 in C. Peter Ripley, ed., *The Black Abolitionist Papers*, Vol. III: *The United States, 1830–1846* (Chapel Hill: The University of North Carolina Press, 1991), pp. 102–3, 105–6. © 1991 by The University of North Carolina Press. Used by permission of the publisher.

14.2 Excerpt from David Walker, *Appeal to the Coloured Citizens of the World*, ed. Peter Hinks (University Park, PA: Penn State Press, 2000), pp. 30–3.

15.2 Gary E. Moulton, ed., *The Papers of Chief John Ross, Vol. 1: 1807–1839* (Norman: University of Oklahoma Press, 1985), pp. 277–9. © 1985 by University of Oklahoma Press. Reprinted with permission from the University of Oklahoma Press.

15.3 Herbert Weaver and Kermit L. Hall, eds., *Correspondence of James K. Polk*, Vol. III: *1835–1836* (Nashville: Vanderbilt University Press, 1975), pp. 64–5.

16.2 Excerpt from Henry Clay to Francis Brooke, November 3, 1838, in Robert Seager, ed., *The Papers of Henry Clay, Vol. 9: The Whig Leader, January 1, 1837–December 31, 1843* (Lexington: University Press of Kentucky, 1988), pp. 245–6.

17.1 Excerpt from Clifford Merrill Drury, ed., *Where Wagons Could Go: Narcissa Whitman and Eliza Spalding* (Lincoln: University of Nebraska Press, 1997), pp. 121–4, 126–7. © 1963 by the Arthur H. Clark Company. Reprinted with permission from the University of Nebraska Press.

19.2 Excerpt from Allan Peskin, ed., *Volunteers: The Mexican War Journals of Private Richard Coulter and Sergeant Thomas Barclay, Company E, Second Pennsylvania Infantry* (Kent, OH: The Kent State University Press, 1991), pp. 142–3, 145–51.

Epilogue 2 John W. Blassingame, ed., *The Frederick Douglass Papers. Series One: Speeches, Debates, and Interviews*, Vol. 2: *1847–1854* (New Haven, CT: Yale University Press, 1982), pp. 170–4. © 1982 by Yale University Press. Reprinted with permission from Yale University Press.

Introduction: Traveling the Early American Republic

The inauguration of George Washington as President of the United States had many meanings. For the people in attendance in New York City on that April day, it was a magnificent celebration. A military procession accompanied by both houses of Congress, a 13-gun salute to represent every state in the new union, and a long parade of New York's most prominent politicians, merchants, and mechanics made for a grand occasion. The cheering crowd pressed into Broad Street to catch a glimpse of Washington, who appeared on a balcony of Federal Hall to take the first presidential oath of office since the ratification of the young nation's new Constitution. To many observers, this was a festive, nationalistic event that marked the beginning of a new era. But the speech Washington actually gave to the joint houses of Congress immediately afterwards offered a more somber tone. He began by referring to his "conflict of emotions," claming that "no event could have filled me with greater anxieties" than the notification that he had been elected. Serving as the first citizen in a republican form of government, or, in his words, the "experiment entrusted to the hands of the American people," would be a difficult venture. Eyewitness accounts mention Washington's plain brown suit and awkward hand gestures that made his speech less than thrilling. After he finished his brief address, he left for private meditation. New York City, undaunted by Washington's anxiety toward the task at hand, celebrated for hours more. A new president, a new nation, and a new century were about to begin in earnest.

The spectacle of this inauguration celebration must have been impressive to a large degree; but imagine that a traveler had to set out from that portentous scene to embark on a tour of the United States in 1789. A few miles from Manhattan Island, Americans lived and worked in dramatically different circumstances. The small farms that dotted the landscape of rural New York, New Jersey, and Connecticut were more common features on the American landscape in 1789 than the tall church spires and crowded streets of New York City. The rhythm and flow of everyday life for these rural Americans provided a stark contrast to the quick pace of urban life. Crops needed to be planted, weeded, and harvested on a regular basis and, since homes lacked modern amenities, the keeping of a house could be equally demanding. Life on an American farm in the Early Republic was hard work from sun-up to sun-down with little time for diversions. Although the population in rural areas was dispersed, these farmers and small townspeople were by no means isolated from each other. Court days, elections, and regular markets all allowed the opportunity for interaction. But it is important to remember that as most Americans lived and worked on farms in 1789, the "average" life would bear little resemblance to that of the urban Manhattanites listening to Washington's speech and would seem especially foreign to Americans living today.

As the traveler ventures further out from the site of Washington's Inaugural, they would likely move through cities that rivaled New York City in size. Boston, Philadelphia, and Baltimore all had the kind of cultural and economic institutions – bustling wharves, banks, counting rooms, and small manufacturing shops – that made American cities centers of commerce and industry. These cities, like New York, served as important destinations for the flow of goods and people from the surrounding countryside. Wheat, corn, tobacco, and other products of the land made their way from farm to market along poorly graded roads and unevenly improved waterways. These journeys were often measured in days, rather than hours. But for the citizens of Massachusetts, Pennsylvania, and Maryland, the political and economic stability promised by the new Constitution seemed to portend well for the future after 1789. There was no way to know exactly which American cities or towns would become preeminent, so residents across the rapidly growing northeast might optimistically look forward to a day when their hometown would grow into the region's next mighty metropolis.

To the south, the American landscape took on yet another look. By 1789, slavery was a familiar institution in most of the United States, but the concentration of enslaved African-Americans would be conspicuous to the traveler once they made their way into southern Maryland and then Virginia. Small farms do not disappear as our traveler ventures further south, but they are accompanied by much larger spreads along the Chesapeake Bay and its feeder rivers. Rather than a network of towns and large cities, self-contained agricultural communities, commonly known as "plantations," start to dominate the landscape. Black labor serves as the linchpin of this economy, and some plantations have hundreds of African-American slaves working and living on their land. They raise familiar crops such as wheat and corn, but the further south one goes, the more distinctly regional crops such as rice or lowland cotton also appear. By the time a traveler in 1789 reached South Carolina or Georgia, the prevalence of plantation society would have seemed all-encompassing. To be sure, southern cities such as Charleston or Savannah served as important economic and cultural centers in the South, but the true driving force behind southern society at the time of Washington's Inaugural would have been the slave-based plantations of the countryside.

If our traveler took a hard right turn in Georgia and began to work toward the Northwest, yet another distinct change in landscape would begin to become apparent. The large plantations on the eastern shore give way to small hardscrabble farms manned by Scotch–Irish emigrants on the pied-mont, and soon numerous villages of Native Americans would appear amidst the forested terrain. Creek, Cherokee, or Choctaw Indians maintained sig-nificant power over the western sections of the South. If we continue to move north along the Appalachian Mountains, these nations would give way to those of the Miami, Shawnee, and Delaware. Today many might lump these peoples into a general category of "Native Americans," but these nations are and were distinct and, as of 1789, manifested a variety of conflicting attitudes toward the newly created United States. Some advocated a peaceful coexistence with the ever-increasing numbers of white settlers looking to homestead in their lands; others doubted whether these new arrivals could be trusted. Whatever their attitude, it is important to remember that these Native American nations – not Washington's federal government – held the de facto reins of power in the Appalachians and westward.

As we complete the loop on our way back to the scene of Washington's Inaugural, the traveler would cross through the rolling hills of western Pennsylvania and New York. Even as Anglo-American settlers become more concentrated than Native Americans on the trail, these white folks do not seem as wedded to the idea of a centralized government as their cohorts to the east. In fact, many western farmers appear downright resent-ful of the power and influence that large cities seem to exert in their respective states. Western Pennsylvanians are not alone in this regard; the more modest hinterland of Massachusetts was only two years removed from a military insurrection led by Revolutionary War officer Daniel Shays at the time of Washington's Inaugural. They believed that they knew firsthand how fragile a republican form of government could be when confronted with a power-hungry eastern elite. They might share their "anxiety" over its future, but they expressed it in a way that was more roughly hewn than President Washington suggested in that gentle speech in April.

This imagined full circuit of the United States in 1789 reveals the many challenges of understanding the Early American Republic. On the one hand, the Inaugural of President George Washington represents a singular moment of nation building. The first Chief Executive taking the oath of office amidst cheering crowds and proclaiming his dedication to the "republican experiment" of the United States should rightly be considered a landmark event in the nation's history. Yet, even as Washington delivered his address, significant political, social, and economic differences threatened the fledgling cohesion and stability of the young nation. The future of slavery in the United States, for example, seemed uncertain. Would it continue to serve as the primary labor system in the American South? Or could enslaved African-Americans expect this longstanding colonial institution to be phased out in their lifetime? As Anglo-Americans moved westward, a different sort of challenge accompanied them. Would power remain centered in the well-established cities along the eastern seaboard such as Philadelphia, Boston, or Charleston? Or would western residents demand an equal share of policymaking in the new federal government? And what of the future of Native Americans in the United States? Would these original inhabitants of the land allow the more recent arrivals to live among them and have Anglo-Americans "leading them thus to agriculture, to manufactures, and civilization," as Thomas Jefferson once suggested? Or would conflict, even military clashes, characterize the relationship between these peoples? President Washington had good reason to express his anxiety over his newly acquired position as Chief Executive.

The documents in *The Early American Republic: A Documentary Reader* reflect a multitude of perspectives, and both the tension and the optimism that characterized these early decades of American history. The first chapter, for example, contains not only the text of Washington's Inaugural, but also the voices of Native Americans displeased over recent treaties and disgruntled farmers from western Pennsylvania seeking tax relief. The advantage of taking a firsthand perspective in sorting out the balance between conflict and consensus in the Early Republic is that the reader hears from the participant directly and without the historian acting as the intermediary. Of course, some editorial work is necessary in order to make these voices coherent and manageable, but the goal in this volume is to allow readers to deal with the "raw ore" of historical research up close. It is a messy approach to the subject. At times, the historical actors might seem to contradict themselves. Other times, their message is cloaked within a mass of platitudes. And sometimes the reader might have difficulty discerning the actual point that the actor is trying to make altogether. Like the traveler in 1789 crossing the American landscape, the reader of these documents will find the terrain to be a challenging mix of the familiar and the foreign. But half the fun of traveling should be the journey itself; *The Early American Republic* offers a fascinating trip in this regard.

To extend the traveling metaphor further, the documents in this volume offer a kind of road map of prominent themes and events of the Early American Republic. The different perspectives of 1789 are already familiar, but as the sources venture into the 1790s and early 1800s, the historical landscape begins to change. The vicious political battles between the Federalists and Republicans, sometimes called the First American Party System, are a prominent feature in this journey. As Federalists sought to steer the country toward a future of more concentrated political and economic power, with mighty banks and manufactories, they encountered resistance from Republicans, who imagined a more agrarian nation with a dispersed arrangement of political and economic clout. So the election of Republican Thomas Jefferson in 1800 was the first peaceful transition of power from one party to another, which was no small event. In fact, the changes brought by Jefferson's interpretation of Republican government caused many to refer to his ascendancy to the Chief Executive as the "Revolution of 1800."

Wars make a major impact on any landscape, and the Early Republic was no exception. The United States entered the War of 1812 dreadfully unprepared to fight the European superpower, Great Britain, as well as the multiple Indian nations east of the Mississippi who viewed the outbreak of hostilities as an opportunity to put an end to the Anglo-American invasion of their homelands. However, as the documents here suggest, the military failures gave way to important political and cultural changes that would extend decades after the burned cityscape of the young capital, Washington DC, had been restored in the wake of the British occupation in the summer of 1814. Francis Scott Key's inspired take on the American resistance to the bombardment of Baltimore's Fort McHenry resulted in the "Star Spangled Banner," for example, and General Andrew Jackson's thwarting of the British invasion of New Orleans made him a national hero. Although the War of 1812 ended well enough for white Americans, the Native American nations who allied themselves with the British suffered a serious blow during the struggle. Not only would the physical landscape of the Ohio Valley and the Old Southwest be altered by their absence; the historical one would dramatically change in the decades following the Treaty of Ghent's conclusion of hostilities in 1814.

As the nation recovered from these military clashes, it began to reshape itself in numerous ways. Although the National Road set out to link

Baltimore with the Mississippi River, this federally funded turnpike only reached the Ohio River in 1818 and took 15 years and millions of dollars to make it to Columbus, Ohio. More impressive was New York's Erie Canal, which linked the Great Lakes to the Hudson River in 1825. New York City enhanced its status as a major entrepôt for goods and people as a result of the canal, but towns along its route like Albany, Lockport, and Buffalo also saw dramatic growth. By the 1830s, a spider web of turnpikes, canals, and even railroads integrated the northern states and encouraged a vibrant agricultural and manufacturing economy. To the south, a boom in cotton production triggered growth of a different sort. Americans in the South moved across the fertile terrain of the Old Southwest no less enthusiastically than their northern neighbors, but they most likely were headed to start new plantations there. Many of the migrants of this period traveled not by choice, but chained to each other in slave coffles that made their way across the region. This involuntary migration reshaped the region into one characterized not only by the cash crop cotton, but by slavery, a system that dominated the South's economy, society, and political structure.

Americans altered the physical landscape with their labor; they also tried to rework the moral terrain of the American nation. Here a modern traveler might view alternating views of the familiar and the foreign. Religious renewal, not in short supply in American life today, began to heat up following the massive revival at Cane Ridge, Kentucky in 1801. While religious enthusiasm might seem timeless, the Second Great Awakening, as the Early Republic's spiritual renewal is labeled by historians, often was grounded in particular times and places of intense religious activity, such as the path of the Erie Canal in western New York – called the "Burned Over District" because of the frequency of traveling revivals. Inward spiritual change led many Americans to believe they needed to exert a benevolent impulse on society as well. The movement to curb the large American appetite for liquor, called "temperance" in the language of the Early Republic, gained way with Lyman Beecher's 1825 call for "total abstinence" from intoxication and the formation of the American Society for the Promotion of Temperance soon thereafter. Excluded from the world of business and politics by the norms of the day, many white women used the temperance and other reform movements as a vehicle for public action. As their voices grew in strength, many of them hoped someday to see legal and political equality for women follow. African-American men and women well knew that so long as slavery continued to serve a prominent role in the nation's economy – America's 1.9 million slaves represented 15 percent of the nation's and 34 percent of the South's total population in 1830 – their place in American society would suffer. David Walker, whose account of living in Boston appears in this volume, offered a means for resisting slavery with his 1829 militant call to arms called *An Appeal to the Colored Citizens of the World.* Maria Stewart, who features in this volume as well, and other African-American women added their voices in different, but no less serious, ways. By the time the white editor William Lloyd Garrison started to broadcast the message of radical abolitionism with his Boston newspaper, *The Liberator,* in 1831, the American passion for reform had already reconfigured the landscape of American society.

American politics in the Early Republic seemed no less passionate, if sometimes a bit less earnest. The ascension of Andrew Jackson in 1828 signaled an important change in the way that the American electorate voted for offices of all levels. The wily New York political veteran Martin Van Buren helped develop many of the tactics employed by Jackson's new Democratic Party. Rallies, torchlight parades, and simple symbols such as hickory sticks used to honor Jackson's nickname, "Old Hickory," became effective tools in this new brand of mass politics. As the Jackson Administration pushed its campaign against the US Bank and vigorously pursued the removal of Native Americans across the Mississippi, its opponents rallied around the new Whig Party. Led by the Kentuckian Henry Clay, the Whigs challenged the Democrats in every level of the electoral process. The fiercely competitive Second American Party System of Democrats and Whigs used these new methods of political action, but also employed similar tactics as its predecessor of Federalists and Republicans. For example, partisan newspapers played an active role in shaping the national Democratic and Whig opinions. These parties reached into all levels of American society, and as the New Hampshire newspapers sampled in this volume suggest, political rancor was no less tame at the local level. The election of the Whig William Henry Harrison during the famous "Log Cabin Campaign" of 1840 fulfilled the promise of the Early Republic's new political system with its emphasis on getting out the vote, rallying folks with sloganeering, and avoiding thorny issues like the growing question of slavery and abolition.

The metaphor of traveling the Early Republic wouldn't be complete unless we turned west and set out across the North American continent. Anglo-Americans living during this period fixed their gaze on the West as well, although with no foreknowledge that the territory west of the Mississippi would one day become not only a part of the United States, but the section known as the "heartland" of the nation. Native Americans controlled this region; in fact, in modern-day Texas, Comanches and Apaches were so powerful that the Republic of Mexico invited Anglo-Americans to settle that region to protect its northern frontier. In areas like the Oregon Territory, Native Americans began to see what had been a steady trickle of white settlers in the 1830s turn into a mighty flow a decade later. California, too, was transformed by this migration. Of course, as the United States expanded, it came into conflict not only with Native American nations, but also with Mexico. Although the editor John L. O'Sullivan, writing from the east coast, viewed the conquest of North America as the United States' providential "manifest destiny," others criticized the advent of "American Spread-Eagleism" in the 1840s. However, with the election of the Democrat James K. Polk in 1844, the annexation of Texas and its disputed Mexican boundary became a mandate, and in turn war with the Republic of Mexico soon followed. In the aftermath of that struggle, the United States acquired the territory that comprises the modern-day states of California, New Mexico, Arizona, Nevada, and Utah. Unfortunately, the US also acquired a new controversy over the future of slavery in those lands that would come to dominate the next decade and end with an entirely different war.

By 1849 the United States had a new president, the Mexican War hero Zachary Taylor. Although "Old Rough and Ready" could lead men into battle, his political skills in solving a growing debate over the expansion of slavery seemed limited. This volume includes his inaugural address, not because it is considered a classic work of American rhetoric, but because it demonstrates the lengths to which many politicians went to speak in platitudes rather than grapple with this growing political controversy over the future of slavery. In this regard, the ex-slave Frederick Douglass, whose words in 1849 appear here also, are much more eloquent and to the point. "The American people may be as accurately measured by the character of her great men," Douglass argued, "as the degree of temperature may be determined by the face of the thermometer." But rather than tell you how the words of these men and women illustrate the rich history of the Early American Republic, this volume allows you to decide for yourself and to read those words directly. As you travel through this past, keep in mind the significance not only of the destination, but of the journey itself.

A Brief Note on the Editorial Technique

This volume is meant to present primary sources as close as possible to the form in which the historical actors originally expressed them. At times, changes have been made in the interests of brevity and clarity. Although the fundamental meaning of each document remains true to the source, sometimes the reader might wonder if the deleted or corrected passages shed additional light on the selection's meaning. Since the footnotes provided give the source of the work, the reader is encouraged by all means to find the original document and read it in full. Every editorial decision regarding the manner in which to present a primary source, no matter how small or seemingly insignificant, alters the document. For that reason, serious historians need to trace the text to its original source whenever possible. Keep in mind that this volume was created for clarity and accessibility, and that the selected documents here are not necessarily the authoritative version of the primary source.

Part I   Building the United States

Introduction to Part I

The period following the ratification of the Constitution held both great promise and great danger. A new form of government had been hammered out in the Constitutional Convention, but it was unclear whether the political compromises made in Philadelphia could overcome the divisive forces that threatened the unity of the new nation. Federalists and Anti-Federalists, after all, still held significant differences of opinion in a wide variety of issues. Eventually these political differences would evolve into the First American Party System, comprising Federalists and Republicans. The documents in Part I present the discordant voices of the early United States, illustrating how the nation's first system of political parties attempted to deal with conflict, and the ways in which Thomas Jefferson's 1801 declaration that "We are all republicans: we are all federalists," attempted to unify the nation at the same time that it underwent its first significant political transition.

Chapter 1   Origins

1. First Inaugural Address of George Washington, April 30, 1789[1]

George Washington arrived in the temporary capital of the United States, New York City, with a great deal of fanfare and pageantry, but also with a great deal of concern. When Washington appeared in front of a boisterous crowd on Broad Street on April 30, 1789 the United States was less than a decade old and had just substantially revised the structure of its federal government. The 13-gun salute that erupted immediately after the administration of the oath of office signaled a new era for the new nation and when he entered the Senate Chamber to address the joint houses of Congress, the first President of the United States had the opportunity to establish a number of precedents. First among these was the tone and tenor of the presidential inaugural address, which subsequent presidents have used to lay out both a broad vision of their leadership as well as some specific policy goals. Washington also established a tradition of humility and quiet respect for the office. Eyewitness accounts describe him as dressed in a simple brown suit and some claim he looked uncomfortable throughout his address. After his speech, Washington slipped away to meditate in nearby St. Paul's Church while the festivities in New York City continued into the early hours of the next morning.

---

[1] W. W. Abbot, ed., *The Papers of George Washington. Presidential Series*, Vol. 2: *April–June 1789* (Charlottesville: University Press of Virginia, 1987), pp. 173–7.

Fellow-Citizens of the Senate and of the House of Representatives:
Among the vicissitudes incident to life no event could have filled me with greater anxieties than that of which the notification was transmitted by your order, and received on the 14th day of the present month. On the one hand, I was summoned by my Country, whose voice I can never hear but with veneration and love, from a retreat which I had chosen with the fondest predilection, and, in my flattering hopes, with an immutable decision, as the asylum of my declining years – a retreat which was rendered every day more necessary as well as more dear to me by the addition of habit to inclination, and of frequent interruptions in my health to the gradual waste committed on it by time. On the other hand, the magnitude and difficulty of the trust to which the voice of my country called me, being sufficient to awaken in the wisest and most experienced of her citizens a distrustful scrutiny into his qualifications, could not but overwhelm with despondence one who (inheriting inferior endowments from nature and unpracticed in the duties of civil administration) ought to be peculiarly conscious of his own deficiencies. In this conflict of emotions all I dare aver is that it has been my faithful study to collect my duty from a just appreciation of every circumstance by which it might be affected. All I dare hope is that if, in executing this task, I have been too much swayed by a grateful remembrance of former instances, or by an affectionate sensibility to this transcendent proof of the confidence of my fellow-citizens, and have thence too little consulted my incapacity as well as disinclination for the weighty and untried cares before me, my error will be palliated by the motives which mislead me, and its consequences be judged by my country with some share of the partiality in which they originated.

Such being the impressions under which I have, in obedience to the public summons, repaired to the present station, it would be peculiarly improper to omit in this first official act my fervent supplications to that Almighty Being who rules over the universe, who presides in the councils of nations, and whose providential aids can supply every human defect, that His benediction may consecrate to the liberties and happiness of the people of the United States a Government instituted by themselves for these essential purposes, and may enable every instrument employed in its administration to execute with success the functions allotted to his charge. In tendering this homage to the Great Author of every public and private good, I assure myself that it expresses your sentiments not less than my own, nor those of my fellow-citizens at large less than either. No people can be bound to acknowledge and adore the Invisible Hand which conducts the affairs of men more than those of the United States. Every step by which they have advanced to the character of an independent nation seems to have been distinguished by some token of providential agency; and in the important revolution just accomplished in the system of their united government the tranquil deliberations and voluntary consent of so many distinct communities from which the event has resulted can not be compared with the means by which most governments have been established without some return of pious gratitude, along with an humble anticipation of the future blessings which the past seem to presage. These reflections, arising out of the present crisis, have forced themselves too strongly on my mind to be suppressed. You will join with me, I trust, in thinking that there are none under the influence of which the proceedings of a new and free government can more auspiciously commence.

By the article establishing the executive department, it is made the duty of the President "to recommend to your consideration such measures as he shall judge necessary and expedient." The circumstances under which I now meet you will acquit me from entering into that subject further than to refer to the great constitutional charter under which you are assembled, and which, in defining your powers, designates the objects to which your attention is to be given. It will be more consistent with those circumstances, and far more congenial with the feelings which actuate me, to substitute, in place of a recommendation of particular measures, the tribute that is due to the talents, the rectitude, and the patriotism which adorn the characters selected to devise and adopt them. In these honorable qualifications I behold the surest pledges that as on one side no local prejudices or attachments, no separate views nor party animosities, will misdirect the comprehensive and equal eye which ought to watch over this great assemblage of communities and interests, so, on another, that the foundation of our national policy will be laid in the pure and immutable principles of private morality, and the preeminence of free government be exemplified by all the attributes which can win the affections of its citizens and command the respect of the world. I dwell on this prospect with every satisfaction which an ardent love for my country can inspire, since there is no truth more thoroughly established than that there exists in the economy and course of nature an indissoluble union between virtue and happiness; between duty and advantage; between the genuine maxims of an honest and magnanimous policy and the solid rewards of public prosperity and felicity; since we ought to be no less persuaded that the propitious smiles of Heaven can never be expected on a nation that disregards the eternal rules of order and right which Heaven itself has ordained; and since the preservation of the sacred fire of liberty and the destiny of the republican model of government are justly considered, perhaps, as deeply, as finally, staked on the experiment entrusted to the hands of the American people ...

Having thus imparted to you my sentiments as they have been awakened by the occasion which brings us together, I shall take my present leave; but not without resorting once more to the benign Parent of the Human Race in humble supplication that, since He has been pleased to favor the American people with opportunities for deliberating in perfect tranquillity, and dispositions for deciding with unparalleled unanimity on a form of government for the security of their union and the advancement of their happiness, so His divine blessing may be equally conspicuous in the enlarged views, the temperate consultations, and the wise measures on which the success of this Government must depend.

2. Tickagiska King Addresses President George Washington, May 19, 1789[2]

At the time of Washington's Inaugural, the United States still had quite a few lingering issues with Native American nations all along its western borders. In 1785, representatives of Cherokees, Choctaws, and Chickasaw nations in the Southeast met with American officials. The resulting Treaty of Hopewell ceded significant lands from those three nations to the United States and also set up a western boundary for American settlement. But as Native Americans fronting the young republic quickly discovered, treaties could not stem the flow of white migrants into their land. Some Native Americans advocated armed resistance, whereas others counseled patience and negotiation. At a meeting held in the Cherokee town of Chota in the spring of 1789, various leaders appealed to the United States to recognize their rights by treaty. The transcriber of this and other speeches at Chota, North Carolina politician John Sevier, brought their case to American authorities at the same time that he planned to sell disputed land to white settlers. Such confusion and conflict was common in the Early Republic.

GREAT BROTHER: The great Being above has directed our hearts to listen to the talks of peace, and sorry that ever any misunderstandings arose between us and our white brothers. Our last troubles have been occasioned by our rash inconsiderate young men, who, we doubt, have been too much encouraged by white men in our towns, that pretend you have sent them among us to do us justice and to direct our nation how to manage.

---

[2]   US Senate, *The Southern Tribes*, 1st Cong., 1st sess., S. Doc. 4, Serial ASP07 Ind.aff. 4, August 22, 1789.

There are a great many towns of us that live on Tennessee, Highwassee, Telliquo, and Ammoah, who are near neighbors to the white people, and we wish to live in peace with them.

We hope that Congress has not forgot the treaty last held at Hopewell, South Carolina. We intend to abide by it, and hope Congress will do us justice, as we look up to them for it, and intend to hear their good talks, and also the talks of all them that are joined with them, but will not listen to any others.

BROTHER: At our last treaty, held in South Carolina, we gave up to our white brothers all the land we could any how spare, and have but little left to raise our women and children upon, and we hope you wont let any people take any more from us without our consent. We are neither birds nor fish; we can neither fly in the air, nor live under water; therefore we hope pity will be extended towards us. We are made by the same hand, and in same shape with yourselves.

We send some of our head-men and warriors to you with talk, and to represent the case and circumstance of our nation; and we hope you will settle matters with them to all our satisfaction, and that they may return home to our country with good tidings of peace and friendship; and any thing done by Congress and our representatives will be held safe by us, and fast by us.

We hear that Congress have got strong powers now, and nothing can be spoiled that you undertake to do; this we hear from our elder brother, John Sevier, which makes us glad and we rejoice at the news.

We wish you to appoint some good man to do the business between us and our elder brothers. Let us have a man that don't speak with two tongues, nor one that will encourage mischief or blood to be spilt. Let there be a good man appointed, and war will never happen between us. Such a one we will listen to; but such as have been sent among us, we shall not hear, as they have already caused our nation to be ruined, and come to almost to nothing.

3. Western Pennsylvanians Petition Against Taxes, March 19, 1790[3]

At the same time that President Washington delivered his inaugural address in New York City, many Americans resented the growing financial and political influence of eastern cities. In early 1787, farmers led by Revolutionary War

---

[3] *Pennsylvania Archives*, Series I, Vol. II: *1786–1790* (Philadelphia: J. Severns, 1856), pp. 670–3.

*veterans in western Massachusetts marched on the federal armory at
Springfield Daniel Shays in order to protest an increase in taxes. Shays'
Rebellion was short-lived, but bitterness between western and eastern
residents continued to plague many states. The following petition explains
how tax policy often served as a point of contention. In this case, western
Pennsylvanians complain about a state tax to their own legislature in 1790.
Four years later, western Pennsylvanians marched on Pittsburgh to protest
a federal excise tax on whiskey. President Washington himself led the troops
that put down the Whiskey Rebellion of 1794, but no amount of force could
completely squash the rivalry between easterners and westerners during the
Early Republic.*

To the Honorable the Representatives of the Freemen of Pennsylvania, in
General Assembly met.

The Petition of the Inhabitants of Westmoreland County – Humbly Sheweth.

That your petitioners are greatly aggrieved by the present operation of an
Excise Law, passed on the 19th day of March, 1783, by which we are made
subject a duty of four pence per gallon on all spirituous liquors distilled and
consumed amongst us from the productions of our farms, even for private
and domestic uses. It is generally believed that excise laws, in all nations and
at all periods, have given greater disgust, and created greater tumults
amongst the people, than any other species of taxation ever adopted for
the raising of revenue; we do not hesitate to declare, that this law has
already been productive of all those and many other evils, and that it is
the only one passed since our revolution that has been treated with general
disapprobation, and reflected upon with universal abhorrence and detest-
ation: and such has been the resentment of many of our fellow citizens,
which we are sorry to have occasion to confess, that they have, upon several
occasions, proceeded to unwarrantable lengths in opposing its operations.

We do not deny that we are as strongly rooted in the habits, and as much
addicted to the use of spirituous liquors as our brethren in the eastern part
of the state: having emigrated from among them, we cannot be condemned
for carrying their customs along with us. But independent of habit, we find
that the moderate use of spirits is essentially necessary in several branches of
our agriculture.

In this new country, labourers are exceedingly scarce, and their hire
excessively high, and we find that liquor proves a necessary means of
engaging their service and securing their continuance through the several
important seasons of the year, when the pressing calls of labour must be
attended to, let the conditions be what they may. For those reasons we have
found it absolutely necessary to introduce a number of small distilleries into

our settlements, and in every circle of twenty or thirty neighbours, one of these are generally erected, merely for the accommodation of such neighbourhood and without any commercial views whatever. The proprietor thereof receives the grain (rye only) from the people, and returns the stipulated quantity of liquor, after retaining the toll agreed upon. In this manner we are supplied with this necessary article, much upon the same conditions that our mills furnish us with flour; and why we should be made subject to a duty for drinking our grain more than eating it, seems a matter of astonishment to every reflecting mind.

These distilleries, small and insignificant as they are, have always been classed among the first objects of taxation, and have been highly estimated in the valuation of property. This, we conceive, might fully suffice, without extending revenue to the mean and humble manufacture produced by them.

With as much propriety a duty might be laid on the rye we feed our horses; the bread we eat ourselves, or any other article manufactured from the products of our own farms.

Our remote situation from the channels of commerce, has long ago prohibited the use of all imported liquors amongst us, and as we are aiming at independence in our manner of living, we have neither the abilities or inclination to aspire to their use. We freely resign to our eastern neighbours, whom Providence has placed under the meridian rays of commercial affluence, and whose local situation confer on them many enjoyments which nature has denied to us; and whilst they are revelling in the luxuries of the most bountiful foreign climes, we are perfectly content with the humble produce of our own farms, and it is our only wish to be permitted to enjoy them in freedom.

We beg that we may not be considered as unfriendly to the supporting of a government, which we so highly approve, as that of Pennsylvania. We have too exalted ideas of the blessings deriving from it, to ever suffer such thoughts to harbour in our breasts. The payment of the state tax has always been submitted to with cheerfulness, and paid to the utmost of our abilities. And here we cannot forbear expressing our astonishment at the suspension of a tax so just and equitable in its nature, whilst the excise complained of is continued to be exacted with rigor. We have reason to believe that the produce of this excise will amount to the same, or perhaps exceed that of our state tax, and if we had any security for the net produce thereof getting into the treasury, it would afford some consolation; but from the flagrant delinquency which we have experienced from many of our revenue officers in this county, as well as from a want of confidence in the present excise officer and his security, our fears are greatly awakened upon the present occasion . . .

It is with pleasure that we reflect upon the many instances of liberality and general encouragement which the legislature, as well as many respectable societies, have given through the course of some years past, for rendering ourselves still more independent of foreign nations, by promoting and improving every branch of our own manufacture; we therefore flatter ourselves that the present assembly will no longer suffer a law to remain in existence which is so evidently calculated to counteract the virtuous designs of those respectable bodies, and which proves so universally obnoxious to the people of this western world. We therefore humbly pray, that the several observations herein stated, may be taken into serious consideration, and that the present excise law, so far as it extends to the laying of a duty or imposition of any kind whatever, upon liquors made or distilled from the productions of this state, may be fully and speedily repealed. And your petitioners as in duty bound will pray ...

Chapter 2   The First American Party System

1. A Federalist Appeal to Voters, 1792[1]

President Washington often condemned political parties as divisive and undesirable, yet his administration displayed a Federalist flavor during his two terms as Chief Executive. The lingering conflict over the ratification of the Constitution, moreover, led many Americans to espouse an "Anti-Federalist" wariness toward centralized power. Even though Washington easily won reelection in 1792, political discontent focused on Alexander Hamilton's ambitious financial policies, most notably the chartering of a National Bank and a federal excise tax, as well as the Washington Administration's conservative attitude toward the French Revolution. Nominally led by Washington's Secretary of State, Thomas Jefferson, political dissent crystallized with the formation of Democratic–Republican societies in 1793, signaling a formal opposition movement in American politics. This 1792 handbill is an early example of the Federalist response to criticism of the Washington Administration. Although the author is anonymous, some historians believe that Noah Webster, the ardent Federalist and author of the noted dictionary, wrote the piece. Notice that the text is quite partisan, but there are still candidates listed in both the "Federal" and "Antifederal" columns.

---

[1] "Federalist," *To the Independent Electors of Pennsylvania* (Philadelphia: n.p., 1792). Early American Imprints, 1st series, No. 46586.

To the independent Electors of Pennsylvania

A RECURRANCE to some recent transactions must convince you that unlawful and dangerous combinations of evil minded persons, enemies to the peace and happiness of Pennsylvania, do now exist in various districts of the state, whose object is to impede the operations of the federal government.

These associations have been formed by characters, who, having in vain opposed the ratification of the federal constitution, are now aiming a deadly blow at its administration: and attempting to bring a government into discredit, the uniform tendency of which has been to enrich and dignify Pennsylvania in a degree far exceeding the most sanguine expectations of its best friends – a government which has been eminently propitious to the interests of the various classes of the community, engaged in agriculture, commerce, mechanics, and manufactures.

These incendiary characters in the western parts of the state, supported by the Antifederalists in the other counties, have entered into resolutions (at a public meeting) disgraceful to humanity, subversive of social happiness, and destructive of all civil authority – resolutions replete with deception and sedition, intended to spread the flame of discord through the land, and to poison the minds of the people.

Their avowed purpose is to excite an opposition to the mildest and most rational of governments, and, under the specious, but delusive, pretexts of salutary reform and protection of liberty, to open a wide field of insurrection and anarchy rather than the favorite views of their party should not succeed – Nay, to such an extreme of violence have they proceeded, that, to avert the impending danger, to baffle the plans of a combination full of traitorous designs, the PRESIDENT OF THE UNITED STATES, in discharge of his constitutional duties, and from a paternal regard to the peace, welfare, and safety of the Society, has been under the necessity of issuing his proclamation, to forewarn the people of the dangerous consequences of so daring an outrage on the constitution, as an open hostility to the laws.

It is ardently wished that the wise and virtuous part of the Society would zealously come forward to support the proclamation of our beloved President, by expressing, in a peaceable and legal manner, their attachment to the federal government, their firm determination to support it, and the abhorrence of all seditious writings and factious combinations which aim to subvert it.

These exertions on the part of the people will exhibit a clear and unerring mirror, in which the enemies of the government will view the real and decided sense of the community, and from which they must infer the impotency of their flagitious attempts, and the certainty of exemplary punishment, should they dare to pursue their treasonable and iniquitous plots against the laws constitutionally enacted.

If any additional consideration be required to stimulate their exertions, it will be found in an examination of their names proposed by the federal and antifederal interests to represent the state of Pennsylvania in the Congress of the United States. The first contains the names of Citizens distinguished in their talents and patriotism – and although seven correspondent names are inserted in the last, yet among the other six of the antifederal ticket, the independent Electors of Pennsylvania will notice, with astonishment and indignation, the name of a person, whose conduct, among others, has claimed the animadversion of the mildest government, and extorted a proclamation, the necessity of which every reflecting man and good Citizen must for ever deprecate.

To propose such a man as our Representative is to insult our sense of decency, and to degrade our understanding. – Far be it from the candor of Pennsylvanians to accuse without reason – but it is the part of prudence to judge of men by their friends and associates – and such a judgment, on the present occasion, is justified on every principle of self-preservation. *The Ticket which will be supported by the* Federal *Interest*:

William Findley,
Thomas Hartley,
Daniel Heister,
Frederic Augustus Muhlenburgh,
John W. Kittera,
Gen. William Irvine,
Peter Muhlenburgh,
James Armstrong,
Thomas Fitzsimons,
William Bingham,
Samuel Sitgreaves,
Thomas Scott,
Henry Wynkoop.

The Ticket which will be supported by the Antifederalist *Interest*:

John Smilie,
Jonathan D. Sargeant,
Andrew Gregg,
John Barclay,
William Montgomery,
Charles Thornton,
William Findley,
Thomas Hartley,

Daniel Heister,
Frederic Augustus Muhlenburgh,
John W. Kittera,
Gen. William Irvine,
Peter Muhlenburgh.

A FEDERALIST

2. Abigail Adams on the Partisan Press, June 8, 1797[2]

By the time John Adams replaced George Washington as President of the United States in 1797, disputes over the shape and direction of the federal government crystallized into a political contest between the Federalist and Republican parties. Chief among the opposing voices to Adams's strong Federalist leanings were Benjamin Franklin Bache's Aurora General Advertiser *in Philadelphia and Thomas Adams's* Boston Independent Chronicle. *As First Lady Abigail Adams notes in this excerpt from a letter to her sister, the partisan press attacked her husband's administration for extravagant expenditures and for hiring his son, John Quincy Adams, as a foreign minister. Although she points out some of the journalistic errors (her son's age is misreported – he was actually 30 years old in 1797) and wonders if her brother-in-law, Richard Cranch, could actually get a fair shake in the press, it seems that Abigail ultimately concedes that the First Family is fair game for attacks.*

To day is post day to Quincy, and yesterday we had the Chronical. I think impudent as Bache is the Chronical has more of the true spirit of Satan, for he not only collects the Billingsgate of all the Jacobin papers but he add[s] to it the Lies, falsehoods, calumny and bitterness of his own. For what other purpose could he design that paragraph, that the President was to receive one hundred & 14 thousand dollors for four years? The sallery every one knows is the same Nominal sum granted to President Washington without half its value. The 14 thousand dollors is no more the Presidents than the money voted to Rigg one of the Frigates building. Every dollor of it, is laid out for the use of the United States, and accurate Book accounts kept & vouchers taken, all of which will be regularly renderd in at our quitting the House. The son too, of 23 years old receiving this salary of ten thousand dollars pr year. These salleries are all setled by Law. A Minister Resident has 4 thousand 500 dollars pr year, a Minister plenipotentiary Nine thousand.

[2]   Stewart Mitchell, ed., *New Letters of Abigail Adams, 1788–1804* (Boston: Houghton Mifflin, 1947), pp. 96–7.

He is not pickd out to receive more than any other, but his fault is being the son of the President. This wretched party are sinking very fast; but the mischief of these publications arises from their circulating amongst persons and in places where no inquiry is made into facts. Bache will publish on both sides. I wish Mr. Cranch would make a true statement and see if the wretch would publish it. We give for this very House a thousand pounds a year. President Washington never gave more than 500. And every thing else in the same proportion, nay more than double –. But enough of this. I expected to be vilified and abused, with my whole Family when I came into this situation. Strickly to addhere to our duty, and keep ourselves unprejuced, is the path before us and the curse causeless shall not come. . . .

3. Matthew Lyon Criticizes "Aristocratic" Politics, June 9, 1797[3]

In response to the attacks on Federalist foreign and domestic policies by the partisan press, President Adams signed the Sedition Act into law in 1798. This law provided stiff fines and imprisonment for saying, writing, or printing "any false, scandalous and malicious writings" against the US government. It was designed to squelch the kind of criticism leveled by Republican editors like Matthew Lyon, a Revolutionary War veteran born in Ireland. Working out of Vermont, Lyon eventually rode his radical politics into the House of Representatives, where he constantly assailed Federalists for what he believed to be their aristocratic pretensions. He was physically assaulted by a Federalist colleague, Roger Griswold of Connecticut, and faced censure from his peers. Although a divisive figure, Lyon became a martyr for many Republicans when he was convicted under the Sedition Act and sentenced to prison. He won reelection in 1798 from his jail cell and returned to Congress the following year.

MR. LYON'S SPEECH:–(of Vermont)
This House, gentlemen, has fallen into a very silly custom of leaving their proper business to attend to an absurd and an unnecessary form of waiting on the President in a body. It was also, permit me to say, an absurd thing to dispatch a messenger to him to be informed when he would graciously be ready to receive their address. The address should be sent at once, for it would be paying but a bad compliment to the President to suppose that he is not always ready to receive communications. In fact, it is his duty, and no one will accuse him in a direct way of neglecting it. It is my opinion, therefore, that if the message of this House were sent to the President by

---

[3]   *The Time Piece; and Literary Companion* (New York), June 9, 1797.

a single member, or even by the clerk, it would do every whit as well, as the house going in a body.

Besides, I have another objection. Many members may not wish to go! Such as do not approve of all things in an address, might fear the imputation of inconsistency. As for my own part, I confess I should be ashamed to make one of the figures, in such a piece of mummery.

All this may possibly be owing to my blood not being of that high and refined quality which a certain gentleman present (Mr. Allen) made such a noise about the other day. As to blood, which I am on the subject, I will own that I make no pretensions to older ancestors than other people. In looking over the roll of my ancestry, I have not traced among them any of the couriers of Oliver Cromwell, nor those who *hanged witches*, or punished their horses for working on Sundays. – I have, gentlemen, no such *exalted* pretensions as these to well-born progenitors.

> "*Patres, et genus, et quoe non secimus ipsi*
> *Vix nostra voco. –*
> *Wealth, honour, lineage, titles, or a throne*
> *Are what mankind should fear to call their own.*"

I have, indeed, some pretensions to what I consider to be founded on a much better basis – I am indeed in one sense well-born – I was well born of a stout, hearty, healthy woman, and sprung from the loins of a vigorous healthy man. This is our best title to be called well-born; and where there are simple manners and probity, I know of no pretensions whatever that can go higher.

I am weary of hearing gentlemen talk so much nonsense of your well-borns, or your ill-borns! – Enjoy your dreams, and welcome. – I have for several years past laughed at this ridiculous, this most contemptible of all vanities.

If gentlemen will come forward and tell us they possess personal merit, it is quite another matter; if they tell us they have individually done this or that for their country, or for the good of mankind, then indeed they may boast of being well-born. For my own part, I have a share in the prosperity of this country, the happiness of posterity, and a wish for rational government. In the days of peril and struggle for independence, I was not behind this or that "ditch": I was averse to retiring into the first or last *ditch*. I fought for America, but it was for her LIBERTIES, not for your well-borns, who are ever studying to render us contemptible by unmeaning and useless ceremonies. I move, therefore, "that so much of the resolution of yesterday be rescinded as goes to compel the attendance of such members, on this occasion, as do not wish to attend. –"

This the speaker declared to be contrary to the standing rules of the house.

Mr. LYON *continued*:– "I wish to modify the resolution, that such members as do not choose to attend may not be liable to compulsion." – [*He was informed the stated methods of procedure in the house, did not allow the proposition.*]

"I therefore move personally to be exempted from the ceremony. It is not a light matter with me, standing as I do here one of the Representatives of a free people. In this case I consider myself in the light of a Quaker, and stand upon an exemption from the ceremonial, as much a Friend would if told to take off his hat before a civil magistrate."

Mr. OTIS said as the gentleman (Lyon) appeared to be insane, he would recommend him to be locked up while the house proceeded to the President. He was loudly called to order from several parts of the House.

Mr. DANA said if the Speaker did not think he lessened his dignity by waiting on the President, and several others of the first characters in this country, he did not see how the gentleman could object.

Mr. MACON moved that the House should adjourn to Monday; he meant for his own part to proceed with the address to the President; but still he considered it a matter of ceremony, and not a duty of the members; neither did he think that a member could be subjected to censure for the omission – on the question being put – shall the House now adjourn? it was carried in the negative; and the House thereupon proceeded with the address ...

4. A Massachusetts Farmer Attacks the Federalists, 1798[4]

Although George Washington recommended that Americans steer clear of political parties in his Farewell Address of 1796, the Federalist and Republican parties were well entrenched by the 1790s. William Manning, a Revolutionary War veteran and farmer from Massachusetts, became embroiled in this political debate through his various writings. Manning offered a critique of the Federalists from the perspective of a self-educated citizen-soldier and promoted the ideas of the Republicans. In this brief essay on political parties, Manning links events overseas to the formation of political factions in the United States. In particular, Manning found the signing of Jay's Treaty in 1794, which he alludes to in this document, to be an odious example of the Federalist attachment to the British attempt to squash republican forms of government in Europe, particularly that of France.

[4] Michael Merrill and Sean Wilentz, eds., *The Key of Liberty: The Life and Democratic Writings of William Manning, 'A Laborer,' 1747–1814* (Cambridge, Mass.: Harvard University Press, 1993), pp. 188–9.

Much has been said of late about parties, and many are the names by which they have been described, such as Monarchical and Republican, Aristocratical and Democratical, Royalists and Jacobins, Tories and Whigs, the Few and the Many – all of which names appear to me to describe but two sets of men differing about one and the same thing. The causes of their disputes arise from the conceived difference of interests I have been describing, and the unreasonable desires of the Few to tyrannize over and enslave the Many. The glorious revolution that has lately taken place in France has alarmed the Few to a very high degree. When it first broke out, almost all the kings of Europe openly combined to destroy it or restore monarchy and tyranny again in France. So great was the confidence of success that they agreed among themselves how to divide the territory and spoils. But as the Lord is always on the side of a people contending for their rights and liberties, He so inspired France with wisdom and courage that they have already cut and torn their enemies to pieces, so that the European monarchs have all but one been obliged to make peace with the French on their own terms.

But this has not discouraged that party. They are yet in hopes of effecting by bribery and corruption what they cannot do by force of arms. Their combinations are extended far and wide, and are not confined to Europe and America but are extending to every part of the globe. Gog and Magog are gathered together, to destroy the rights of man and banish liberty from the world. . . .

That there is such an extensive combination in favor of royalty is evident from the great knowledge and great calculations that were made upon it all over Europe and in America long before it took place – for the royal newspapers were full of hints about it. Also its being published in England that twenty of the American senators had agreed to sign the British treaty before ever it arrived here is another piece of evidence of said combinations. Thousands of others might be mentioned.

Therefore, I am strongly led to believe, by the great zeal of our administration to send so many ministers to foreign nations – and the characters they send – and the great opposition made in Congress to granting supplies for that purpose, that they are many of them somewhat engaged in this combination. I also believe that by the great zeal of these parties in America, which appears in the newspapers and the warm debates in Congress, that one party or the other will soon govern, or there will be a scratch for it. Therefore, I conclude that it is high time for the Republicans to unite as well as the Royalists. . . .

Chapter 3   Recasting the American Nation

1. First Inaugural Address of Thomas Jefferson, March 4, 1801[1]

When Thomas Jefferson faced off against John Adams for the presidency in 1800, it was a momentous occasion. The Republican Jefferson and Federalist Adams were among the most prominent of the Founding Generation, but their partisan differences drove a wedge between them and many of their fellow Americans. The campaign was a bitter one, with Federalists accusing Republicans of being radical, godless and in league with French revolutionaries. Republicans countered that the Federalists would prefer a king to a chief executive and favored the rich and powerful at the expense of the small farmer. When the smoke cleared, the Republicans carried the Electoral College, 73 votes to 65 for the Federalists. But confusion reigned when Jefferson's vice-presidential candidate, New York's Aaron Burr, received the same number of votes. The election eventually was thrown to the House and, after 19 tie ballots, Jefferson was finally declared the winner. The Twelfth Amendment (1804) split the vote between presidential and vice-presidential candidates to insure this kind of fracas never occurred again. But nonetheless, it was a bumpy trip to the presidency for Thomas Jefferson. In this context, he delivered his inaugural address on March 4, 1801 in the nation's new capital of Washington, DC.

---

[1] *The Papers of Thomas Jefferson*, Vol. 33: *17 February to 30 April 1801* (Princeton University Press, 2006), pp. 148–52.

Friends & Fellow Citizens,
Called upon to undertake the duties of the first Executive office of our
country, I avail myself of the presence of that portion of my fellow citizens
which is here assembled to express my grateful thanks for the favor with
which they have been pleased to look towards me, to declare a sincere
consciousness that the task is above my talents, and that I approach it
with those anxious and awful presentiments which the greatness of the
charge, and the weakness of my powers so justly inspire. A rising nation,
spread over a wide and fruitful land, traversing all the seas with the rich
productions of their industry, engaged in commerce with nations who feel
power and forget right, advancing rapidly to destinies beyond the reach
of mortal eye; when I contemplate these transcendent objects, and see the
honor, the happiness, and the hopes of this beloved country committed to
the issue and the auspices of this day, I shrink from the contemplation &
humble myself before the magnitude of the undertaking. Utterly indeed
should I despair, did not the presence of many, whom I here see, remind
me, that, in the other high authorities provided by our constitution, I shall
find resources of wisdom, of virtue, and of zeal, on which to rely under all
difficulties. To you, then, gentlemen, who are charged with the sovereign
functions of legislation, and to those associated with you, I look with
encouragement for that guidance and support which may enable us to
steer with safety the vessel in which we are all embarked, amidst the
conflicting elements of a troubled world.

   During the contest of opinion through which we have passed, the anima-
tion of discussions and of exertions has sometimes worn an aspect which
might impose on strangers unused to think freely, and to speak and to write
what they think; but this being now decided by the voice of the nation,
announced according to the rules of the constitution all will of course
arrange themselves under the will of the law, and unite in common efforts
for the common good. All too will bear in mind this sacred principle, that
though the will of the majority is in all cases to prevail, that will, to be
rightful, must be reasonable; that the minority possess their equal rights,
which equal laws must protect, and to violate would be oppression. Let us
then, fellow citizens, unite with one heart and one mind, let us restore
to social intercourse that harmony and affection without which liberty,
and even life itself, are but dreary things. And let us reflect that having
banished from our land that religious intolerance under which mankind
so long bled and suffered, we have yet gained little if we countenance a
political intolerance, as despotic, as wicked, and capable of as bitter and
bloody persecutions. During the throes and convulsions of the ancient

world, during the agonising spasms of infuriated man, seeking through blood and slaughter his long lost liberty, it was not wonderful that the agitation of the billows should reach even this distant and peaceful shore; that this should be more felt and feared by some and less by others; and should divide opinions as to measures of safety; but every difference of opinion is not a difference of principle. We have called by different names brethren of the same principle. We are all republicans: we are all federalists. If there be any among us who would wish to dissolve this Union, or to change its republican form, let them stand undisturbed as monuments of the safety with which error of opinion may be tolerated, where reason is left free to combat it. I know indeed that some honest men fear that a republican government cannot be strong; that this government is not strong enough. But would the honest patriot, in the full tide of successful experiment, abandon a government which has so far kept us free and firm, on the theoretic and visionary fear, that this government, the world's best hope, may, by possibility, want energy to preserve itself? I trust not. I believe this, on the contrary, the strongest government on earth. I believe it the only one, where every man, at the call of the law, would fly to the standard of the law, and would meet invasions of the public order as his own personal concern. – Sometimes it is said that man cannot be trusted with the government of himself. Can he then be trusted with the government of others? Or have we found angels, in the form of kings, to govern him? Let history answer this question.

Let us then, with courage and confidence, pursue our own federal and republican principles; our attachment to union and representative government. Kindly separated by nature and a wide ocean from the exterminating havoc of one quarter of the globe; too high minded to endure the degradations of the others, possessing a chosen country, with room enough for our descendants to the thousandth and thousandth generation, entertaining a due sense of our equal right to the use of our own faculties, to the acquisitions of our own industry, to honor and confidence from our fellow citizens, resulting not from birth, but from our actions and their sense of them, enlightened by a benign religion, professed indeed and practised in various forms, yet all of them inculcating honesty, truth, temperance, gratitude and the love of man, acknowledging and adoring an overruling providence, which by all its dispensations proves that it delights in the happiness of man here, and his greater happiness hereafter; with all these blessings, what more is necessary to make us a happy and a prosperous people? Still one thing more, fellow citizens, a wise and frugal government, which shall restrain men from injuring one another, shall leave them otherwise free to regulate their own pursuits of industry and improvement, and shall not take from the mouth of labor the bread it has earned. This is the sum of good government; and this is necessary to close the circle of our felicities.

About to enter, fellow citizens, on the exercise of duties which comprehend every thing dear and valuable to you, it is proper you should understand what I deem the essential principles of our government, and consequently those which ought to shape its administration. I will compress them within the narrowest compass they will bear, stating the general principle, but not all its limitations. – Equal and exact justice to all men, of whatever state or persuasion, religious or political: – peace, commerce, and honest friendship with all nations, entangling alliances with none: – the support of the state governments in all their rights, as the most competent administrations for our domestic concerns, and the surest bulwarks against anti-republican tendencies: – the preservation of the General government in its whole constitutional vigor, as the sheet anchor of our peace at home, and safety abroad: a jealous care of the right of election by the people, a mild and safe corrective of abuses which are lopped by the sword of revolution where peaceable remedies are unprovided: – absolute acquiescence in the decisions of the majority, the vital principle of republics, from which is no appeal but to force, the vital principle and immediate parent of the despotism: – a well disciplined militia, our best reliance in peace, and for the first moments of war, till regulars may relieve them: – the supremacy of the civil over the military authority: – economy in the public expence, that labor may be lightly burthened: – the honest payment of our debts and sacred preservation of the public faith: – encouragement of agriculture, and of commerce as its handmaid: – the diffusion of information, and arraignment of all abuses at the bar of the public reason: – freedom of religion; freedom of the press; and freedom of person, under the protection of the Habeas Corpus: – and trial by juries impartially selected. These principles form the bright constellation, which has gone before us and guided our steps through an age of revolution and reformation. The wisdom of our sages, and blood of our heroes have been devoted to their attainment: – they should be the creed of our political faith; the text of civic instruction, the touchstone by which to try the services of those we trust; and should we wander from them in moments of error or of alarm, let us hasten to retrace our steps, and to regain the road which alone leads to peace, liberty and safety ...

Relying then on the patronage of your good will, I advance with obedience to the work, ready to retire from it whenever you become sensible how much better choices it is in your power to make. And may that infinite power, which rules the destinies of the universe, lead our councils to what is best, and give them a favorable issue for your peace and prosperity.

2. A New Name for the United States? 1803[2]

*In 1800 the United States of America had grown to encompass 16 states
and 5.3 million residents. As a young and expanding nation, the US struggled
to forge its own political path separate from the traditional European
powers such as Great Britain, France, or Spain. In the early nineteenth century
Dr. Charles Mitchell of New York City suggested that a new name,
"Fredonia," would also help the United States forge a distinct identity.
Although Dr. Mitchell was quite serious about his proposal, lexicographer
John Pickering described the idea as "deservedly ridiculed" in 1816.
Perhaps the idea does seem bizarre to us today, but Mitchell's idea speaks to
the newness of the American nation and the various ideas for its improvement
in the public sphere. After all, in 1789 the Senate agreed to use the title,
"His Highness the President of the United States of America, and Protector
of the Liberties." The House of Representatives rejected that title as too
aristocratic, but that struggle suggests that "Fredonia" was not the only
strange idea swirling around the political culture of the Early Republic.*

THE portion of terraqueous globe comprehended by the great Lakes, the
Saint Lawrence, the Ocean and the Mississippi, has no general denomin-
ation by which it can be conveniently distinguished in geography. Its sub-
divisions and local names are appropriate enough and sufficiently well
understood. But there is still wanting one broad and universal appellation,
to designate and characterize the whole appropriated and unappropriated
territory of the United States.

It was a great oversight in the Convention of 1787, that they did not give
a name to the country for which they devised a frame of government.
Its citizens are suffering every day for lack of such a generic term. Destitute
of a proper name for their own soil and region, they express themselves
vaguely and awkwardly on the subject. By some it is termed "United States;"
this however is a *political*, and not a *geographical* title. By others it is called
"America," and the inhabitants "Americans." But these epithets equally
belong to Labrador and Paraguay and their natives. "New England" and
"New-Englanders" are two uncouth terms applied by certain other writers
and speakers. In some parts of Europe, we have been distinguished as
"Anglo-Americans;" and this appellation is in some respects worse, and in
no respect better than either of the others.

---

[2]   *The Monthly Anthology, and Boston Review Containing Sketches and Reports of Philosophy,
Religion, History, Arts, and Manners* 1 (June 1804), pp. 342–5.

What are we to do? Are we never to have a geographical distinction? Is the land to be forever called "United States," and its people "United States men?" And even then, on a supposition that the union should cease must the region it occupies be nameless? It is in the power of the people to find and adopt fitting names for their country and themselves, by common consent. These ought to be expressive, concise, nervous and poetical. And any new word possessing these qualities, may serve to designate *this part of the planet we inhabit* – From such a word as a radical term, all others proper for distinguishing the people, &c. may be derived.

To supply this sad deficiency in our geographical and national nomenclature, the following project is respectfully submitted to the consideration of our map-makers, engravers, printers, legislators and men of letters. The authors of it are citizens of the United States, and are zealous for their prosperity, honour, and reputation. They wish them to possess a name among the nations of the earth. They lament that hitherto and at present the country is destitute of one.

Let the extent of land ceded to our nation by the treaty of 1783, be distinguished henceforward on charts, globes, and in elementary books by the name of

FREDON:

the etymology of this is obvious and agreeable: it may mean a *free-gift*; or any *thing done freely*; or *the land of free privileges and doings*. This is the proper term to be employed in all grave, solemn, and prose compositions, and in ordinary conversation. It is better adapted than "Albion" is to England.

If, however, any of the favorites of the Muses desire a poetical name for this tract of earth, it is easy to supply them with one which sounds and pronounces to great advantage. Such an one is

FREDONIA:

which will meet the ear more excellently than Italia, Gallia, Parthia, Hispania, Germania, or even Britannia itself. – America and Columbia will retain their present signification of extending to the whole Western hemisphere.

The citizens and inhabitants of the United States when spoken of generally, without reference to any particular state, may be known and distinguished as

FREDONIANS:

And that such a person being asked in Europe or any other part of the world, from what country he comes or to what nation he belongs, may correctly and precisely answer that he is a FREDONIAN. And this will meet the ear much more nobly than "a Frenchman, a Spaniard, a Portuguese," "a Turk" and the like.

Again, a monysyllablic name is perfectly easy to be obtained from the same root; and to him who thinks the last word too long or lofty, it will be wholly at his option to call himself

FREDE;

and in this respect he will put himself on a par with a "Mede" and "a Swede." Moreover, should an adjective be desired to qualify expressions and facilitate discourse, there is such a thing immediately ready for use in

FREDISH;

and thereby, we can speak of "a Fredish ship," or a "Fredish man," or a "Fredish manufacture or production," after the same manner and according to the same rule, by which we employ the adjectives, *British, Spanish, Danish, Turkish, Turkish*, and the like. Thus, our nation is in possession of a *prosaic* word for its whole territory, FREDON; a *poetical* word for the same, FREDONIA; a *grave and sonorous* generic title for its people, property and relations, FREDONIA; a *short and colloquial appellation*, FREDE; and a convenient universal epithet, FREDISH. A language so rich and copious is scarcely to be found; and it is hoped our citizens will make the most of it.

In case any of our countrymen should wish to express himself according to this novel dialect, the following is offered as an example, alluding to a recent subject of public discussion.

"It has been a favourite object with a certain class of men to involve FREDON in a war with Spain, France or both of them, about the right of deposit on the Mississippi. The outrageous conduct of the Intendant at New-Orleans was indeed very provoking, but the FREDONIAN SPIRIT, though roused by just indignation, was too temperate and magnanimous to rush immediately to arms. It was thought most wise and politic for the administration to attempt a negociation in the first instance, and accordingly, one of the FREDISH ships was ordered to be got in readiness to carry an envoy extraordinary from America to Europe. Should war become necessary for the national honour and security, our public enemies will find to their sorrow that the FREDES will make brave soldiers and gallant sailors. Never will they quit the hardy contest until their deeds shall be worthy of being recorded in immortal verse, equally honourable to the bards and the heroes of FREDONIA."

The radical word is also well adapted to songs and rhymes. And this is a great convenience and felicity in a national point of view. Observe, how prettily our poets can make it jingle: for instance, if the subject is warlike, then

> "Their Chiefs, to glory lead on
> The noble sons of FREDON."

Or if it is moral sublimity,

> "Nor Plato, in his PHÆDON
> Excels the Sage of FREDON."

Should it be commercial Activity,

> "All Nations have agreed on
> The Enterprize of FREDON."

Perhaps it may refer to our exports; why then

> "The Portuguese may feed on
> The wheat and maize of FREDON."

It may be desirable to celebrate our Agriculture, as in the following distich,

> "No land so good as FREDON
> To scatter grain and seed on."

On the supposition that a swain wishes to compliment his country-women, he may inform them that

> "The graceful Nymphs of FREDON
> Surpass all Belles we read on."

And indeed if it is his desire to ejaculate in a serious strain, it may be written

> "In this fair land of FREDON
> May right and justice be done."

We give these as samples of what may be accomplished in this way, adding that the poet may easily contrast his country with SWEDEN, or compare it to EDEN, if he is puzzled for a rhyme.

On the whole, we recommend these words to the serious consideration and speedy adoption of our fellow-citizens; that our common and beloved portion of the earth, may thereby acquire a NAME, and be famous among the NATIONS.

M.

3. Rules of Etiquette in Jefferson's White House, 1803[3]

Whereas European courts had an extensive list of rules and protocol, it was unclear to many Americans just how a "republican" government should receive diplomats, heads of state, and other dignitaries. Just as the Chief Executive went by the simple title "Mr. President," should the other trappings of state be similarly austere? President Jefferson insisted on informality at his White House, going so far as to receive the first minister of Great Britain, Anthony Merry, to the United States in his everyday clothes and slippers. This caused a great controversy, which was heightened when Jefferson allowed a free-for-all in seating to occur at a White House dinner according to his principles of "pêle mêle," or "to mix" in French. In the end, the bruised egos of various European ministers were soothed, but not before the Jefferson Administration codified its informal rules of etiquette in late 1803.

RULES OF ETIQUETTE

I. In order to bring the members of society together in the first instance, the custom of the country has established that residents shall pay the first visit to strangers, and, among strangers, first comers to later comers, foreign and domestic; the character of stranger ceasing after the first visit. To this rule there is a single exception. Foreign ministers, from the necessity of making themselves known, pay the first visit to the ministers of the nation, which is returned.

II. When brought together in society, all are perfectly equal, whether foreign or domestic, titled or untitled, in or out of office.

All other observances are but exemplifications of these two principles.

I. 1st. The families of foreign ministers, arriving at the seat of government, receive the first visit from those of the national ministers, as from all other residents.

2d. Members of the Legislature and of the Judiciary, independent of their offices, have a right as strangers to receive the first visit.

II. 1st. No title being admitted here, those of foreigners give no precedence.

2d. Differences of grade among diplomatic members, give no precedence.

[3]   Paul Leicester Ford, ed., *The Works of Thomas Jefferson*, Volume X (New York: G. P. Putnam's Sons, 1905), pp. 47–8.

3d. At public ceremonies, to which the government invites the presence of foreign ministers and their families, a convenient seat or station will be provided for them, with any other strangers invited and the families of the national ministers, each taking place as they arrive, and without any precedence.

4th. To maintain the principle of equality, or of *pêle mêle*, and prevent the growth of precedence out of courtesy, the members of the Executive will practice at their own houses, and recommend an adherence to the ancient usage of the country, of gentlemen in mass giving precedence to the ladies in mass, in passing from one apartment where they are assembled into another.

Discussion Questions

1. How do "outsiders" like Native Americans, western farmers, or political radicals fashion their appeals to government? What reasoning do they use to express their grievances? Do they seem to be speaking the same language of politics used in other documents in Part I?

2. Do the documents in Part I give a clear vision of the policies advocated by the Federalist or Republican parties in the 1790s and early 1800s? Why or why not? What do they reveal about the First American Party System?

3. Compare the inaugural addresses of George Washington and Thomas Jefferson. Are they essentially similar or distinct? What is the rhetorical style used in these early inaugural addresses? Do you find them effective in understanding each president's vision?

4. Do the documents speak to the "newness" of the American nation? In what ways? Is it difficult for contemporary readers to place themselves within the context of this generation of Americans?

5. If you were forced to select one of these documents as "representative" of the legacy of the American Revolution, which one would you choose? Was the text of the document or the author of the document more important to your selection?

Part II   Clashes East and West

Introduction to Part II

In the first decade of the nineteenth century, the United States sought to exert its influence both in its vast western territory and in the Atlantic Ocean. Clashes with both Native Americans and Great Britain soon followed. The War of 1812 had its inglorious military moments, but also many fascinating political and cultural ones. The United States saw its invasion of Canada fall apart, its coast blockaded, and its capital occupied and burned. Yet, this war also provided the great military victory over the British at New Orleans, the reassertion of American independence, and the inspiration behind "The Star Spangled Banner." The collapse of both Native American resistance in the Ohio Valley and the Federalist Party are more ambivalent, if no less momentous, legacies of the War of 1812. So even though the shooting war lasted about two and a half years, the significance of the struggle reaches across the decades of the Early American Republic and beyond.

Chapter 4   Whose Land?

1. Lewis and Clark Make American Claims in the "Great West," August 1805[1]

In 1803 France sold its claims on the 828,000 square miles between the Rocky Mountains and the Mississippi River to the United States for $15 million, or about four cents per acre. Although on paper, the Louisiana Purchase nearly doubled the size of the nation, American officials knew very little about their newly acquired territory. In the spring of 1804, President Thomas Jefferson commissioned the Corps of Discovery, led by Meriwether Lewis and William Clark, to explore this new land claim and map out land routes to the Pacific Ocean. Along the way, the Lewis and Clark expedition encountered many Native American nations who cared little for the land transfer hammered out in Paris a few years earlier. When the expedition returned to St. Louis in 1806, they brought back a wealth of new geographic, biological, and cultural knowledge of what would become the great American Midwest. They also learned that the Native Americans still held the balance of power in this vast region. One of the travelers in the Corps was Private Joseph Whitehouse, a member of the US 1st Infantry at Kaskaskia when he joined Captain Lewis on the expedition. Whitehouse kept a journal of the events, in which he offered terse observations on the everyday routines of crossing the American continent and negotiating with a variety of different peoples. In this brief excerpt from his journal, Private Whitehouse describes the Corps' encampment in the mountains of southwestern Montana and an encounter with the Shoshone.

---

[1]   Gary Moulton, ed., *The Journals of the Lewis and Clark Expedition*, Vol. 11: *The Journals of Joseph Whitehouse, May 14, 1804–April 2, 1806* (Lincoln: University of Nebraska Press, 1997), pp. 279–80.

Wednesday August 21st [1805] We had a hard white frost this morning, the water that stood in small Vessells froze, and some Deer Skins which was spread out wet last night, was froze stiff this morning, & the Ink froze in the pen at Sun rise; The morning was clear & got pleasant, One of the hunters went out hunting on horse back & 4 of our Men were sent down the River to dig a hole or Cashe to deposit some of our baggage in. At 8 oClock A.M. some of the party found Ice in some standing water ¼ of an inch thick, In the evening we carried the baggage that was to be left at the Cashe, or hole that was dug, in order to deposit it there. The evening was dark, & Captain Lewis thought it best to have it done at that time, so that the Indians that were at our Camp, should not mistrust, or discover that we were going to bury anything at this place.

Thursday 22nd August 1805. a white frost & cold as usal in the morning. our hunter returned late last night. had killed a faun deer, and informed us that he fell among a party of Indians which were troublesome as they took his gun & rode off he rode after them and got his gun from out of an Indians hand. Their was Several Squaws which had considerable of their kinds of foods and Skins. they went and left it all he took it and brought it in with him. a clear pleasant morning three men wen to finish in hideing the baggage. the men at Camp employed dressing their deer Skins & making their mockasons &c. I am employed makeing up their leather Shirts & overalls. about 11 oClock A.m. one tribe of the Snake nation 50 odd in nomber arived here on horse back some women & children. They have now come over the dividing ridge to trade their horses &c. with us. Capt. Lewis counciled with them made 2 of them chiefs, and told them that we had come to open the way and try to make peace among the red people, and that they would be Supplyed with goods and necessaries, if they would catch beaver and otter and Save their Skins which the white people were fond of and would trade with them as Soon as times would admit &c. Capt. Lewis traded with them & bought 3 horses & 2 mules or half mules, for a little marchandize &c. we being out of fresh meat & have but little Salt meat we joined and made a fish drag out of willows tyed bunches of them together and made it long enofe to reach across the River, and Caught with it 520 different kinds of fine pane fish. we divided them with the natives. Gave them a mess of boiled corn which they were fond of. they appear to be verry kind and friendly. we trade with them for dressed mountn. rams Skins and otter Skins &c. our Interpreter & wife came over with them & were all Scarce off for provisions killed nothing but one or 2 mountain Sheep & rabits &c. they all Camp with us and are peaceable, so not attempt to Steel any thing. borrow nothing but what they return. they appear to live in fear of other nations who are at war with them, but Capt. Lewis tells them that these other nations promise to let them alone and if they do not, their Great father will Send them arms and ammunition to defend themselves with, but rather that they would live in peace &c . . .

2. Tecumseh Speaks Out Against American Policy in the Old Northwest, August 20, 1810[2]

In 1794, Native Americans resisting white invasion of their lands suffered a crushing defeat at the hands of American armed forces at the Battle of Fallen Timbers. The following year, representatives of these defeated nations signed the Treaty of Greenville, which ceded large portions of the "Old Northwest" (the area north of the Ohio and east of the Mississippi rivers) to the United States. Tensions between whites and Native Americans in this territory continued to simmer in the decade that followed. The Shawnee political leader Tecumseh renewed hopes of resisting white expansion by joining with his spiritualist brother Tenskwatawa to reject cultural and political accommodation with Anglo-Americans. When selected Native American leaders ceded 2.5 million acres of land to the United States in the Treaty of Fort Wayne (1809), Tecumseh rallied his increasing number of allies in the Old Northwest to join forces against the United States. In this speech to William Henry Harrison, the governor of the Indiana Territory, Tecumseh cites the abuse of the Greenville and Fort Wayne treaties and rejects the idea that individual leaders could negotiate land cessions to the United States.

Brother, I wish you to listen to me well. I wish to reply to you more explicitly as I think you do not clearly understand what I before said to you. I shall explain it again . . .

You ought to know that after we agreed to bury the tomahawk at Greenville we then found new fathers in the Americans who told us they would treat us well, not like the British who gave us but a small piece of pork every day.

I want now to remind you of the promises of the white people. You recollect that the time the Delawares lived near the white people (Americans) and satisfied with the promises of friendship and remained in security, yet one of their towns was surprised and the men, women and children murdered.

[2]   Indiana Historical Society Digital Collections, http://images.indianahistory.org/u?/dc007,19.

The same promises were given to the Shawnees flags were given to them and were told by the Americans that they were now children of the Americans. These flags will be as security for you; if the white people intend to do you harm hold up your flags and no harm will be done you. This was at length practised and the consequence was that the person bearing the flag was murdered with others in their village. How my Brother after this conduct can you blame me for placing little confidence in the promises of our fathers the Americans?

Brother, since the peace was made you have killed some of the Shawnees, Winebagoes, Delawares and Miamies and you have taken our lands from us, and I do not see how we can remain at peace with you if you continue to do so. You have given goods to the Kickapoos for the sale of their land which has been the cause of many deaths among them. You have promised us assistance but I do not see that you have given us any.

You try to force the red people to do some injury. It is you that is pushing them on to do mischief. You endeavour to make distinctions. You wish to prevent the Indians to do as we wish them: to unite and let them consider their land common property of the whole.

You take tribes aside and advise them not to come into this measure and until our design is accomplished we do not wish to accept of your invitation to go and visit the President.

The reason I tell you this is you want by your distinctions of Indian tribes in allotting to each a particular track of land to make them to war with each other. You never see an Indian come and endeavour [to] make the white people do so. You are continually driving the red people when at last you will drive them into the great Lake where they can't eat eather or stand or work.

Brother, you ought to know what you are doing with the Indians. Perhaps it is by direction of the President to make those distinctions. It is a very bad thing and we do not like it. Since my residence at Tippecanoe we have endeavoured to level all the distinctions to destroy village chiefs by whom all mischief is done. It is they who sell our land to the Americans. Our object is to let all our affairs be transacted by warriors ...

Brother, it has been the object of both myself and brother from the beginning to prevent the lands being sold. Should you not return the land it will occasion us to call a great council that will meet at the Huron Village where the council fire has already been lighted. At which those who sold the land shall be called and shall suffer for their conduct.

Brother, I wish you would take pity on all the red people and do what I have requested ...

3. An Artist's Depiction of Scalping during the War of 1812, 1812[3]

Although the formal declaration of war targeted Great Britain, the majority of fighting in the War of 1812 actually occurred between American and Native American forces. The image shown in Figure 1 is a possible response to a Pottawatomie attack on the garrison at Fort Dearborn in modern-day Chicago that occurred on August 15, 1812. That battle, like many others in the War of 1812, came about as local Native Americans, allied with the British, sought to remove the American presence from the Old Northwest. The widespread rumor that British officers paid bounties on American scalps fueled much of the animosity in the western theatres of the War of 1812, and is depicted in this image.

Figure 1 An artist's depiction of scalping during the War of 1812.
Source: Harpweek: American Political Prints, http://loc.harpweek.com/

---

[3] Harpweek: American Political Prints, http://loc.harpweek.com/

Transcription of text:

"Arise Columbia's Sons and forward press,
Your Country's wrongs call loudly for redress;
The Savage Indian with his Scalping knife,
Or Tomahawk may seek to take your life;
By bravery aw'd they'll in a dreadful Fright,
Shrink back for Refuge to the Woods in Flight;
Their British leaders then will quickly shake,
And for those wrongs shall restitution make."

Chapter 5   Conflict on Many Fronts

1. James Madison Justifies War with the British, June 1, 1812[1]

Although William Henry Harrison's victory at Tippecanoe in 1811 quelled the threat of Tecumseh's pan-Indian movement on the nation's western boundary, the United States was far from secure. The European powers' refusal to respect American neutrality on the high seas became a thorn in the side of the Early Republic. Western and southern politicians, known as the "War Hawks," denounced the policies of Great Britain in the Atlantic and argued that British agents supported Native American resistance in the West. After the failure of trade embargos and negotiations to settle the issue, many Republicans argued that an armed conflict was the only answer. Federalists largely opposed a war with Great Britain, but in 1812 they lacked the political clout in Washington to prevent it. In this context, President James Madison laid out the case for war in the following message to Congress. On June 18, the United States formally declared war against Great Britain.

... Without going back beyond the renewal in 1803, of the war in which Great Britain is eng[a]ged, and omitting unrepaired wrongs of inferior magnitude; the conduct of her Government presents a series of acts, hostile to the United States, as an Independent and neutral nation.

[1]   J. C. A. Stagg et al., *The Papers of James Madison. Presidential Series, Vol. 4: 5 November 1811–9 July 1812 With a Supplement 5 March 1809–19 October 1811* (Charlottesville: University Press of Virginia, 1999), pp. 432–3, 436–7.

British cruisers have been in the continued practice of violating the American flag on the great high way of nations, and of seizing and carrying off persons sailing under it; not in the exercise of a Belligerent right founded on the Law of Nations against an Enemy; but of a municipal prerogative over British subjects. British jurisdiction is thus extended to neutral vessels, in a situation where no laws can operate but the law of nations, and the laws of the Country to which the vessels belong; and a self-redress is assumed, which, if British subjects were wrongfully detained an along concerned, is that the substitution of force, for a resort of the responsible sovereign, which falls within the definition of War. Could the seizure of British subjects, in such cases, be regarded as within the exercise of a Belligerent right, the acknowledged laws of war, which forbid an article of captured property to be adjudged, without a regular investigation before a competent Tribunal, would imperiously demand the fairest trial, where the sacred rights of persons were at issue. In place of such a trial, these rights are subjected to the will of every petty commander.

The practice, hence, is so far from affecting British subjects alone that under the pretext of searching for these, thousands of American Citizens, under the safeguard of public law, and of their national flag, have been torn from their country, and from every thing dear to them; have been dragged on board ships of war of a foreign nation; and exposed, under the siverities of their discipline, to be exiled to the most distant and deadly climes, to risk their lives in the battles of their oppressors, and to be the melancholy instruments of taking away those of their own brethren.

Against this crying enormity, which Great Britain would be so prompt to avenge; if committed against herself, the United States have, in vain, exhausted remonstrances and expostulations: And that no proof might be wanting of their conciliatory dispositions, and no pretext left for a continuance of the practice, the British Government was formally assured of the readiness of the United States to enter into arrangements, such as could not be rejected, if the recovery of British subjects were the real and the sole object. The communication passed without effect.

British cruisers have been in the practice also, of violating the rights and the peace of our Coasts. They hover over and harass our entering and departing Commerce. To the most insulting pretensions, they have added the most lawless proceedings in our very harbors; and have wantonly spilt American blood, within the sanctuary of our territorial jurisdiction. The principles and rules enforced by that nation when a neutral nation, against armed vessals of Belligerents hovering near her coasts, and disturbing her commerce, are well known. When called on, nevertheless, by the United States to punish the greater offenses committed by her own vessels, her Government has bestowed on their commanders, additional marks of honor and confidence ...

In reviewing the conduct of Great Britain towards the United States, our attention is necessarily drawn to the warfare just renewed by the Savages, on one of our extensive frontiers; a warfare which is known to spare neither age nor sex, and to be distinguished by features peculiarly shocking to humanity. It is difficult to account for the activity, and combinations, which have for some time been developing themselves among tribes in constant intercourse with British traders and garrisons, without connecting their hostility with that influence; and without recollecting the authenticated examples of such inter-positions, heretofore furnished by the officers and agents of that Government.

Such is the spectacle of injuries and indignities which have been heaped upon our Country: and such the crisis which its unexampled forbearance and conciliatory efforts have not been able to avert. It might at least have been expected, that an enlightened nation, if less urged by moral obligations, or invited by friendly dispositions on the part of the United States would have found, in its true interest alone, a sufficient motive to respect their rights and their tranquility on the high seas, that an enlarged policy would have favored that free and general circulation of Commerce, in which the British nation is at all times interested, and which in times of war, is the best alleviation of its calamities to herself, as well as to other Belligerents; and, more especially, that the British Cabinet, would not, for the sake of a precarious and surreptitious intercourse with hostile markets, have persevered in a course of measures, which necessarily put at hazard the invaluable market of a great and growing Country, disposed to cultivate the mutual advantages of an active commerce.

Other Councils have prevailed. Our moderation and conciliation, have had no other effect than to encourage perseverance, and to enlarge preten-sions. We behold our seafaring Citizens still the daily victims of lawless violence commited on the great common and high way of nations, even within sight of the Country which owes them protection. We behold our vessels, freighted with the products of our soil and industry, or returning with the honest proceeds of them, wrested from their lawful destinations, confiscated by prize courts, no longer the organs of public law, but the instruments of arbitrary Edicts; and their unfortunate crews dispersed and lost, or forced, or inveigled in British ports, into British fleets: whilst arguments are employed, in support of these aggressions, which have no foundation but in a principle equally supporting a claim, to regulate our external commerce, in all cases whatsoever.

We behold, in fine, on the side of Great Britain a state of war against the United States; and on the side of the United States, a state of peace towards Great Britain.

Whether the United States shall continue passive under these progressive usurpations, and these accumulating wrongs; or, opposing force to force in defence of their national rights, shall commit a just cause into the hands of the Almighty disposer of events; avoiding all connections which might entangle it in the contests or views of other powers, and preserving a constant readiness to concur in an honorable re-establishment of peace and friendship, is a solemn question, which the Constitution wisely confides to the Legislative Department of the Government. In recommending it to their early deliberations, I am happy in the assurance, that the decision will be worthy the enlightened and patriotic Councils, of a virtuous, a free, and a powerful Nation ...

2. The Hartford Convention Denounces the War, December 15, 1814[2]

By late 1814, the war against the British was not going well for the United States. The occupation of the new capital of Washington DC, the setbacks in Canada, and the impending invasion of New Orleans all undermined American morale. Federalists in New England lacked enthusiasm for the fight in 1812; two years later their spirits were at an all-time low. By December of 1814, delegates from Connecticut, Rhode Island, New Hampshire, Vermont, and Massachusetts convened at Hartford, Connecticut to discuss remedies for the situation. Some delegates pressed for secession and a separate peace with Great Britain, but instead the Hartford Convention proposed a series of resolutions designed to limit the power of the federal government. Critics charged that the Federalists were simply angry at their diminished role in national policymaking. In this excerpt from the proceedings of the Hartford Convention, the delegates explain their dissatisfaction with both the justification and prosecution of the War of 1812.

REPORT, &c.

The delegates from the legislatures of the states of Massachusetts, Connecticut, and Rhode Island, and from the counties of Grafton and Cheshire, in the state of New-Hampshire, and the county of Windham in the state of Vermont; assembled in convention, beg leave to report the following result of their conference.

The convention is deeply impressed with a sense of the commission which they were appointed to execute, of devising the means of defence against

[2]   *Niles' Weekly Register*, January 14, 1815.

dangers, and of relief from oppressions proceeding from the acts of their own government, without violating constitutional principles, or disappointing the hopes of a suffering and injured people. To prescribe patience and firmness to those who are already exhausted by distress, is sometimes to drive them to despair, and the progress towards reform by the regular road, is irksome to those whose imaginations discern, and whose feelings prompt to a shorter course. But when abuses reduced to system and accumulated through a course of years have pervaded every department of government, and spread corruption through every region of the state, when these are clothed with the forms of law, and enforced by an executive whose will is their source, no summary means of relief can be applied without recourse to direct and open resistance. This experiment, even when justifiable, cannot fail to be painful to the good citizen; and the success of the effort will be no security against the danger of the example. Precedents of resistance to the worst administration are eagerly seized by those who are naturally hostile to the best. Necessity alone can sanction a resort to this measure; and it should never be extended in duration or degree beyond the exigency, until the people, not merely in the fervor of sudden excitement, but after a full deliberation, are determined to change the constitution ...

Again, the experiment of the powers of the constitution, to regain its vigor, and of the people to recover from their delusions, has been hitherto made under the greatest possible disadvantages arising from the state of the world. The fierce passions which have convulsed the nations of Europe, have passed the ocean, and finding their way to the bosoms of our citizens, have afforded the administration the means of perverting public opinion, in respect to our foreign relations, so as to acquire its aid in the indulgence of its adherence. Further, a reformation of public opinion, resulting from dear bought experience in the southern and Atlantic states, at least, is not to be despaired of. They will have felt, that the eastern states cannot be made exclusively the victims of a capricious and impassioned policy. They will have seen that the great and essential interests of the people, are common to the south and to the east. They will realize the fatal errors of a system, which seeks revenge for commercial injuries in the sacrifice of commerce, and aggravates by needless wars, to an immeasurable extent, the injuries it professes to redress. They may discard the influence of visionary theorists, and recognize the benefits of a practical policy. Indications of this desirable revolution of opinion among our brethren in those states, are already manifested, while a hope remains of its ultimate completion, its progress should not be retarded or stopped, by exciting fears which must check these favorable tendencies and frustrate the efforts of the wisest and best men in those states, to accelerate this propitious change.

Finally, if the union be destined to dissolution, by reason of the multiplied abuses of bad administrations, it should, if possible, be the work of peaceable times, and deliberate consent. Some new form of confederacy should be substituted among those states, which shall intend to maintain a federal relation to each other. Events may prove that the causes of our calamities are deep and permanent. They may be found to proceed, not merely from the blindness of prejudice, pride of opinion, violence of party spirit, or the confusion of the times; but they may be traced to implacable combinations of individuals, or of states, to monopolize power and office, and to trample without remorse upon the rights and interests of commercial sections of the union. Whenever it shall appear that these causes are radical and permanent, a separation by equitable arrangement, will be preferable to an alliance by constraint, among nominal friends, but real enemies, inflamed by mutual hatred and jealousies, and inviting by intestine divisions, contempt and aggression from abroad. But a severance of the union by one or more states, against the will of the rest, and especially in time of war, can be justified only by absolute necessity. These are among the principal objections against precipitate measures tending to disunite the states, and when examined in connection with the farewell address of the father of his country, they must, it is believed, be deemed conclusive.

Under these impressions, the convention have proceeded to confer and deliberate upon the alarming state of public affairs, especially, as affecting the interests of the people who have appointed them for this purpose, and they are naturally led to a consideration, in the first place, of the dangers and grievances which menace an immediate or speedy pressure, with a view of suggesting means of present relief; in the next place, of such as are of a more remote and general description, in the hope of attaining future security...

Without pausing at present to comment upon the causes of the war, it may be assumed as a truth, officially announced, that to achieve the conquest of Canadian territory, and to hold it as a pledge for peace, is the deliberate purpose of administration. This enterprize, commenced at a period when government possessed the advantage of selecting the time and occasion for making a sudden descent upon an unprepared enemy, now languishes in the third year of the war. It has been prosecuted with various fortune, and occasional brilliancy of exploit, but without any solid acquisition. The British armies have been recruited by veteran regiments. Their navy commands Ontario. The American ranks are thinned by casualties of war. Recruits are discouraged by the unpopular character of the contest, and by the uncertainty of receiving their pay.

In the prosecution of this favorite warfare, administration have left the exposed and vulnerable parts of the country destitute of all efficient means of defence. The main body of the regular army has been marched to the frontier. The navy has been stripped of a great part of its sailors for the service of the lakes. Meanwhile the enemy scours the sea-coast, blockades our ports, ascends our bays and rivers, makes actual descent in various and distant places, holds some by force, and threatens all that are assailable, with fire and sword. The sea-board of four of the New-England states, following its curvatures, presents an extent of more than seven hundred miles, generally occupied by a compact population, and accessible by a naval force, exposing a mass of people and property to the devastation of the enemy, which bears a great proportion of the residue of the maritime frontier of the United States. This extensive shore has been exposed to frequent attacks, repeated contributions and constant alarms. The regular forces detached by the national government for its defence, are mere pretexts for placing officers of high rank in command. They are besides confined to a few places, and are too insignificant in number to be included in any computation ...

If the war be continued, there appears no room for reliance upon the national government for the supply of those means of defence, which must become indispensable to secure these states from desolation and ruin. Nor is it possible that the states can discharge this sacred duty from their own resources, and continue to sustain the burden of the national taxes. The administration, after a long perseverance in plans to baffle every effort of commercial enterprize, had fatally succeeded in their attempts at the epoch of the war. Commerce, the vital spring of New England's prosperity, was annihilated. Embargoes, restrictions, and the rapacity of revenue officers, had completed its destruction. The various objects for the employment of productive labor, in the branches of business dependent on commerce, have disappeared. The fisheries have shared its fate. Manufactures, which government has professed an intention to favor and to cherish, as an indemnity for the failure of these branches of business, are doomed to struggle in their infancy with taxes and obstructions, which cannot fail most seriously to affect their growth. The specie is withdrawn from circulation. The landed interest, the last to feel these burdens, must prepare to become their principal support, as all other sources of revenue must be exhausted. Under these circumstances, taxes of a description and amount unprecedented in this country, are in a train of imposition, the burden of which must fall with the heaviest pressure upon the states east of the Potomac. The amount of these taxes for the ensuing year, cannot be estimated at less than five millions of dollars upon the New England states, and the expenses of the last year for defence in Massachusetts alone, approaches to one million of dollars.

From these facts, it is almost superfluous to state the irresistible inference that these states have no capacity of defraying the expense requisite for their own protection, and, at the same time, of discharging the demands of the national treasury.

The last inquiry, what course of contact ought to be adopted by the aggrieved states, is in a high degree momentous. When a great and brave people shall feel themselves deserted by their government, and reduced to the necessity either of submission to a foreign enemy, or of appropriating to their own use, those means of defence which are indispensable to self preservation, they cannot consent to wait passive spectators of approaching ruin, which it is their power to avert, and to resign the last remnant of their industrious earnings, to be dissipated in support of measures destructive of the best interest of the nation.

This convention will not trust themselves to express their conviction of the catastrophe to which such a state of things inevitably tends. – Conscious of their high responsibility to God and their country, solicitous for the continuance of the Union, as well as the sovereignty of the states, unwilling to furnish obstacles to peace – resolute never to submit to a foreign enemy, and confiding in the Divine care and protection, they will, until the last hope shall be extinguished, endeavor to avert such consequences . . .

3. An Eyewitness Account of the Battle of New Orleans, 1816[3]

Although the War of 1812 contained many military setbacks for the United States, the successful defense of New Orleans became one of the most renowned events of the struggle. As 10,000 British troops, led by Sir Edward Pakenham, advanced on the city in the winter of 1814–15, General Andrew Jackson quickly assembled a defense force from the regular US Army, militiamen from Tennessee, Kentucky, and Mississippi, free African-Americans, and even local pirates. After enduring a prolonged shelling, the 4,000 American defenders awakened on the morning of January 8, 1815 to see the British forces advancing in an all-out assault. This eyewitness account comes from the pen of Arsène Lacarrière Latour, a French architect living in New Orleans at the time of the battle. Jackson recruited Latour to be the principal engineer of the defensive works and as a kind of liaison between his American forces and the French-speaking creoles of New Orleans. It is unclear exactly where Latour was stationed during the events of January 8, but in his Historical Memoir *published in 1816 he claims to have witnessed the battle firsthand.*

---

[3]   Gene A. Smith, ed., Arsène Lacarrière Latour, *Historical Memoir of the War in West Florida and Louisiana* (The Historic New Orleans Collection and University Press of Florida, 1999), pp. 107–11.

... on the 7th, shortly after night-fall, we distinctly heard men at work in the enemy's different batteries; the strokes of hammers gave "note of preparation," and resounded even within our lines; and our out-posts informed us that the enemy was re-establishing his batteries: his guards were re-enforced about sunset, probably with a view to cover the movements of the troops. In our camp all was composure; the officers were ordered to direct their subalterns to be ready on the first signal. Half the troops passed the night behind the breastwork, relieving each other occasionally. Every one waited for the day with anxiety and impatience, but with calm intrepidity, expecting to be vigorously attacked, and knowing that the enemy had then from twelve to fifteen thousand bayonets to bring into action, besides two thousand sailors and some marines.

A little before daybreak, our out-post came in without noise, having perceived the enemy moving forward in great force.

At last the dawn of day discovered to use the enemy occupying two-thirds of the space between the wood and the Mississippi. Immediately a Congreve rocket went off from the skirt of the wood, in the direction of the river. This was the signal for the attack. At the same instant, the twelve-pounder of battery No. 6, whose gunners had perceived the enemy's movement, discharged a shot. On this all his troops gave three cheers, formed in close column of about sixty men in front, in very good order, and advanced nearly in the direction of battery No. 7, the men shouldering their muskets, and all carrying fascines, and some with ladders. A cloud of rockets preceded them, and continued to fall in showers during the whole attack. Batteries Nos. 6, 7, and 8, now opened an incessant fire on the column, which continued to advance in pretty good order, until, in a few minutes, the musketry of the troops of Tennessee and Kentucky, joining their fire with that of the artillery, began to make an impression on it, which soon threw it into confusion. It was at that moment that was heard the constant rolling fire, whose tremendous noise resembled rattling peals of thunder. For some time the British officers succeeded in animating the courage of their troops, and making them advance, obliqueing to the left, to avoid the fire of battery No. 7, from which every discharge opened the column, and mowed down whole files, which were almost instantaneously replaced by new troops coming up close after the first: but these also shared the same fate, until at last, after twenty-five minutes continual firing, through which a few platoons advanced to the edge of the ditch, the column entirely broke, and part of the troops dispersed, and ran to take shelter among the bushes on the right. The rest retired to the ditch where they had been when first perceived, four hundred yards from our lines.

There the officers with some difficulty rallied their troops, and again drew them up for a second attack, the soldiers having laid down their knapsacks at the edge of the ditch, that they might be less incumbered.

And now, for the second time, the column, recruited with the troops that formed the rear, advanced. Again it was received with the same rolling fire of musketry and artillery, till, having advanced without much order very near our lines, it last broke again, and retired in the utmost confusion. In vain did the officers now endeavor, as before, to revive the courage of their men; to no purpose did they strike them with the flat of their swords, to force them to advance: they were insensible to every thing but danger, and saw nothing but death which had struck so many of their comrades.

The attack on our lines had hardly begun, when the British commander-in-chief, the honourable sir Edward Pakenham, fell a victim to his own intrepidity, while endeavoring to animate his troops with ardour for the assault. Soon after his fall, two other generals, Keane and Gibbs, were carried off the field of battle, dangerously wounded. A great number of officers of rank had fallen: the ground over which the column had marched, was strewed with the dead and the wounded. Such slaughter on their side, with no loss on ours, spread consternation through their ranks, as they were now convinced of the impossibility of carrying our lines, and saw that even to advance was certain death. In a word, notwithstanding the repeated efforts of some officers to make the troops form a third time, they would not advance, and all that could be obtained from them, was to draw them up in the ditch, where they passed the rest of the day.

Some of the enemy's troops had advanced into the woods towards the extremity of our line, to make a false attack, or to ascertain whether a real one were practicable. These the troops under general Coffee no sooner perceived, than they opened on them a brisk fire with their rifles, which quickly made them retire. The greater part of those who, on the column's being repulsed, had taken shelter in the thickets, only escaped our batteries to be killed by our musketry. During the whole hour that the attack lasted, our fire did not slacken for a single moment; and it seemed as though the artillery and musketry vied with each other in vivacity . . .

By half after eight in the morning, the fire of the musketry had ceased. The whole plain on the left, as also the side of the river, from the road to the edge of the water, was covered with the British soldiers who had fallen. About four hundred wounded prisoners were taken, and at least double that number of wounded men escaped into British camp; and, what might perhaps appear incredible, were there not many thousands ready to attest the fact, is that a space of ground, extending from the ditch of our lines to that on which the enemy drew up his troops, two hundred and fifty yards in length, by about two hundred in breadth, was literally covered with men, either dead or severely wounded. About forty men were killed in the ditch, up to which they had advanced, and about the same number were there made prisoners. The artillery of our lines kept up a fire against the enemy's batteries and troops until two o'clock in the afternoon. By the disposition of his troops, the enemy appeared to apprehend lest we should make a sortie, and attack him in his camp. The soldiers were drawn up in ditches, in several parallel lines, and all those who had been slightly wounded, as soon as their wounds were dressed, were sent to join their corps, to make their number of effective men seem greater, and show a firm countenance. The enemy's loss on the left bank, in the affair of the 8th January, was immense, considering the short duration of the contest, the ground, and the respective number of the contending forces. According to the most probable accounts, it cannot have amounted to less than three thousand men in killed, wounded, and prisoners. The number of officers who fell that day is a much greater loss in proportion, owing to the necessity they were under of exposing themselves in the brunt of the battle, to encourage the men, and lead them on to the desperate assault. Our loss was comparatively inconsiderable, amounting to no more than thirteen in killed and wounded, on the left bank of the Mississippi. . . .

Discussion Questions

1. Do the documents concerning the relations between the United States and Native American nations suggest that conflict was inevitable? Do the documents offer a fair perspective of the Native American worldview? Why or why not?
2. If you only had the documents from Chapter 4 as evidence, what would you say were the true causes of the War of 1812? Do you think that your conclusion runs counter to popular conceptions of the war's causes today?
3. Do you find evidence in these documents of the tensions mentioned in Part I? Is there evidence of a coherent vision of the "American Nation" on the eve of and during the War of 1812? Do you think that the war helped crystallize notions of American nationalism?

Part III   The Postwar Nation Looks Forward

Introduction to Part III

Some historians refer to the period following the War of 1812 as the "Era of Good Feelings." Although the nation did see stability in its international boundaries and a reduction in partisan strife as the Federalist Party faded into obscurity, these years were hardly placid ones. In fact, the United States saw a great deal of conflict in the decade or so following the war. Rather than fighting a foreign military foe, Americans struggled with spirituality, morality, economic hardship, and the slavery question during this time – hardly a period deserving of the "good feelings" sobriquet.

Chapter 6   The Year 1819 in Image and Verse

1. A Poem about a Panic, 1819[1]

The four years of peace following the end of the War of 1812 brought impressive economic growth. The American economy soared as the high demand for cotton, grain, and meat in European markets gave farmers ample reason to expand their purchases of land and, in the southern states, slaves. But when the price of American cotton fell in late 1818, the speculative bubble burst. Land purchased on credit fell in value and an alarming number of defaults hit American credit markets the following year. The newly chartered Second Bank of the United States attempted to stop the hemorrhaging by calling in loans to state-chartered banks, particularly those in the South and West that had issued loans far beyond their means. The so-called "Panic of 1819" was in fact a severe depression in which thousands of Americans suffered financial ruin. One of the biggest targets of scorn in the hard times were banks, some of which had lent freely and irresponsibly during the boom times. This poem from Philadelphia's Port-Folio lampoons the failure of small, western banks and their inability to exchange – or "redeem" in the parlance of the day – their issued notes for actual hard currency.

---

[1] *The Port-Folio* 7 (March 1819), p. 248.

THE BANKS; OR WESTERN MELODIES – No. 1
Air – Oh! blame not the bard.

Oh! blame not the banks if they fly to suspension
    Where *Av'rice* lies carelessly smiling at *Shame*;
They would have done better, and 'twas their intention
    T'have paid the last dollar, and died in a flame.
That box which now languishes lone in the corner,
    Might have yielded delight to the countryman's heart,
And the teller, alive to the impulse of honour,
    Would have paid it with gladness, and seen it depart.

But alas! for the banks; their fame is gone by,
    And that credit is *broken* which used but to *bend*,
O'er their fall, each director in secret must sigh,
    For 'tis interest to love them, but *shame* to defend.
Unpriz'd are their notes, or at ten per cent selling,
    Unhonour'd at home, unredeem'd on demand:
But still they've a merit – I joy in the telling,
    They're taken for *pork*, though rejected for land.

Then blame not the banks, though they cease to redeem
    (We should try to forget what we never can heal)
Oh! furnish the dust; let the dollars but gleam
    Through the gloom of their vaults, and mark how they'd feel!
That instant they'd pay! on demand they'd throw down
    The branch paper so lov'd, or the gold so ador'd,
While the eagle, the dollar, and old Spanish crown
    Would jingle in concert, and shine on the board.

But their glory is gone! ev'ry dog has his day,
    Yet their fame (such as 'tis) shall abide in my songs,
Not e'en in the hour when my heart is most gay,
    Will I cease to remember their *notes* or their wrongs.
The stranger in passing each village shall say,
    (As he eyes the sad spot with his hand on his breast)
THERE ONCE STOOD A BANK! but unable to pay,
    It suspended itself, and has now gone to rest!!

OHIO BARD

2. Americans on Their Way to a Camp Revival, 1819²

In the late summer of 1801, about 20,000 Americans gathered at Cane Ridge, Kentucky. They were there to hear emotional sermons and calls to repent of their sins and renew their spirituality in the presence of fellow evangelical Christians. This large meeting – ten times the size of Lexington, Kentucky's largest city – is the symbolic starting point of the Second Great Awakening. Across the United States, religious revivals called upon sinners to replenish their personal relationship with God. Thousands of Americans attended these revivals, drawing the curiosity of many foreign observers, who often commented on the religious zeal displayed by most Americans of the Early Republic. The Second Great Awakening was a grassroots religious movement in that many Americans rejected older, hierarchical church structures and turned to the strong emotional appeals made by preachers at revivals. As this artist demonstrates (in Figure 2), camp meetings were raucous, informal affairs that combined huge crowds in pastoral settings. As revivals became familiar events across the United States, it became clear that American religious life had been reinvigorated and would play a role in the future course of the nation.

Figure 2 Americans on their way to a camp revival.
Source: Library of Congress, Washington, DC.

² "Camp Meeting of the Methodists in N. America," by M. Dubourg, *c.*1819. Library of Congress Print.

3. A Satirist Looks at the American Militia, 1819[3]

On paper the American militia was the bulwark of republican power, but the recent hostilities against Great Britain had proved them to be less than stellar military units. All able-bodied white male citizens of the United States between the ages of 18 and 45, according to the Militia Act of 1792, were members of their local militia. States varied in their service demands, but in the years following the War of 1812, the mandatory drill was limited to two days a year. These "militia musters" often involved as much politicking, drinking, and horseplay as they did serious military training. The growing notion of political equality among white male Americans, moreover, undermined the authority of militia officers in the eyes of their soldiers. In this print, the satirist David Claypoole Johnston pokes fun at the American militia system by depicting the call-out of a Philadelphia unit after a boisterous crowd disrupted an attempt to launch a balloon in nearby Spring Garden. Johnston lampoons the unmilitary bearing of the politically appointed mounted officers and the fact that immigrants often served in the militia, and also includes commentary from a pair of African-American boys observing the event. To hammer home the absurdity of the event, Johnston reprints some lines from John Milton's Paradise Lost, *an epic poem depicting the struggle between God and Lucifer. Along with religious revivals, militia musters demonstrated how new ideas about individuality and equality could substantially transform longstanding American institutions during the Early Republic. This particular print was so popular that Johnston updated it and reprinted several times in his distinguished career.*

---

[3] "A Militia Muster: Drawn by Busybody, Engraved by Nobody, Published by Somebody for Anybody & Everybody." Copperplate Etching by David Claypoole Johnston, Philadelphia, 1819. American Antiquarian Society, Worcester, Massachusetts.

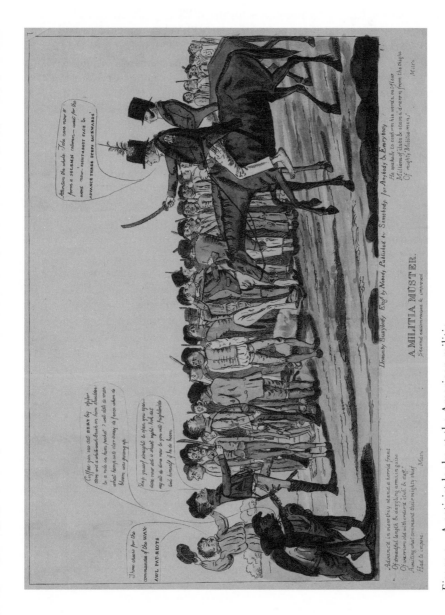

Figure 3 A satirist looks at the American militia.
Source: American Antiquarian Society, Worcester, Mass.

Dialogue:

[*Man waving hat*]:	"Three cheers for the WAX-AWL PAT-RIOTS"
[*African-American child on left*]:	"Cuffee you see dat BERY big ofsifer dere wid a white-wash brush on him shoulder & a rule in him pocket? Well dats de man wat hemp us to clarr away de fence when do bloom was guang up"
[*Non-commissioned officer on left*]:	"Keep youself straight & open your eyes – dare now dat is shust right – look dat way all de dime now & you vill frighten de tevil himself if he do koom."
[*Officer on horse*]:	"Attention the whole. Take care now to form a SOL-EMN column – wait for the word now – RIGHT ABOUT FACE & ADVANCE THREE STEPS BACKWARDS"

Quotes from Milton's *Paradise Lost*:
[On left side]

> Advanc'd in view they stand a horrid front
> Of dreadful length & dazzling arms, in guise
> Of warriors old with order'd "club" & "staff,"
> Awaiting what command their mighty chief
> Had to impose

[On right side]

> He spake & to confirm his words, out flew
> Millions of "clubs & stars" draw from the thighs
> Of mighty Milita-men

Chapter 7   The Future Course of the Republic?

1. John C. Calhoun Promotes Federal Internal Improvements, February 4, 1817[1]

In 1816, Congress chartered the Second Bank of the United States with the strong support of nationalistic politicians from the South and West – some of the same folks who had made up the "War Hawks" contingent advocating war with Great Britain in 1812. Rather than conquer a foreign opponent, however, these nationalists now advocated the conquest of time and space through the construction of federally funded internal improvements. This idea had first been broached in 1807 when Albert Gallatin, Thomas Jefferson's Secretary of the Treasury, set out a plan for a $16.6 million network for the construction of canals, improved rivers, and turnpikes to span the United States. A decade later, John C. Calhoun of South Carolina wanted to use $1.5 million bonus and future stock earnings paid to the government by the Second Bank to fund such a system. Although Calhoun would later make a name for himself as an ardent supporter of states' rights, his support of the "Bonus Bill" of 1817 revealed his strong belief that improved lines of transportation were essential for the new nation's future. President Madison vetoed the "Bonus Bill," but the controversy over publicly funded internal improvements continued to rage in Congress and state houses throughout the Early Republic. In this speech delivered to the House of Representatives in February of 1817, Calhoun outlines his argument for the political significance of internal improvements.

---

[1] E. B. Williston, comp., *Eloquence of the United States*, vol. 3 (Middletown, CT: E. & H. Clark, 1827), pp. 255–65.

... when I reflect how favorable is the present moment, and how confessedly important a good system of roads and canals is to our country, I may reasonably be sanguine of success. At peace with all of the world; abounding in pecuniary means; and, what is of the most importance, and at what I rejoice as most favorable to the country, party and sectional feelings, immerged in a liberal and enlightened regard to the general concerns of the nation – such, are the favorable circumstances under which we are now deliberating. Thus situated, to what can we direct our resources and attention more important than internal improvements? What can add more to the wealth, the strength, and the political prosperity of our country? The manner, in which facility and cheapness of intercourse adds to the wealth of a nation, has been so often and ably discussed by writers on political economy, that I presume the House to be perfectly acquainted with the subject. It is sufficient to observe, that every branch of national industry, agricultural, manufacturing and commercial, is greatly stimulated and rendered by it more productive. The result is, that it tends to diffuse universal opulence. It gives to the interior the advantages possessed by the parts most eligibly situated for trade. It makes the country price, whether in the sale of raw products, or in the purchase of the articles for consumption, approximate to that of the commercial towns. In fact, if we look into the nature of wealth we will find, that nothing can be more favorable to its growth, than good roads and canals ... Let it not be said that internal improvement may be wholly left to the enterprise of the states and of individuals. I know, that much may justly be expected to be done by them; but in a country so new, and so extensive as ours, there is room enough, for all the general and state governments and individuals, in which to exert their resources. But many of the improvements contemplated are on too great a scale for the resources of the states or individuals; and many of such a nature, that the rival jealousy of the states, if left alone, might prevent. They require the resources and the general superintendence of this government to effect and complete them. But there are higher and more powerful considerations why Congress ought to take charge of this subject. If we were only to consider the pecuniary advantages of a good system of roads and canals; it might indeed admit of some doubt whether they out not to be left wholly to individual exertions; but when we come to consider how intimately the strength and political prosperity of the republic are connected with this subject, we find the most urgent reasons why we should apply our resources to them. In many respects, no country of equal population and wealth, possesses equal materials of power with ours. The people, in muscular power, in hardy and enterprising habits, and in lofty and gallant courage, are surpassed by none. In one respect, and, in my opinion, in one only, are we materially weak.

We occupy a surface prodigiously great in proportion of our numbers. The common strength is brought to bear with great difficulty on the point that may be menaced by an enemy. It is our duty, then, as far as in the nature of things it can be effected, to counteract this weakness. Good roads and canals, judiciously laid out, are the proper remedy. In the recent war, how much did we suffer for the want of them? Beside the tardiness and the consequential inefficacy of our military movements, to what an increased expense was the country put for the article of transportation alone? In the event of another war, the saving in this particular, would go far towards indemnifying us for the expence of construction the means of transportation ...

... We are great, and rapidly, I was about to say, fearfully growing. This is our pride and our danger, our weakness and our strength. Little does he deserve to be intrusted with the liberties of this people, who does not raise his mind to these truths. We are under the most imperious obligation to counteract every tendency to disunion. The strongest of all cements is, undoubtedly, the wisdom, justice, and, above all, the moderation of this House; yet the greatest subject on which we are now deliberating, in this respect, deserves the most serious consideration. Whatever impedes the intercourse of the extremes with this, the centre of the republic, weakens the union. The more enlarged the sphere of commercial circulation, the more extended that of social intercourse; the more strongly we are bound together, the more inseparable are our destinies. Those who understand the human heart best, know how powerfully distance tends to break the sympathies of our nature. Nothing, not even dissimilarity of language, tends more to estrange man from man. Let us then bind the republic together with a perfect system of roads and canals. Let us conquer space. It is thus the most distant part of the republic will be brought within a few days' travel of the centre; it is thus that a citizen of the west will read the news of Boston still moist from the press.

The mail and the press are the nerves of the body politic. By them the slightest impression made on the most remote part, is communicated to the whole system; and the more perfect the means of transportation, the more rapid and true the vibration. To aid us in this great work, to maintain the integrity of this republic, we inhabit a country presenting the most admirable advantages. Belted around, as it is, by lakes and oceans, inter-sected in every direction by bays and rivers, the hand of industry and art is tempted to improvement. So situated, blessed with a form of government at once combining liberty and strength, we may reasonably raise our eyes to the most splendid future, if we only act in a manner worthy of our advantages. If, however, neglecting them, we permit a low, sordid, selfish, and sectional spirit to take possession of this House, this happy scene will vanish. We will divide, and, in its consequences, will follow misery and despotism. ...

2. The American Colonization Society Appeals to Congress, 1820[2]

During the Early Republic, the idea of "colonization" became an early, if rather conservative, plan to undermine slavery. After slaves became free through sale or voluntary manumission, advocates of colonization maintained that free African-Americans could not assimilate into white society and needed to be repatriated to Africa. In 1816, advocates of this type of anti-slavery founded the American Colonization Society (ACS). Five years later, the ACS founded a colony on the west coast of Africa that they named Monrovia, after President James Monroe, a prominent member of the ACS. In this petition to Congress, the ACS outlines its position on the "problem" of free African-Americans and cites the positive impact of their colonization scheme on the suppression of the slave trade before asking for recognition and financial support from the federal government.

TO THE HONORABLE THE SENATE AND HOUSE OF
REPRESENTATIVES OF THE UNITED STATES.

The President and Board of Managers of the American Colonization Society, respectfully represent that, being about to commence the execution of an object to which their views have been long directed, they deem it proper and necessary to address themselves to the legislative council of their country. They trust that this object will be considered, in itself, of great national importance, will be found inseparably connected with another, vitally affecting the honor and interest of this nation, and leading, in its consequences, to the most desirable results ...

The last census shews the number of the free people of color of the United States, and their rapid increase. Supposing them to increase in the same ratio, it will appear how large a proportion of our population will, in the course of even a few years, consist of persons of that description.

No argument is necessary to shew that this is very far indeed from consti-tuting an increase of our physical strength; nor can there be a population, in any country, neutral as to its effects upon society. The least observation shews

[2]   *Memorial of the President and Board of Managers of the American Colonization Society,* 16th Cong., 1st Sess., H.Doc. 63, serial 35, February 3, 1820.

that this description of persons are not, and cannot be, either useful or happy among us; and many considerations, which need not be mentioned, prove, beyond dispute, that it is best, for all the parties interested, that there should be a separation; that those who are now free, and those who may become so hereafter, should be provided with the means of attaining to a state of respectability and happiness, which, it is certain, they have never yet reached, and, therefore, can never be likely to reach in this country.

Several of the States, deeply interested in this subject, have already applied to the general government; and, concurring in the views of your memorialists, both from the considerations of justice towards themselves and humanity towards the colored people, have expressed, to the general government, their desire that a country should be procured for them, in the land of their forefathers, to which such of them, as should choose to avail themselves of the opportunity, might be removed. It has been the one single object of the Society, which your memorialists represent, to effect this end. They have made the most cautious and particular inquiries, as to the practicability of such a plan and its prospects of success, both in this country and in Africa, and they are warranted in declaring, that there are no difficulties which they do not confidently expect will be easily overcome by a moderate exertion of discretion and perseverance ...

No nation has it so much in its power to furnish proper settlers for such an establishment as this; no nation has so deep an interest in thus disposing of them. By the law passed at the last session, and before referred to, the captives who may be taken by our cruisers, from the slave ships, are to be taken to Africa, and delivered to the custody of agents appointed by the President. There will then be a settlement of captured negroes upon the coast, in consequence of the measures already adopted. And it is evidently most important, if not necessary, to such a settlement, that the civilized people of color, of this country, whose industry, enterprise, and knowledge of agriculture, and the arts, would render them most useful assistants, should be connected with such an establishment.

When, therefore, the object of the Colonization Society is viewed, in connection with that entire suppression of the slave trade, which your memorialists trust it is resolved shall be effected, its importance becomes obvious and extreme. The beneficial consequences resulting from success in such a measure, it is impossible to calculate. To the general cause of humanity, it will afford the most rich and noble contribution, and for the nation that regards that cause, that employs its power in its behalf, it cannot fail to procure a proportionate reward. It is by such a course that a nation secures to itself the protection and favor of the Governor of the world. Nor are there wanting views and considerations, arising from our peculiar political institutions, which would justify the sure expectation of the most signal blessings to ourselves from the accomplishment of such an object. If one of these consequences shall be the gradual, and almost imperceptible, removal of a national evil, which all unite in lamenting, and, for which, with the most intense, but hitherto hopeless anxiety, the patriots and statesmen of our country have labored to discover a remedy, who can doubt, that, of all the blessings we may be permitted to bequeath to our descendants, this will receive the richest tribute of their thanks and veneration? ...

3. Maine Answers the "Missouri Question," 1820[3]

When Missouri petitioned for statehood in 1819, it threatened the delicate political balance between the existing 11 slave and 11 free states. Although it had been a slaveholding territory, New York Representative James Tallmadge offered an amendment to the legislation admitting Missouri to the Union only if a plan of gradual emancipation was included in the package. That particular initiative failed, but the controversy over Missouri's admission raged in Washington, signaling a severe division between southern and northern delegations. "But this momentous question," former president Thomas Jefferson wrote in 1820, "like a fire bell in the night, awakened and filled me with terror. I considered it at once as the knell of the Union." Eventually cooler heads prevailed and the so-called "Missouri Compromise" joined together that state's admission as a slave state, a ban on slavery in the territories north of Missouri's southern boundary (the 36° 30' north latitude), and the admission of Maine as a free state. The immediate political crisis was averted, yet some lingering resentment toward the extension of the slavery question remained in both northern and southern circles. In this poem, an anti-slavery author expresses his dissatisfaction with Maine's unintentional partnership with Missouri in cooling sectional tensions in 1820.

MAINE NOT TO BE COUPLED WITH THE MISSOURI QUESTION

IF the South will not yield, to the West it be known,
That Maine will declare for a *King* of her own;
And *three hundred thousand* of freemen demand
The justice bestow'd on each State in the land.

---

[3]   Timothy Claimright, *Maine Not To Be Coupled with the Missouri Question* (Brunswick, ME, n.p., 1820). From the Library of Congress Ephemera Collection.

Free whites of the East are not blacks of the West,
And Republican souls on this principle rest,
That if no respect to their rights can be shown,
They know how to vindicate what are their own.
Their patriot zeal has been ever express'd;
Their enterprize, Europe has often confess'd. –
They are founded on freedom, humanity's right,
Ordained by God against slavery to fight.
And Heaven born liberty sooner than yield,
The whites of Missouri shall dress their own field.
We are hardy and healthy, can till our own soil,
In labour delight; make a pleasure of toil.
They spurn at our climate; yet live in a bog:
We enjoy fair, cold weather; they grope in a fog.
We fly in our sleighs; they wallow in mire,
O'erwhelmed with musquitoes; we sing by our fire.
We have port and potatoes, fish, mutton, and beef;
Fill'd with agues, to physic, they fly for relief.
They too lazy to work, drive slaves, whom they fear;
We school our own children and brew our own beer.
We do a day's work and go fearless to bed;
Tho' lock'd up, they dream of slaves, who they dread.
We have learn'd too much wisdom to emigrate west,
As poor souls returning, too well can attest.
We this principle hold, as fixed, as fate,
Independent of them, *we will be a State*. –
While we sail in fine ships, they paddle a float,
The best of their navy a flat bottom'd boat.
A bushel of corn they often are glad
To exchange for a cod, or poor shotten shad:
And without their slaves, how long would it take
To shell corn enough to purchase one hake?
We have coffee and salt and tea the year round;
Six bushels of corn, they must pay for a pound.
By sea and by land never idle or stingy,
Our houses are fill'd with the products of India.
And if a cold season, we all have a notion,
John Codline will bring us a fish from the ocean.
While we grant they can live on lean smok'd hams,
We fear not starvation on lobsters and clams.
Our bays are alive with geese, ducks, and widgeons,
And every scarce year our woods swarm with pigeons.

They may boast of fine pastures as much as they please,
But we stand unrival'd in butter and cheese.
They may boast of their blacks; we boast of our plenty,
And swear to be free, eighteen hundred and twenty.
South and West, now be honest, to MAINE give her due,
If you call her a child, she's an Hercules too.
A Sister in Union, admit her as free;
To be coupled with slaves, she will never agree.

TIMOTHY CLAIMRIGHT
Brunswick, Jan. 1820

Discussion Questions

1. Would you say that the average American in 1819 would be optimistic or
    pessimistic about the nation's future? How do the documents from 1819 use
    humor to get their argument across? Do you think this is an effective technique?
2. Compare John C. Calhoun's call for a federal system of internal improvements
    with the poem about banks from the Panic of 1819. What do these documents
    tell us about the American economy in the postwar years? How does Calhoun
    combine patriotism with economic growth?
3. Using the two documents dealing with the slave question in this chapter,
    what would you say are the major concerns of anti-slavery Americans in 1820?
    Do they contain a moral, political, or economic indictment of slavery? How do
    you think a slaveholder would respond to either document?
4. What do the documents in Part III reveal about the role of government in the
    lives of Americans during the Early Republic? Do you think that they portray
    government as an active or passive force? Do they reveal a faith in the ability
    of public institutions to effect positive change?

Part IV   The Work of a New Republic

Introduction to Part IV

In the decades following the War of 1812, the United States began to expand in a number of areas. The physical boundaries of the nation remained the same, but travel became easier as turnpikes and canals transformed muddy roads and shallow waterways into vibrant avenues of commerce. The advent of better transportation routes helped kick-start an economy that had been in limbo since the crippling British blockade during the war. Americans had always worked hard in the home and in the fields; now they added a new category of factory labor into the mix. With the growth of travel, commerce, and industry, the population of cities swelled to unprecedented numbers. To be sure, older places like Boston, New York City, Philadelphia, and Baltimore remained at the forefront of urban development. But the cities of the West like Cincinnati, St. Louis, and New Orleans allowed urbanization to occur in the nation's interior during the Early Republic. The ways in which Americans of all classes, colors, and creeds responded to these new developments varied, and one thing was certain: the nation would never be the same again.

Chapter 8   A Nation on the Move

1. A Western Editor Endorses "Old Hickory," June 14, 1824[1]

*With the demise of the Federalist Party in the wake of the War of 1812,
the Republican Party stood virtually unchallenged in national politics.
The method of selecting presidential nominees in this one-party system was
a caucus composed of the sitting Republicans in Congress. Known as "King
Caucus," this system rewarded political connections and maneuvering more
than it selected candidates for their popular appeal. James Monroe of Virginia
easily won two terms with the backing of the caucus – in 1820 he ran
practically unopposed. But broader suffrage laws in the states and growing
discontent with "King Caucus" eroded support for this undemocratic
nomination method. In 1824 two-thirds of the Republican caucus announced
that they would not attend the meeting and no single Republican candidate
emerged. Andrew Jackson, the hero of the Battle of New Orleans and a
symbol of the growing political power of western and southern states, was
among the many potential candidates, as was John C. Calhoun, now President
Monroe's Secretary of War. After a pivotal state convention in Pennsylvania,
however, Calhoun became Jackson's vice-presidential candidate. One of
Calhoun's most stalwart western supporters, Duff Green of St. Louis,
followed him into the Jackson camp. The following editorial from Green's
St. Louis Enquirer emphasizes the popular support for Jackson and the
rejection of an elite political culture. Duff Green rode his support of
Jackson all the way back east to Washington DC where he edited a
pro-Jackson newspaper entitled* The United States Telegraph, *and helped*

---

[1]   *St. Louis Enquirer,* June 14, 1824.

*elect "Old Hickory" to the White House in 1828. They eventually had a major
fallout, but not before Green had helped usher in a new era of partisan politics
that would transform the American electoral landscape.*

All who profess to know any thing of legislation, admit the great bearing
which executive influence has on matters pending before Congress. Having
convinced ourselves, that a revision of the Tariff and a system of internal
improvement were essential to our national prosperity, it was natural for us
to prefer a candidate for the Presidency whose identity with those interests,
and whose prospect of success justified the union of those favorable to them
in his support – In addition to considerations growing out of the early stand,
taken in behalf of these great principles of national policy, and his preeminent qualifications and public services, we found Mr. Calhoun the advocate
of measures which involved the prosperity of Missouri. His able reports on
the Indian affairs gave testimony of his intimate knowledge of our interests,
and a wish to secure them; we did not hesitate to declare our preference for
him as a candidate for Presidency. This preference was natural & grew out
of his public acts.

The nomination of Gen. Jackson for President, and Mr. Calhoun for Vice
President, by the people of Pennsylvania, has arranged Mr. Calhoun from
the list of candidates – this was consistent with the principle upon which
their friends had always acted; the Presidency was "neither to be sought nor
rejected." The question was before the people, and to them it was always
submitted. That a large majority of the friends of Mr. Calhoun, should unite
in support of Gen. Jackson, was to be expected for the most obvious of
reasons; they, acting upon principle, were willing to give up their preference
for men, to secure the great interests involved. The growing popularity of
Gen. Jackson and his known opinions on these great questions produced a
simultaneous expression of public sentiment in his favor. Our preference
for him is induced by the same reasons, and avowed with the same frank-
ness that governed our support for Mr. Calhoun. – We have no personal
acquaintance with him – we have no favored friend to introduce us in case of
his election, nor have we any thing to hope individually by his promotion –
nor have the great mass of the people among whom his warm supporters are
to be found. It is the people, who pay the taxes and fight for the country,
who support him; the regulars of Wellington scoffed at the *raw militia*,
placed as a guard for the beauty and booty of New Orleans; and some of the
regulars of King Caucus, scoff at those raw politicians who now dare to
place themselves under the banners of the same General, to guard our
constitution and perpetuate our liberties. Our course has been consistent;

we shall persevere; we have the people for our support, & will not swerve from our duty for fear of consequences. Our adversaries have been liberal in their abuse, not only of us but of those who think with us and are disposed to act in concern with us. Such insinuations will recoil with redoubled force on their authors.

2. The Erie Canal Hits the American Stage, 1830[2]

When New York's mayor, DeWitt Clinton, proposed that the State of New York construct a canal linking the Hudson River to the Great Lakes in 1817, critics derisively called it "Clinton's Big Ditch." Despite the skeptics, New York completed the Erie Canal in 1825. It was the most expensive public works project in the nation's brief history, but also one of the most celebrated. Travel times and shipping costs plummeted. Older states like Pennsylvania and Virginia rushed to produce statewide public works projects and even relative newcomers like Ohio and Indiana fell to the "canal mania" by the 1830s. William Dunlap immortalized the project in 1830 by writing a drama to accompany a massive moving diorama of various scenes along the Hudson and the Erie Canal. Dunlap's play, A Trip to Niagara, was written explicitly for the famous Bowery Theater in New York City. There is little action or plot in A Trip to Niagara. Instead, the characters representing various nationalities comment on the scenery – in this case the moving diorama – and the import of the Erie Canal. Rough, stereotypical dialects of "Dutch" (German), Irish, and French accents abound in the play. One character goes by the sobriquet "John Bull," but in this particular scene he is disguised as a local, or "Yankee" native. Although confusing and arcane to modern ears, contemporary audiences would have found the various caricatures both familiar and humorous.

SCENE 4.

The little falls of the Mohawk. A view of the stupendous rocks, through which the river flows. A part of the town. The canal and the aqueduct crossing the river. Enter WENTWORTH, AMELIA, and other travelers. Travelers pass over the stage, and go off.

---

[2] William Dunlap, *A Trip to Niagara: or, Travellers in America. A Farce, in Three Acts* (New York: E.B. Clayton, 1830), pp. 42–7.

Ame: This is delightful, brother.

Went: Is it?

Ame: The opportunity we so frequently have, of stepping from the canal-boat, and thus walking on the bank, adds to the pleasure derived from the ever changing scenery that is presented to us.

Went: Pleasure! To be dragged along upon a muddy ditch, hour after hour, in constant dread of lifting your head above your knees for fear of having it knock'd off your shoulders by a bridge!

Ame: But your head is safe, now, nothwithstanding the Frenchman's razor, and the canal bridges, and you must admire this great patriotic work – this union of the inland seas with the Atlantic Ocean.

Went: What is this, to the work of the Duke of Bridgewater.

Ame: Let praise be given, where praise is due. There are two names, which will live in the memories of Americans, as long as they can appreciate the blessings that flow in a rapid interchange of every good from one extreme of their republic to the other. Fulton and Clinton. And I hope that the gratitude of their countrymen, will not only be shown to their names and memories, but to their children, and their children's children.

Went: Where's Doolittle? I begin to like that fellow. He sees things as I do.

Ame: We left him talking with a Dutchman. Here he comes.

Enter BULL as JONATHAN

Bull: What do you think that tarnation Mohawk Dutchman says?

Went: Praises the great canal, I suppose.

Bull: No. He says, "Effer since Glinton gut de pig canawl, de peef ant putter of de Sharmanflats ave falt fifty bur shent: ant dey pring all de tam dings to New-York, all de vay from Puffalo, ant de tuyvil knows vere."

Ame: Ha, ha, ha! Fault finding every where. Brother, I will walk on. [*Exit Amelia*]

Went: I dare say he is right. But Mr. Doolittle, when shall we get to the wilderness?

Bull: Ah, that's what every body says. But these curst creatures have spoilt all that. What with their turnpike roads, and canals, they have gone, like tarnal fools as they are, and put towns and villages, gardens and orchards, churches and schools, and sich common things, where the woods and wild beasts and Indians and rattle-snakes ought to have ben. Shall I tell you what my uncle Ben said?

Den: [Without.] Stop a bit Mr. Wintwort! Stop a bit.

Bull: He thinks the yellow fever is at his heels.

Enter DENNIS

Den: Ah! Sure enough it is you! I've cotch you at least! And now I may fale safe again, any how!

Went: Safe! why, what has happened?

Den: Why you know the *first* time I came with you, I came *last*, and I didn't come at all you know *before*, becase the boat left me *behind*.

Bull: So, you came *first* at *last*, *after* all; and you didn't come at all, because you were *behind before*.

Den: That's it. [*To Wentworth*.] Who may this civil, *clare-spoken* gentleman be?

Went: Mr. Doolittle. One of the natives of this country. A Yankee.

Den: O! a Yankee. You nivver have the faver among yoursilves, you natives, but only kape it for us of the ould country.

Bull: Now, you, I wonder how we should keep it if we never have it? That would be cute – I guess.

Den: I thought, once, I would be made a native myseif, that I might be safe.

Went: But you were born in Ireland, you know.

Den: What signifies *that*? And haven't I seen Irishmen all the way as I came along, and they told me they were made natives. But, now, how could you lave me Mr. Wintwort?

Went: I thought we had lost you, friend.

Den: Not at all; it was I lost my passage. But I wouldn't be left any more, any how, and so I went aboard of the nixt boat that wint off, thinking I would catch you, but she happend to go t'other way, and where do you think they took me to, of all places in the world?

Went: That I can't tell.

Den: How should you, if you don't know? Will then, they carried me to the place where they put all the yellow faver people at, I suppose to keep one another in countenance.

Bull: What? To the quarantine ground!

Den: That's it. "What place is that?" says I. "It's the hospital for the faver," says he. "And sure you wouldn't put me there?" says I. "That's as you like," says he. "The divvil a bit of like, nor will I go ashore at all." And so I wouldn't till they brought me back again to York.

Bull: That was a Yankee trick. What them there sarpents call a joke.

Went: So you went ashore at York?

Den: I did. But not on the land. I went ashore on the river. I landed on a boat, for I took up my board and lodging in the stame-boat for Albany; and I made sure to get a bert in the fore-castle, that I mightn't be behind all this long way.

Went: And so followed me all this long way?

Den: That I did. For I thought that you would be the most likely way to overtake you. And I thought I would have your protection, sure I would, 'till I get safe into his Majesty's dominions. And I axt for you at Albany, and they said you had gone on up the canal.

Went: They remembered me?

Den: Yes. Says they. "The man that grumbles at every thin." "That's Mr. Wintwort," says I.

Bull: I told you what the Yankees were.

Den: So, by the powers, I've been riding in a boat behind tree horses a day and night to catch you – and here your are going a fut all the time.

Went: Our boat is ahead.

Den: Then you are behind this time.

Bull: See, Mister, what ignorant creeturs these Yankees are [*Points to a sign by a hovel of a tavern.*] T.R.O.F. for horses to drink out of.

Den: Sure enough. And they might be so azily spelt it right, by only putting another *ef* at the end.

Bull: True. I see you are a scholar.

Den: I was once – when I was a little boy.

Went: But, Dennis, my good fellow, you must want money by this time, after traveling so far.

Den: O fait the stame-boat was chape enough, any how; and when I came to the canal, I work'd my passage.

Went: Work'd your passage?

Den: Yes. It was my own proposal. For I found my dollars grow light. "Work your passage, Pat," says a civil man, like that gentleman, [pointing to Bull,] laughing all the time. "You are the man I want," says he. "That's what they all say," says I. So I went on board, and when the boat started again, they put me ashore to lade the horses.

Bull: Yankee, again, forever!

Went: And you walk'd all the way before the horses?

Den: I'll tell you. "Pat, how do you like sailing in the canal-boat?" says the civil grinning gentleman, like that [pointing to Bull.] "Fait," says I, "if it was not for the name of the thing, I'm thinking I might as well be walking a fut."

Bull: Ha, ha, ha! and what said the Yankee?

Den:	"Stip aboard," says he, "and take some bafe and whiskey; you shall work the rest of your passage wid your tathe."
Bull:	Well done, both Pat and Yankee! I see the boat is crossing the river on that unnatural thingumbob they call an aqueduct; and if we don't hurry a bit, we shall be left.
Den:	Lift in this place! it would be horrible!
Bull:	Wouldn't it [*Exeunt – while the canal-boat is seen crossing the river on the aqueduct.*]

3. An Englishwoman Remembers Her First Illinois Winter, 1848[3]

By 1830, the population of the United States had reached 12.7 million. Although some of this increase was due to the nation's high birth rate, European immigration accounted for a great deal of the growth in the Old Northwest. As Native American resistance to white settlement waned in the years following the War of 1812, more and more settlers flowed in to new states like Ohio, Indiana, and Illinois. Illinois saw migrants flow in from the Erie Canal into the Great Lakes and others steamed up the Mississippi to settle its western counties. As a result, the population of Illinois nearly tripled from 1820 to 1830. Edward and Rebecca Burlend were tenant farmers who migrated to the United States from rural Yorkshire in 1831. They immediately settled into their homestead in Pike County in western Illinois. The description of their first winter there is told from Rebecca's perspective, but was transcribed and edited by her husband, Edward, in the 1848 pamphlet entitled A True Picture of Emigration: Or Fourteen Years in the Interior of North America.

During the time we were at lodgings we had felt ourselves dependent, and looked forward with anxious expectation to the time when we might again taste the sweets and independence of home, and those enjoyments which are only to be expected at one's fireside. That period had now arrived. We had indeed a house such as I have already described, but we had no furniture except two large boxes, two beds, and a few pots and cooking utensils; besides, our provisions were just finished. Till this time we had been using principally the remains of biscuits, &c., purchased at New Orleans. The

---

[3] Rebecca and Edward Burlend, *A True Picture of Emigration: Or Fourteen Years in the Interior of North America* (London: G. Berger, 1848), pp. 24–6, 28–30.

first wants of nature must be first attended to: whether we had a chair to sit on or not, something to eat we must have. Our nearest neighbor lived about a half-a-mile from us, and we were at least two miles and a-half from any place at which flour was sold; thither, however, my husband went, and as our money was growing scarce, he bought a bushel of ground Indian corn, which was only one-third the price of wheaten flour; it was there sold for thirty cents a bushel. Its taste is not pleasant to persons unaccustomed to it; but as it is wholesome food, it is much used for making bread. We had now some meal, but no yeast, nor an oven; we were therefore obliged to make sad paste, and bake it on our frying pan on some hot ashes. We procured a little milk of our nearest neighbor, Mr. Paddock, which, on account of the severe frosts that prevail in Illinois, we generally received in lumps of ice.

Thus we lived the first few weeks at our new estate. Hasty pudding, sad bread, and a little venison which we had left, were our ordinary food. The greater part of my husband's time was spent in cutting and preparing wood for our fires. About this time we made further purchases of a cow and calf, for which we paid fourteen dollars, a young mare, which cost us twenty dollars, two pigs, and a shallow flat-bottomed iron pan, with a cover to it, to bake in. This is the common, and indeed the only kind of oven used in Illinois. It is vulgarly called a skellit. To make it hot it is immersed in glowing embers, the lid is then removed till the dough is put in; it is then replaced and ashes again thrown over it, till the cake is baked. Hence it will be perceived that a quantity of bread beforehand is unknown in Illinois: their custom is to bake a cake to each meal, which is generally very good; eggs and milk being so plentiful, are regularly used in their bread, along with a little celeratus to lighten it, whereby it becomes very rich and nutritive.

The Illinois settlers live somewhat differently from the English peasantry; the former have only three meals a-day, and not much variety in them: bread, butter, coffee, and bacon, are always brought to the table, but fresh meat is a rarity, and is never obtained as in England by going to a butcher for it. In Illinois the farmers all kill their own cattle, and salt what is not used immediately; sometimes, however, they distribute portions among neighbors, with the view of receiving as much again when they kill theirs. It is by no means uncommon for an old settler to have a couple of fowls, ducks, a goose, or a turkey to dinner; and, generally speaking, everybody has plenty of plain good food ...

Nothing can be more beautiful than a field of Indian corn in full blossom, and perhaps nothing in nature displays the munificence of Providence more strikingly than this matchless plant. In order to supply our cattle with winter meat, we applied to Mr. Paddock, our nearest neighbor, who sold us part of a field unreaped; some of it we cut down and took home, the rest we allowed to stand and turned our cattle to it. The reader may think it strange that we should turn cattle into the fields in the depth of winter, especially as the winters are there more severe than in England; it is however the regular custom: the cattle are inured to it, as they are never kept up any part of the year, either day or night. The two pigs we had bought we were obliged to kill shortly after we purchased them, as we wanted them for our own use, and we wished to spare the small stock of Indian corn we had on hand. The reader must also know that our money was nearly done: I believe we had not more than four or five dollars remaining; part of it we were obliged to spend in sulphur, to cure what is called the Illinois mange, from which we were all suffering.

This complaint invariably attacks new settlers, shortly after their arrival, and is a complete scourge until it is removed. The body breaks out all over in little spots, attended with intolerable itching. It is generally attributed to the change of water, but as theirs possesses no peculiarity of taste, I cannot understand how that can be the cause. We were soon cured after using the sulphur, and never felt anything more of it.

We have already seen that considerable labour is required to prepare fuel, as a good fire in America is essential during the winter season. The frosts are intensely keen, a wide river is sometimes iced over in a single night, so as to be unnavigable. Every thing of a fluid nature, exposed to the weather, is formed into a solid. For two or three months the milk freezing as soon as it is taken from the cows, affords no cream, consequently no butter. It is nevertheless possible to obtain butter, by keeping the churn near the fire, and churning cream and milk both together; but as this method is exceedingly troublesome it is seldom practiced. The nights in winter are at once inexpressibly cold, and poetically fine. The sky is almost invariably clear, and the stars shine with a brilliancy entirely unknown in the humid atmosphere of England. Cold as it was, often did I, during the first winter, stand at the door of our cabin, admiring their luster and listening to the wolves, whose howlings, among the leafless woods at this season, are almost unceasing. These animals are numerous in America; and, unless the sheep be regularly folded, their depredations are extensively injurious, as they lacerate the throats of nearly all the flock; sometimes also they will seize young pigs, but as they fear the old ones, unless they are impelled by hunger, these animals are not much in danger. The timid submissive sheep is always their favorite prey. The reader will perceive we had not much intercourse with the rest of the world. For a while no one seemed to notice us, except Mr. B., our neighbor Mr. Paddock, and one Mr. Burns, who lived about two miles off (all are *Misters* in America.) ...

In this manner we spent our first winter; we had plenty of work; our amusements even tended to advantage. Great numbers of quails frequented our home-stead to feed on our small stock of Indian corn; we caught several of them with snares, which were excellent eating. My husband also shot a few rabbits, of which there are vast numbers in America. We likewise saw several deer, but as we had no rifle, we could not kill any. We observed several kinds of birds, which we had not before seen, one in particular, which we took to be a species of turkey, engaged our attention; my husband tried several times to kill one, without effect. One Saturday, however, he was successful, and brought home his game with as much apparent consciousness of triumph, as if he had slain some champion hydra of the forest. The following day we expected Mr. B., who by this time had received his money, to dine with us. We accordingly dressed our bird, and congratulated ourselves with the idea of having our countryman to dine with us on fine boiled turkey. Sunday morning arrived, and in due time our turkey was in the pot boiling for dinner. Mr. B. came; we told him how happy we were on account of the treat we were going to give him. He was surprised at our story, as those birds are difficult to obtain with a common fowling-piece, and desired to see the feet and head. But the moment he saw them, he exclaimed "it's a buzzard," a bird which, we subsequently learnt, gormandizes any kind of filth or carrion, and consequently is not fit to be eaten. We were sorely disappointed; our turkey was hoisted in the yard, and we were obliged to be contented with a little bacon, and a coarse Indian corn pudding, for which our stomachs were not altogether unprepared, although recently in anticipation of more sumptuous fare. The reader may think we were stupid not to know a turkey; the bird in question is very much like one, and indeed on that account is called in Illinois a turkey-buzzard.

As spring approached we felt some symptoms of those hopes which had animated us in England with reference to our success as emigrants . . .

4. Charles Ball Describes Moving in the Slave Trade, 1837[4]

Not all movement in the growing United States was voluntary. The internal slave trade boomed during the 1830s, as new states like Alabama, Mississippi, and Louisiana absorbed 288,000 slaves into their growing cotton plantations. The slave trade destroyed one-half of antebellum slave families. Slaves sold

[4]   Charles Ball, *Slavery in the United States: A Narrative of the Life and Adventures of Charles Ball, A Black Man* (New York: John S. Taylor, 1837), pp. 83–5, 92–3, 99–102.

"down the river" to Louisiana endured the long journey by ship or overland by
"coffle" to the massive market in New Orleans. Once there, they were put on
the auction block and sold to the highest bidder. Most of what we know about
the experience of moving in this trade comes from the narratives written by
ex-slaves following their escape. The following account comes from Charles
Ball, a slave sold away from his mother at an early age, raised in Maryland,
and then sold away from his own wife and children to Georgia as an adult.
Ball eventually escaped slavery, but his narrative written in 1837 describes the
experience of traveling through South Carolina in the internal slave trade
during the early years of its growth.

... It was manifest, that I was now in a country, where the life of a black man was no more regarded than that of an ox, except as far as the man was worth the more money in the market. On all the plantations that we passed, there was a want of live stock of every description, except slaves, and they wore deplorably abundant.

The fields were destitute of every thing that deserved the name of grass, and not a spear of clover was anywhere visible. The few cattle that existed, were browsing on the boughs of the trees, in the woods. Every thing betrayed a scarcity of the means of supplying the slaves, who cultivated the vast cotton-fields, with a sufficiency of food. We travelled this day more than thirty miles, and crossed the Catawba river in the afternoon, on the bottoms of which I saw, for the first time, fields of rice, growing in swamps, covered with water. Causeways were raised through the low-lands in which the rice grew, and on these, the road was formed on which we travelled. These rice-fields, or rather swamps, had, in my eyes, a beautiful appearance. The rice was nearly two feet in height above the water, and of a vivid green colour, covering a large space, of at least a hundred acres. Had it not been for the water, which appeared stagnant and sickly, and swarmed with frogs and thousands of snakes, it would have been as fine a sight as one need wish to look upon. After leaving the low grounds along the river, we again entered plantations of cotton, which lined the roads on both sides, relieved, here and there, by corn-fields, and potato-patches. We stopped for the night at a small tavern, and our master said we were within a day's journey of Columbia.

We here, again, received boiled rice for supper, without salt, or any kind of seasoning; a pint was allotted to each person, which we greedily devoured, having had no dinner to-day, save an allowance of corn-cakes, with the fat of about five pounds of bacon, extracted by frying, in which we dipped our bread. I slept soundly after this day's march, the fatigues of the body having, for once, overcome the agitations of the mind. The next day, which was, if my recollection is accurate, the ninth of June, was the last of our journey before our company separated; and we were on the road before the stars had disappeared from the sky. Our breakfast, this morning, consisted of bacon soup, a dish composed of corn meal, boiled in water, with a small piece of bacon to give the soup a taste of meat. For dinner we had boiled Indian peas, with a small allowance of bacon. This was the first time that we had received two rations of meat in the same day, on the whole journey, and some of our party were much surprised at the kindness of our master; but I had no doubt that his object was to make us look fat and hearty, to enable him to obtain better prices for us at Columbia ...

Throughout the whole journey, until after we were released from our irons, he had forbidden us to converse together beyond a few words in relation to our temporary condition and wants; and as he was with us all day, and never slept out of hearing of us at night, he rigidly enforced his edict of silence. I presume that the reason of this prohibition of all conversation, was to prevent us from devising plans of escape; but he had imposed as rigid a silence on himself as was enforced upon us; and after having passed from Maryland to South Carolina, in his company, I knew no more of my master, than, that he knew how to keep his secrets, guard his slaves, and make a close bargain. I had never heard him speak of his home or family; and therefore had concluded that he was an unmarried man, and an adventurer, who felt no more attachment for one place than another, and whose residence was not very well settled; but, from the large sums of money which he must have been able to command and carry with him to the north, to enable him to purchase so large a number of slaves, I had no doubt that he was a man of consequence and consideration in the place from whence he came.

In Maryland, I had always observed that men, who were the owners of large stocks of negroes, were not averse to having publicity given to their names; and that the possession of this species of property even there, gave its owner more vanity and egotism, than fell to the lot of the holders of any other kind of estate; and in truth, my subsequent experience proved, that without the possession of slaves, no man could ever arrive at, or hope to rise to any honourable station in society; – yet, my master seemed to take no pride in having at his disposal the lives of so many human beings. He never spoke to us in words of either pity or hatred; and never spoke of us, except to order us to be fed or watered, as he would have directed the same offices to be performed for so many horses, or to inquire where the best prices could be obtained for us. He regarded us only as objects of traffic and the materials of his commerce; and although he had lived several years in Carolina and Georgia, and had there exercised the profession of an overseer, he regarded the southern planters as no less the subjects of trade and speculation, than the slaves he sold to them . . .

We had no beds of any kind to sleep on, but each one was provided with a blanket, which had been the companion of our travels. We were left entirely at liberty to go out or in when we pleased, and no watch was kept over us either by night or day.

Our master had removed us so far from our native country, that he supposed it impossible for any of us ever to escape from him, and surmount all the obstacles that lay between us and our former homes. He went away immediately after we were established in our new lodgings, and remained absent until the second evening about sundown, when he returned, came into our shed, sat down on a block of wood in the midst of us, and asked if any one had been sick; if we had got our clothes clean; and if we had been supplied with an allowance of rice, corn, and butter. After satisfying himself upon these points, he told us that we were now at liberty to run away if we chose to do so; but if we made the attempt we should most certainly be re-taken, and subjected to the most terrible punishment. "I never flog," said he, "My practice is to *cat-haul*; and if you run away, and I catch you again – as I surely shall do – and give you one cat-hauling, you will never run away again, nor attempt it." I did not then understand the import of cat-hauling, but in after times, became well acquainted with its signification.

We remained in this place nearly two weeks, during which time our allowance of food was not varied, and was regularly given to us. We were not required to do any work; and I had liberty and leisure to walk about the plantation, and make such observations as I could upon the new state of things around me. Gentlemen and ladies came every day to look at us, with a view of becoming our purchasers; and we were examined with minute care as to our ages, former occupations, and capacity of performing labour. Our persons were inspected, and more especially the hands were scrutinized, to see if all the fingers were perfect, and capable of the quick motions necessary in picking cotton. Our master only visited us once a day, and sometimes he remained absent two days; so that he seldom met any of those who came to see us; but, whenever it so happened that he did meet them, he laid aside his silence and became very talkative, and even animated in his conversation, extolling our good qualities, and averring that he had purchased some of us of one colonel, and others of another general in Virginia; that he could by no means have procured us, had it not been that, in some instances, our masters had ruined themselves, and were obliged to sell us to save their families from ruin; and in others, that our owners were dead, their estates deeply in debt, and we had been sold at public sale; by which means he had become possessed of us. He said our habits were unexceptionable, our characters good, and that there was not one amongst us all who had ever been known to run away, or steal any thing from our former masters. I observed that running away, and stealing from his master, were regarded as the highest crimes of which a slave could be guilty; but I heard no questions asked concerning our propensity to steal from other people besides our masters, and I afterwards learned, that this was not always regarded as a very high crime by the owner of a slave, provided he would perpetrate the theft, so adroitly as not to be detected in it ...

Chapter 9   Work at Home, Factory, and Field

1. Lydia Maria Child on the Family Economy and Soapmaking, 1830[1]

Although it was only sporadically rewarded with cash payment, women's labor in the household provided the economic foundation for American families in the Early Republic. In many rural households, for example, women worked to provide food, clothing, and shelter for their families and also produced goods such as cheese, canned preserves, millinery, and garments in exchange for cash. Despite the proscriptive literature that increasingly described men as living in the rough-and-tumble political and business world and women residing in the more placid "domestic" sphere, women's labor was ubiquitous in the Early Republic. Even middle-class families that could ostensibly afford this gendered division of labor relied upon the work of women for survival. In these two selections from her 1830 guide to household management entitled The Frugal Housewife, *Lydia Maria Child offers both a theoretical approach to domestic economy and some more concrete tips on how to manufacture an essential commodity, soap, in the home. As such, it provides a strong reminder of how much mental and physical labor was required of women during this time.*

---

[1] Lydia Maria Child, *The Frugal Housewife: Dedicated to Those Who Are Not Ashamed of Economy* (Boston: Carter and Hendee, 1830), pp. 3–8, 24–5.

THE true economy of housekeeping is simply the art of gathering up all the fragments, so that nothing be lost. I mean fragments, of *time*, as well as *materials*. Nothing should be thrown away so long as it is possible to make any use of it, however trifling that use may be; and whatever be the size of a family, every member should be employed either in earning, or saving money.

"Time is money." For this reason, cheap as stockings are, it is good economy to knit them. Cotton and woollen yarn are both cheap; hose that are knit wear twice as long as woven ones; and they can be done at odd minutes of time, which would not be otherwise employed! Where there are children, or aged people, it is sufficient to recommend knitting that it is an *employment*.

In this point of view, patchwork is good economy. It is indeed a foolish waste of time to tear cloth into bits for the sake of arranging it anew in fantastic figures; but a large family may be kept out of idleness, and a few shillings saved by thus using scraps of gowns, curtains, &c.

In the country, where grain is raised, it is a good plan to teach children to prepare and braid straw for their own bonnets, and their brothers' hats.

Where turkeys and geese are kept, handsome feather fans may as well be made by the younger members of a family, as to be bought. The earlier children are taught to turn their faculties to some account, the better for them and for their parents.

In this country, we are apt to let children romp away their existence, till they get to be thirteen, or fourteen. This is not well. – It is not well for the purses and patience of parents; and it has a still worse effect on the morals and habits of the children. *Begin early* is the great maxim for everything in education. A child of six years old can be made useful; and should be taught to consider every day lost in which some little thing has not been done to assist others.

Children can very early be taught to take all the care of their own clothes.

They can knit garters, suspenders, and stockings; they can make patchwork and braid straw; they can make mats for the table, and mats for the floor; they can weed the garden, and pick cranberries from the meadow, to be carried to market.

Provided brothers and sisters go together, and are not allowed to go with bad children, it is a great deal better for the boys and girls on a farm to be picking blackberries at six cents a quart, than to be wearing out their clothes in useless play. They enjoy themselves just as well; and they are earning something to buy clothes, at the same time they are tearing them.

It is wise to keep an exact account of all you expend – even of a paper of pins. This answers two purposes; it makes you more careful in spending money; and it enables your husband to judge precisely whether his family live within his income. No false pride, or foolish ambition to appear as well as others, should ever induce a person to live one cent beyond the income of which he is certain. If you have two dollars a day, let nothing but sickness induce you to spend more than nine shillings; if you have one dollar a day, do not spend but seventy five cents; if you have half a dollar a day, be satisfied to spend forty cents.

To associate with influential and genteel people with an appearance of equality, unquestionably has its advantages; particularly where there is a family of sons and daughters just coming upon the theatre of life; but like all other external advantages, these have their proper price, and may be bought too dearly. They who never reserve a cent of their income, with which to meet any unforeseen calamity, "pay too dear for their whistle," whatever temporary benefits they may derive from society. Self-denial, in proportion to the narrowness of your income, will eventually be the happiest and most respectable course for you and yours. If you are prosperous, perseverance and industry will not fail to place you in such a situation as your ambition covets; and if you are not prosperous, it will be well for your children that they have not been educated to higher hopes than they will ever realize.

If you are about to furnish a house, do not spend all your money, be it much, or little. Do not let the beauty of this thing, and the cheapness of that, tempt you to buy unnecessary articles. Doctor Franklin's maxim was a wise one, "nothing is cheap that we do not want." Buy merely enough to get along with, at first. It is only by experience that you can tell what will be the wants of your family. If you spend all your money, you will find you have purchased many things you do not want, and have no means left to get many things, which you do want. If you have enough, and more than enough, to get everything suitable to your situation, do not think you must spend it all, merely because you happen to have it. Begin humbly. As riches increase, it is easy and pleasant to increase in hospitality and splendour; but it is always painful and inconvenient to decrease.

After all, these things are viewed in their proper light by the truly judicious and respectable. Neatness, tastefulness, and good sense, may be shown in the management of a small household, and the arrangement of a little furniture, as well as upon a larger scale; and these qualities are always praised, and always treated with respect and attention. The consideration which many purchase by living beyond their income, and of course living upon others, is not worth the trouble it costs. The glare there is about this false and wicked parade is deceptive; it does not in fact procure a man valuable friends, or extensive influence. More than that, it is wrong – morally wrong, so far as the individual is concerned; and injurious beyond calculation to the interests of our country. To what are the increasing beggary, and discouraged exertions of the present period owing? A multitude of causes have no doubt tended to increase the evil; but the root of the whole matter is the extravagance of all classes of people! We never shall be prosperous, till we make pride and vanity yield to the dictates of honesty and prudence! We never shall be free from embarrassment, until we cease to be ashamed of industry and economy! Let women do their share towards reformation – Let their fathers and husbands see them happy without finery; and if their husbands and fathers have (as is often the case) a foolish pride in seeing them decorated, let them gently and gradually check this feeling, by showing that they have better and surer means of commanding respect – Let them prove by the exertion of ingenuity and economy, that neatness, good taste, and gentility, are attainable without great expense ...

In early childhood, you lay the foundation of poverty or riches, in the habits you give your children. – Teach them to save everything, – not for their *own* use, for that would make them selfish – but for *some* use. Teach them to *share* everything with their playmates; but never allow them to *destroy* anything.

I once visited a family where the most exact economy was observed; yet nothing was mean, or uncomfortable. It is the character of true economy to be as comfortable and genteel with a little, as others can be with much. In this family, when the father brought home a package, the older children would, of their own accord, put away the paper and twine neatly, instead of throwing them in the fire, or tearing them to pieces. If the little ones wanted a piece of twine to play scratch-cradle, or spin a top, there it was, in readiness; and when they threw it upon the floor, the older children had no need to be told to put it again in its place.

The other day, I heard a mechanic say, "I have a wife and two little children; we live in a very small house; but, to save my life, I cannot spend less than twelve hundred a year." Another replied, "You are not economical; I spend but eight hundred." I thought to myself, – "Neither of you pick up your twine and paper." A third one, who was present, was silent; but after they were gone, he said, "I keep house, and comfortably too, with a wife and children, for six hundred a year; but I suppose they would have thought me mean, if I had told them so." I did not think him mean; it merely occurred to me that his wife and children were in the habit of picking up paper and twine.

Economy is generally despised as a low virtue, tending to make people ungenerous and selfish. This is true of avarice; but it is not so of economy.

The man who is economical, is laying up for himself the permanent power of being useful and generous. – He who thoughtlessly gives away ten dollars, when he owes a hundred more than he can pay, deserves no praise, – he obeys a sudden impulse, more like instinct than reason: it would be real charity to check this feeling; because the good he does may be doubtful, while the injury he does his family and creditors is certain. True economy is a careful treasurer in the service of benevolence; and where they are united, respectability, prosperity, and peace will follow ...

SOAP

In the city I believe it is better to exchange ashes and grease for soap; but in the country, I am certain it is good economy to make one's own soap. If you burn wood, you can make your own lye; but the ashes of coal is not worth much. Bore small holes in the bottom of a barrel, place four bricks around, and fill the barrel with ashes. Wet the ashes well, but not enough to drop; let it soak thus three or four days; then pour a gallon of water in every hour or two, for a day or more, and let it drop into a pail or tub beneath. Keep it dripping till the color of the lye shows the strength is exhausted. If your lye is not strong enough, you must fill your barrel with fresh ashes, and let the lye run through it. Some people take a barrel without any bottom, and lay sticks and straw across to prevent the ashes from falling through. Three pounds of grease should be put into a pail full of lye. The great difficulty in making soap 'come' originates in want of judgment about the strength of the lye. One rule may be safely trusted – If your lye will bear up an egg, or a potato, so that you can see a piece of the surface as big as ninepence, it is just strong enough. If it sink below the top of the lye, it is too weak, and will never make soap; if it is buoyed up half way, the lye is too strong; and that is just as bad. A bit of quick lime thrown in while the lye and grease are boiling together is of service. When the soap becomes thick and ropy carry it down cellar in pails and empty it into a barrel.

Cold soap is less trouble, because it does not need to boil; the sun does the work of fire. The lye must be prepared and tried in the usual way. The grease must be tried out, and strained from the scraps. Two pounds of grease, (instead of three) must be used to a pailful, unless the weather is very sultry, the lye should be hot when put to the grease. It should stand in the sun, and be stirred every day. If it does not begin to look like soap, in the course of five or six days, add a little hot lye to it; if this does not help it, try whether it be grease that it wants. Perhaps you will think cold soap wasteful because the grease must be strained; but if the scraps are boiled thoroughly in strong lye, the grease will all float upon the surface, and nothing be lost ...

2. Two Views on the Morality of Capitalism in the Early Republic, 1834 and 1836[2]

In the years following the War of 1812, more and more men and women found work in the nation's growing manufacturing sector. In varied locations such as the cotton mills of New England, shipyards in Baltimore, Maryland, and iron furnaces in western Virginia, Americans fueled the growth of the nation's industrial economy. Attitudes toward this development were ambivalent, as many wondered if republican values could coexist with permanent wage labor. The use of young middle-class women in the New England textile factories offered one way of reconciling new industrial values with the needs of a good republican population. Work for these "Lowell Girls" was intended to be temporary and have little impact on the wider population. But as the use of wage labor spread to encompass various trades once controlled by proprietary artisans, questions arose about the long-term effects upon a nation founded on political equality and republican virtue.

In these two accounts – the first an appeal for worker consumer cooperatives and the second a tribute to textile magnate Samuel Slater – the authors provide very different views of the emerging capitalist economy.

ADDRESS, &c. (1834)

... What are the privations we endure for a scanty subsistence? What are the daily fatigues of body and mind we are doomed to suffer for a mere pittance: and whom do our excessive toil enrich? Not ourselves.

The privations we are subjected to, are, the privation of property, of plenty, of recreation and rest, and the cultivation of mind. If these are denied, the practice of this system will prove them to be facts in the result of its operation on the members. But we have the evidence at hand.

Whose are those dwellings we inhabit? They belong to the rich! Who built them? The working poor! What did we get for those stately mansions now inhabited by the idle rich? Nothing! We, as a body of producers of wealth, lived upon our own and each other's wealth! – Then what has became of that which we received of them as an equivalent for our labor? We had to give it up to them again for house rent and profit added to goods for that purpose, and to make up the losses they met with from honest as

[2] "A Philanthropist," *An Address to Farmers, Mechanics, and Laborers* (Philadelphia, 1834) pp. 3–6; George S. White, *Memoir of Samuel Slater, The Father of American Manufactures* (Philadelphia, 1836), pp. 113–20.

well as dishonest men – swindlers, counterfeiters, and other knaves, caused by the madness of speculation! And what has become of the surplus, exclusive of the houses? Oh! they issued an extra quantity of paper from the *bank*, sufficient to cover the whole, and so bought it all up? And did we ever get any thing for our paper money from them? Oh, yes! – They raised our rents by way of a reward, and the profits on the goods we used, and so drew it all back again. Well, what became of it then? They gave it to the workmen who built the house for them! What did they do with it? They gave it to the store-keepers and lumber-men, in order to furnish themselves with food and raiment, and materials to build more houses for the rich! Did they give a profit on these goods? Yes, and a large profit, too, to enable these middle men to pay their rent, and other extra expenses? Then all of these middle men cannot get rich, at least very soon: no, but very few of them get rich. They are the veriest dupes of the whole lot of working men; they fight with their workmen, scratch and claw every body for money to give the rich, or for the inexpressible pleasure of counting change – generally frightened almost out of their wits, for fear the whole of it will finally slip through their fingers, without leaving a mark or a vestige of it behind. By this, we may perceive that nearly all our surplus labor regularly and systematically falls into the possession of the idle rich.

But, why should we not stop off this copious stream from their basket and their store, to fill our own, seeing it is ours by right of production, as they have no right to it, except they can give us as much for it as will confer as many benefits on us, as our labor productions did upon them. If these was done the trade would be fair and equal: then the house we lived in might be ours.

Why should we not own the house we occupy, in preference to him who never produced the value of an apple in his life, or did as much good to society as the value of a pound of coffee. Do you think such a distribution of property among the frugal industrious could harm society? If it could I should like to know how?

It could not take a thing from any one which was properly his, nor prevent any one from obtaining that which he or they were properly entitled to. But we are frequently prevented from working, however justly we may be entitled to it, and the benefits arising therefrom.

We who produce every thing which is of indispensable utility, ought to enjoy as much as they who produce none of these things. They enjoy all the pleasures of literature, without loss on their part, when we eat of the crumbs that fall from their lips. This is not all; we have to pay them richly for every morsel of literary honey that drops from their comb. Why should we not be equal with them? Surely they could find no fault ...

MORAL INFLUENCE OF MANUFACTURING
ESTABLISHMENTS (1836)

... Manufacturing establishments become a blessing or a curse according to the facilities which they create for acquiring a living, to the necessary articles which they provide, and the general character which they produce. To set up and encourage the manufacturing of such articles, the use and demand of which produces no immoral tendency, is one of the best and most moral uses which can be made of capital. The moral manufacturer, without the power or disposition to overreach, is in reality a benefactor. The acquisition of wealth in this way, is the most laudable. In point of benevolence and real worth of character, it claims a decided advantage over the cent per cent process of accumulation. Some have not the requisite ability to carry on manufacturing establishments; capital, then, with great propriety is loaned to those who have. The moral influence of a community is not promoted by creating or submitting to a manufacturing, or any other aristocracy, solely in the pursuit of interest, in which selfishness is wont to predominate.

The manufacturing interest, in a flourishing state, naturally creates power and wealth. The value of labor and the value of money are then at his disposal; but, in this free country there is a sufficient counteracting influence to keep up the price of labor and to equalize the prices of their commodities with the value of the products of the earth. Without such a resisting power, a few would abound in wealth and influence, while the multitude would be in poverty and reduced to servitude. But there always exists a counteracting influence in the rival establishments, and the general spirit of enterprise ...

The dependence between the employed and the employers should be mutual. But by employing vicious, improvident, and indigent characters, the dependence falls mostly on one side – yet it is a benefit to the community that such a class should find employment and support. Though in some countries, oppression ensues, poverty and vice show their dismal and disorderly features, and then the honest, upright, and intelligent, are driven from the establishment, and perhaps from the employment; better things can be spoken of in this country, where the honest, upright, and intelligent, have always a preference. Such are leaving the old world, they are disappearing, and many of them are in the west, engaged in other employments. Pursuing such a policy, by and by, only the dregs are left, and then without looking for the cause of all the mischief. On a candid enquiry, it is seen to be the abuse, and therefore not chargeable to a proper use.

Slater, the founder of the cotton manufacture in America, abundantly demonstrated, that under right management, they had no immoral tendency. On the contrary, he made it appear, that they might be serviceable to the most moral purposes. Following the plan instituted by Arkwright & Strutt in England, taking the oversight of the instruction and morals of those he employed, and instituting and keeping up schools, he successfully combated the natural tendency of accumulating vice, ignorance and poverty. Such remedies not only prevented their occurrence, but had a tendency to remove them, when they actually existed.

Industry, directed by honest and intelligent views in moral pursuits, and honourably rewarded, holds a very high rank among moral causes. To maintain good order and sound government, it is more efficient than the sword or bayonet ...

In the present happy conditions of the manufacturing districts, there are no advantages enjoyed by the rich, that are not reciprocated with the poor. Labour was never better paid, and the labourer more respected, at any period, or in any part of the world, than it is at present among us. And that man is not a friend to the poor who endeavors to make those dissatisfied with their present condition, who cannot hope, by any possibility of circumstances, to be bettered by a change. This is emphatically *the poor man's country* ...

3. Henry Bibb Describes Slave Labor in the Cotton Fields, 1849[3]

At the same time that northern Americans debated the merits and shortcomings of wage labor during the 1830s, more than two million Americans lived and worked as slaves. Comprising roughly a third of the southern population, African-American slaves were indispensable to the rapid expansion of the cotton trade during the Early Republic. By the 1830s and 1840s, the brutal, sunup-to-sundown routine of plantation labor created the most valuable export crop in the United States. The internal slave trade, described in the earlier document from Charles Ball, provided the impetus for the "cotton boom" by diffusing the slave population across the Deep South. The results were as profitable for slave owners as they were miserable for their slaves, as the states of Alabama, Mississippi, and Louisiana alone provided more than half the nation's cotton in 1834. Henry Bibb was born into slavery in Kentucky, but the slave trade carried him to several southern states over the course of his life. He eventually escaped slavery and became an abolitionist speaker during the 1840s. In this excerpt from his self-published narrative, he provides an account of work on a cotton plantation in Louisiana.

[3] Henry Bibb, *Narrative of the Life and Adventures of Henry Bibb* (New York: Published by the Author, 1849), pp. 114–18.

... I was not used quite as bad as the regular field hands, as the greater part of my time was spent working about the house; and my wife was the cook.

This country was full of pine timber, and every slave had to prepare a light wood torch, over night made of pine knots, to meet the overseer with, before daylight in the morning. Each person had to have his torch lit, and come with it in his hand to the gin house, before the overseer and driver, so as to be ready to go to the cotton field by the time they could see to pick out cotton. These lights looked beautiful at a distance.

The object of blowing the horn for them two hours before day, was, that they should get their bit to eat, before they went to the field, that they need not stop to eat but once during the day. Another object was, to do up their flogging which had been omitted over night. I have often heard the sound of the slave driver's lash on the backs, of slaves, and their heart-rending shrieks, which were enough to melt the heart of humanity, even among the most barbarous nations of the earth.

But the Deacon would keep no overseer on his plantation, who neglected to perform this every morning. I have heard him say that he was no better pleased than when he could hear the overseer's loud complaining voice, long before daylight in the morning, and the sound of the driver's lash among the toiling slaves.

This was a very warm climate, abounding with musquitos, galinippers and other insects which were exceedingly annoying to the poor slaves by night and day, at their quarters and in the field. But more especially to their helpless little children, which they had to carry with them to the cotton fields, where they had to set on the damp ground along from morning till night, exposed to the scorching rays of the sun, liable to be bitten by poisonous rattle snakes which are plenty in that section of the country, or to be devoured by large alligators, which are often seen creeping through the cotton fields going from swamp to swamp seeking their prey.

The cotton planters generally, never allow a slave mother time to go to her house, or quarter during the day to nurse her child; hence they have to carry them to the cotton fields and tie them in the shade of the tree, or in clusters of high weeds about in the fields, where they can go to them at noon, when they are allowed to stop work for one half hour. This is the reason why so very few slave children are raised on these cotton plantations, the mothers have no time to take care of them – and they are often found dead in the field for want of care of their mothers. But I never was eye witness to a case of this kind, but have heard many narrated by my slave brothers and sisters, some of which occurred on the deacon's plantation.

Their plan of getting large quantities of cotton picked is not only to extort it from them by the lash, but hold out an inducement and deceive them by giving small prizes. For example; the overseer will offer something worth one or two dollars to any slave who will pick out the most cotton in one day; dividing the hands off in three classes and offering a prize to the one who will pick out the most cotton in each of the classes. By this means they are all interested in trying to get the prize.

After making them try it over several times and weighing what cotton they pick every night, the overseer can tell just how much every hand can pick. He then gives the present to those that pick the most cotton, and then if they do not pick just as much afterward they are flogged.

I have known the slaves to be so much fatigued from labor that they could scarcely get to their lodging places from the field at night. And then they would have to prepare something to eat before they could lie down to rest. Their corn they had to grind on a hand mill for bread stuff, or pound it in a mortar; and by the time they would get their suppers it would be midnight; then they would herd down all together and take but two or three hours rest, before the overseer's horn called them up again to prepare for the field.

At the time of sickness among slaves they had but very little attention. The master was to be the judge of their sickness, but never had studied the medical profession. He always pronounced a slave who said he was sick, a liar and a hypocrite; said there was nothing the matter, and he only wanted to keep from work.

His remedy was most generally strong red pepper tea, boiled till it was red. He would make them drink a pint cup full of it at one dose. If he should not get better very soon after it, the dose was repeated. If that should not accomplish the object for which it was given, or have the desired effect, a pot or kettle was then put over the fire with a large quantity of chimney soot, which was boiled down until it was as strong as the juice of tobacco, and the poor sick slave was compelled to drink a quart of it.

This would operate on the system like salts, or castor oil. But if the slave should not be very ill, he would rather work as long as he could stand up, than to take this dreadful medicine.

If it should be a very valuable slave, sometimes a physician was sent for and something done to save him. But no special aid is afforded the suffering slave even in the last trying hour, when he is called to grapple with the grim monster death. He has no Bible, no family alter, no minister to address to him the consolations of the gospel, before he launches into the spirit world. As to the burial of slaves, but very little more care is taken of their dead bodies than if they were dumb beasts ...

Chapter 10   A New Urban America

1. Frances Trollope Describes Cincinnati, 1832[1]

Although established cities like Boston, New York, Philadelphia, and Baltimore all grew during the Early Republic, relatively new cities also began to boom in the western states. One of the most remarkable stories of rapid urban growth was Cincinnati, which had grown from a small village of 1,000 residents in 1802 to 10,000 by 1820. Emigrants continued to flow into the city, so that by the time of this firsthand account in 1830, nearly 25,000 Americans called it home. City boosters of the 1820s used the word "Queen City" to describe Cincinnati, but the city's role in meatpacking also gave it the more inelegant nickname of "Porkopolis." Whatever you called it, Cincinnati, along with Pittsburgh, Chicago, St. Louis, and New Orleans, was one of the fastest growing urban areas in the United States. In 1828 and 1829, the English novelist Frances Trollope and her family lived in Cincinnati. After their attempts to develop a retail business there failed, Trollope returned to England and produced an unflattering account of the United States entitled Domestic Manners of the Americans. *In this brief excerpt describing her arrival in Cincinnati, only a slight bit of the bile that characterized much Trollope's account of her travels is evident.*

... We reached Cincinnati on the 10th of February. It is finely situated on the south side of a hill that rises gently from the water's edge; yet it is by no means a city of striking appearance; it wants domes, towers, and steeples;

---

[1] Frances Trollope, *Domestic Manners of the Americans* (New York: Vintage Books, 1949 [1832]), pp. 35–6, 38–41.

but its landing-place is noble, extending for more than a quarter of a mile; it is well paved, and surrounded by neat, though not handsome buildings. I have seen fifteen steam-boats lying there at once, and still half the wharf was unoccupied.

On arriving we repaired to the Washington Hotel, and thought ourselves fortunate when we were told that we were just in time for dinner at the table d'hôte; but when the dining-room door was opened, we retreated with a feeling of dismay at seeing between sixty and seventy men already at table. We took our dinner with the females of the family, and then went forth to seek a house for our permanent accommodation ...

We were soon settled in our new dwelling, which looked neat and comfortable enough, but we speedily found that it was devoid of nearly all the accommodation that Europeans conceive necessary to decency and comfort. No pump, no cistern, no drain of any kind, no dustman's cart, or any other visible means of getting rid of rubbish, which vanishes with such celerity in London, that one has no time to think of its existence; but which accumulated so rapidly at Cincinnati, that I sent for my landlord to know in what manner refuse of all kinds was to be disposed of.

"Your Help will just have to fix them all into the middle of the street, but you must mind, old woman, that it is the middle. I expect you don't know as we have got a law what forbids throwing such things at the sides of streets; they must just all be cast right into the middle, and the pigs soon takes them off."

In truth the pigs are constantly seen doing Herculean service in this way through every quarter of the city; and though it is not very agreeable to live surrounded by herds of these unsavoury animals, it is well they are so numerous, and so active in their capacity of scavengers, for without them the streets would soon be choked up with all sorts of substances in every stage of decomposition.

We had heard so much of Cincinnati, its beauty, wealth, and unequalled prosperity, that when we left Memphis to go thither, we almost felt the delight of Rousseau's novice, "un voyage à faire, et Paris au bout!" – As soon, therefore, as our little domestic arrangements were completed, we set forth to view this "wonder of the west," this "prophet's gourd of magic growth," – this infant Hercules;" and surely no travelers ever paraded a city under circumstances more favourable to their finding it fair to the sight. Three dreary months had elapsed since we had left the glories of London behind us; for nearly the whole of that time we had beheld no other architecture than what our ship and steam-boats had furnished, and excepting at New Orleans, had seen hardly a trace of human habitations. The sight of bricks and mortar was really refreshing, and a house of three stories looked splendid. Of this splendour we saw repeated specimens, and moreover a brick church, which, from its two little peaked spires, is called the two-horned church. But alas! the flatness of reality after the imagination has been busy! I hardly know what I expected to find in this city, fresh risen from the bosom of the wilderness, but certainly it was not a little town, about the size of Salisbury, without even an attempt at beauty in any of its edifices, and with only just enough of the air of a city to make it noisy and bustling. The population is greater than the appearance of the town would lead one to expect. This is partly owing to the number of free Negroes who herd together in an obscure part of the city, called little Africa; and partly to the density of the population round the paper-mills and other manufactories. I believe the number of inhabitants exceed twenty thousand.

We arrived in Cincinnati in February, 1828, and I speak of the town as it was then; several small churches have been built since, whose towers agreeably relieve its uninteresting mass of buildings. At that time I think Main-street, which is the principal avenue, (and runs through the whole town, answering to the High-street of our old cities), was the only one entirely paved. The *troittoir* is of brick, tolerably well laid, but it is inundated by every shower, as Cincinnati has no drains whatever. What makes this omission the more remarkable is, that the situation of the place is calculated both to facilitate their construction and to render them necessary. Cincinnati is built on the side of a hill that begins to rise at the river's edge and were it furnished with drains of the simplest arrangement, the heavy showers of the climate would keep them constantly clean; as it is, these showers wash the higher streets, only to deposit their filth in the first level spot; and this happens to be in the street second to importance to Main-street, running at right angles to it, and containing most of the large warehouses of the town. This deposit is a dreadful nuisance, and must be productive of miasma during the hot weather.

The town is built, as I believe most American towns are, in squares, as they call them; but these squares are hollow. Each consists, or is intended to consist, when the plan of the city is completed, of a block of buildings fronting north, east, west, and south; each house communicating with an alley, furnishing a back entrance. This plan would not be a bad one were the town properly drained, but as it is, these alleys are horrible abominations, and must, I conceive, become worse with every passing year.

To the north, Cincinnati is bounded by a range of forest-covered hills, sufficiently steep and rugged to prevent their being built upon, or easily cultivated, but not sufficiently high to command from their summits a view of any considerable extent. Deep and narrow water-courses, dry in summer, but bringing down heavy streams in winter, divide these hills into many separate heights, and this furnishes the only variety the landscape offers for many miles round the town. The lovely Ohio is a beautiful feature wherever it is visible, but the only part of the city that has the advantage of its beauty is the street nearest to its bank. The hills of Kentucky, which rise at about the same distance from the river, on the opposite side, form the southern boundary to the basin in which Cincinnati is built.

On first arriving, I thought the many tree-covered hills around, very beautiful, but long before my departure, I felt so weary of the confined view, that Salisbury Plain would have been an agreeable variety. I doubt if any inhabitant of Cincinnati ever mounted these hills so often as myself and my children; but it was rather for the enjoyment of a freer air than for any beauty of prospect, that we took our daily climb. These hills afford neither shrubs nor flowers, but furnish the finest specimens of millepore in the world; and the watercourses are full of fossil productions ...

2. A Poem Composed to Cholera, 1832[2]

Among the biggest challenges to urban life in the Early Republic was the debilitating effect of disease. Closely packed populations and only rudimentary ideas about public health produced devastating results. Cholera epidemics, for example, ripped through the eastern seaboard in 1832 and again in 1849, killing thousands of Americans. The urban poor seemed particularly susceptible to cholera. On a single day in July of 1832, 100 people in New York City died of cholera, 95 of whom were buried in paupers' graves. Many elite observers linked the spread of disease to perceived overindulgence in food, drink, and sexual activity among the working classes of the city. This added a strong moral dimension to the campaign to eradicate cholera. This poem, written by a minister from Lansingburg, New York, was attached to a broadside printed by the Massachusetts Legislature in 1837 that denounced the consumption of alcohol.

- I
  AT length the Cholera is come,
  To desolate the land; –
  It sweeps its thousands to the tomb –
  Who can its power withstand?

[2] From *An eulogium on rum ... Printed for the benefit of the Mass. Legislature* (Boston, 1837?), in the Printed Ephemera Collection, Library of Congress, Washington, DC.

- 2

With what rapidity it spreads!
From town to town it goes;
Now here, now there, its way it threads,
How fast the judgment flows!!

- 3

It spares no age, but young and old,
Fall victims to its power;
The timid, and the fearless bold,
Alike it doth devour.

- 4

No skill its progress can arrest,
And no physician save
The people from the dreadful pest,
That sweeps them to the grave.

- 5

Before another sun goes down,
Scores will be call'd away
Of this disease – we of this town
Are liable as they.

- 6

New-York's vast city shares the woe,
And Philadelphia weeps
The ravage of the deadly foe,
Who there his harvest reaps.

- 7

Death's sceptre waves o'er many a place,
Devoted to his power;
To seize his prey behold him haste, –
With him a busy hour.

- 8

Alarm and dread fill every breast,
The stoutest courage quails;
For ne'er was known such dire distress,
Where'er the scourge prevails.

- 9

Nor youthful bloom, nor manly prime,
Nor childhood's smiling age,
Can save from death the shortest time,
Or stay the tyrant's rage.

- 10

Mourning and grief, distress and pain,
Wring every fibre, where

The Cholera hath its hundreds slain –
One scene of dark despair.

● 11
Great God! the dreadful scourge remove,
Do thou in mercy spare;
We own 'tis just thou shouldst reprove,
But make us still thy care.

● 12
Frown not in judgment on the land,
Although our sins are great;
Rebuke us with a pitying hand,
The pestilence abate.

● 13
O may we turn to thee, our God,
And of our sins repent;
Nor longer go the downward road,
Till judgments thus are sent.

● 14
Our favor'd country hath gone on,
In pride and wickedness;
Regardless of that Holy One,
Who doth with favors bless.

● 15
Repent, proud people of your ways,
And for forgiveness sue;
And God will lengthen out your days,
And mercy grant to you.

● 16
The avenging angel will be stay'd,
And health will be restor'd;
Compassion ever is display'd
To those who seek the Lord.

3. A Raucous Omnibus Ride in New York City, 1839[3]

*If American cities were ill-planned, crowded, and susceptible to epidemics,
one wonders why anyone chose to live in them. The excitement and many
economic, cultural, and culinary opportunities of urban life, however, proved*

---

[3] "Harry Franco" [Charles Frederick Briggs], "A Ride in an Omnibus," *The Knickerbocker;
or New York Monthly Magazine* 14 (December 1839), pp. 542–7.

a powerful magnet for burgeoning American cities. In New York City, for
example, affluent residents could eat a meal at Delmonico's restaurant, see
Shakespeare performed at the famous Bowery Theatre, and then take in
a drink or a late-night snack at the various taverns and oyster cellars that
dotted Manhattan. These attractions eventually drew a national following as
newspapers and other periodicals spread word of both the rewards and the
dangers of urban living. One example of the ways in which the fast pace of the
city proved both exciting and treacherous is found in this account of an
impromptu omnibus race down New York's famous Broadway. Written by
Charles Frederick Briggs, a journalist who often wrote under the pseudonym
"Harry Franco," this work of fiction provides a brief tour of the main sights of
New York at the same time that it describes the exhilaration of the race.

However improbable the assertion may appear to the Broadway belles and
the Bowery boys, it is nevertheless unquestionably true, that there are many
men and women in the world, who have never travelled in an omnibus. I am
aware that the very name of the vehicle seems to imply that they carry all
the world; but still it must be regarded as a mere figure of speech, and not
taken in its literal sense. In Cockaigne, where the carriage and its name
both had their origin, the impropriety of the OMNI has long since been
acknowledged, and the citizens of that classic land make use of the BUSS
only; and it is a matter of some wonder, that our travelled countrymen have
not introduced the improvement here. Taking it for granted, then, that there
are, even among the distant readers of the KNICKERBOCKER, some
who have never enjoyed the luxury of a ride down Broadway, in one of
these convenient vehicles, I design, in this present writing, to narrate, for
their especial benefit, some of the pleasures of that delightful manner of
travelling.

It was near the close of one warm afternoon in the decline of summer, that
I emerged out of one of the elegant streets in the upper part of the city
of New-York, and stepped upon the newly-laid flagging of Broadway, just
as a long white carriage, drawn by four horses of as many different colors,
and with a figure of Minerva painted upon its central panel, started for a
little spot of verdure at the lower end of the city, called, by way of a joke, the
"Bowling Green." The driver of this vehicle, raising himself in his seat, gave
a preliminary flourish with his whip, and looking behind him, caught sight
of my weary-looking limbs, and gave me an invitation to ride, by making a
peculiar sweep with his uplifted elbow; I answered the invitation by lifting
up my fore finger, upon which he checked his horses, and I entered the
carriage, and found that it contained no one but an elderly lady, opposite
whom I sat down. Our driver was a tall, thin young man, with a whitish hat

upon his head, and a cigar in his mouth. His whole dress was in admirable keeping – a perfect study for MOUNT, the genius of Stoney Brook; and there was a reckless glance in his eye, that would have well become the ambitious Phaeton, the day on which we set fire to the world by his careless driving.

We jogged along at an easy rate, passing the white towers of the University on our left, and the square stone tower of the Church of the Messiah on our right; and leaving the beautiful granite church, with a marble alter and a wooden steeple, and numerous other architectural wonders, behind us. But suddenly there came dashing along behind us an opposition line, from the neighborhood of Union Square, as that tasteful oval is called. The carriage was a deep crimson, with a great profusion of gilding; and it was drawn by four mettlesome bay horses. The driver was a buckish-looking individual, with a glossy black hat, and a bob-tailed green coat. He also had a newly lighted cigar in his mouth, and altogether his appearance was saucy in the extreme. He was about to dash past us, without the smallest acknowledge-ment of our existence, when our driver gave a sudden crack with his whip, and started his cattle into a pretty brisk trot; for drivers of omnibuses, like drivers of quills and bargains, do not like to be distanced in a race with a rival; and therefore it was quite natural that he should make freer use of his whip than he before had done.

Just at this moment, a couple of young ladies stopped on the crossing, and motioned our driver to stop; but without giving the slightest heed to their wishes, he gave a loose to his reins, and contrived, by a free use of his whip, and an incessant ejaculation of crack phrases, which are presumed to be very gratifying to horses, to keep up the speed of his divers-colored cattle. At the first bound of the omnibus, I found myself plump in the lap of the lady passenger, who seemed disposed to take my sudden intrusion upon her premises as no joke; but scarcely was I seated on my own side again, than another sudden bound sent the lady herself quite as suddenly into my arms. We were now square on the score of visits; so she regained her good humor as soon as circumstances would allow, and said something very "smart;" but I could not understand a syllable of it . . .

"A stern chase is a long chase," is an old saying with sailors; and I see no reason why it should not come to be a proverb among omnibus drivers. Our present case certainly afforded a very pretty illustration of its truth. We were decidedly inferior to our consort in point of metal; but having the lead, we continued to keep it without great difficulty. On which ever side he might endeavor to pass, our driver would very adroitly prevent him, by heading his horses directly across his path. Fortunately, there is a city ordinance against driving omnibusses on the side-walk, or we might have been compelled to submit to a defeat. Every now and then the heads of the "leaders" of the opposition would intrude themselves into the door of our omnibus, and giving a disdainful toss, would half cover us with foam. Then the lady would shriek, the horses would snort, the drivers would swear, crack would go their whips, crash would go something, and away we would fly again ... I forgot all my fears, now, and thought only of victory. Indeed, I should have valued a broken arm no more than the paring of a finger-nail. I was afraid of nothing but defeat. In the height of my anxiety, I put my head out of the window, and shouted to the driver to crack on; and the lady, who had turned pale with fright when we first set out, was now flushed with excitement, and she clapped her hands together in high glee, every time we got an advantage on our pursuer. Suddenly I heard a crash and a shout, and turning my head, I saw two well-dressed gentlemen sprawling in the middle of the street, and a pair of grays flying away with a half-demolished dear-born-wagon. Men, I thought, had no business to venture themselves in Broadway in such slight things; and probably so thought our driver, for he never turned his head to see what damage he had done, but continued to urge on his horses at the top of their speed ...

If my feelings were excited before, they reached their calenture now. The humanity of my driver had enlisted my sympathies strongly in his behalf, while the ferocious looks and profane expressions of the opposition, caused me to exult in his defeat. Away we flew like lightening, and gained the next corner without doing any other damage than overturning the oyster-stand of a one-legged old sailor, who appeared to regard his loss of a few oysters and a bottle of red peppers, with a degree of chagrin which I thought was greatly disproportioned to the occasion ...

As we were fast approaching the end of our journey, the efforts of the rivals increased in vigor. They hallooed, they swore, they cursed, they stamped; they whipped their horses, and then brandished their whips at each other; and if we did not increase, we certainly did not diminish our speed; while the interest, if possible, grew more exciting at every moment. But soon a new difficulty arose. The lady wanted to alight at Lispenard-street, but the driver was proof against the admonitions of the check-string. The lady had no wish to travel so far out of her way as Bowling Green, but the driver was too intent on the race to allow a passenger to alight, and thereby give his antagonist an opportunity of beating him. And I must confess that I was highly delighted with his spirit; and forgetting for the moment, that I was a member of a temperance society, I determined to treat him to a julap, so soon as we should reach the end of our journey. The lady continued to tug away at the check-string, but the only reply our gallant driver made was, "No you don't!" – and by putting the end of his thumb to his nose, and gently fanning the air with his extended fingers; and then seizing his whip again, he made it crack over the ears of his smoking leaders. The lady at last threw herself back in despair, as we rattled past the little dusty hole called, in derision, Contoit's Garden, and the great lumbering, greenish-brown pile of bricks opposite, called, by way of an experiment in bombast, the "Carlton House" ...

Chance, now, as in many a renowned contest, must determine the victory, for the crowd of carriages thickens fast. It is an easy matter to overturn an old apple-woman, or even a dandy phaeton; but a loaded dray presents an obstacle that, like the will of the people, must be respected. And here, too, are numerous pyramids of bricks, which care no more for an omnibus than do the pyramids of the desert for old Time, who has whetted his scythe upon them for a longer period than men know of.

If oaths and curses could avail any thing, we should have been distanced long since. The opposition has exhausted the swearer's vocabulary a dozen times; but our gallant driver spurs on his cattle with a good-natured hulla-baloo, which contrasts favorably with the savage ferocity of his rival. We catch a glimpse of time-honored Columbia College, and its noble elms, and we are again on the cobbles. Goodness, what a change! It is like laying down Tom Moore, and taking up doctor M'Henry!

Crash! smash! The drivers swear, the horses plunge, the lady screams; but there is no great damage, only one corner of the omnibus torn off. Away we go, without heeding it. Here is our triumph! All the world is looking at us. What a moment! We are almost a length ahead of the opposition! Twenty dandies, with cigars in their mouths, and small tufts of hair on their upper lips, are gazing at us from the steps of the Astor House. A whole drove of little folks, who have been treated to a sight of the wonders in Scudder's Museum, clap their little hands with delight, as we rush past. All the coachmen on the Park stand mount their boxes to look at us; and a mettle-some grey horse, with a militia officer on his back, takes fright, and scampers down Barclay-street, in fine style. Away we fly, past St. Paul's Church, with our pursuer hard upon our heels, splashing and dashing, slam-bang, and mingling with dirt-carts, oyster-carts, and milk-wagons, until we get inex-tricably interlocked with a whole caravan of brokers' and bankers' clerks, fleeing from Wall-street and throwing off steam like a locomotive. Our driver waxes moderate in the use of his whip and his oaths. The excitement is fast cooling; and after repeated struggles to get clear, we at last have the mortification of seeing the opposition drive past us, and we reach Bowling Green just two minutes after him.

After all, what is the use of striving to out-race our fellows in this world? If we win, our spirits have all evaporated in the contest; and if we lose, we have nothing but mortification for our exertions. With such reflections, I stepped out of the omnibus, and left my fair fellow traveller disputing with the driver about her fare; for she very justly refused to pay for her ride back down, unless he would agree to take her back to the place of her destination, free of charge.

Discussion Questions

1. What do the documents in Part IV reveal about the difference between free and slave labor? When slaves moved and worked, was the experience fundamentally different from that of their free counterparts? Why or why not?

2. Consider the pieces that discuss travel in its various forms. Do they emphasize the process of travel or the ultimate destination? Do you think that this is an important distinction? Do they reveal a distinctly *American* approach to travel?

3. What audience do you think that the firsthand accounts of work were trying to reach? Are they simply trying to describe an existing approach to labor? Or, do you think that there is a proscriptive element to these accounts? In other words, are the pieces trying to alter existing habits of work?

4. One of the most important factors pulling rural Americans to cities was the idea that urban areas offer a more exciting life. Do you think that the firsthand accounts of urban life here convey that sense of excitement? Are there any caveats to the thrill of urban living that show up here?

5. If you were a European trying to describe American society to your peers like Frances Trollope does in her account of Cincinnati, is it possible to select another document from this chapter that you would use to convey the essential character of the American nation? What do you think a foreign reader would find most unusual? What might they find most universal?

Part V   Renewal and Reform

Introduction to Part V

At the same time that Americans experienced dramatic economic growth, they also witnessed an upsurge in spiritual and moral awareness. If roads, canals, and factories offered a physical form of improvement, so could "improvement" occur through religious and moral reform. The zeal of the evangelical revivals in the early nineteenth century inspired the idea that a "Second Great Awakening" was revitalizing American religion in the same way that the First Great Awakening energized believers a century earlier. If the soul could undergo some renewal, some argued, then the purification of the body must follow. Temperance societies levied an all-out attack on alcohol abuse that carried over into various aspects of dietary and sexual reform as well. Just as individual humans could undergo improvement, so did some reformers of the Early Republic attempt to remake American society into a more perfect form. Missionary societies, labor reformers, utopian communities, and other causes all struggled to convince Americans of the significance of their individual movement. Out of this zeal for improvement in its various forms came the most controversial reform movement of the Early Republic, abolitionism. Originating in the African-American community, the crusade against slavery rankled white southerners and northerners alike for most of this period. As a lasting influence on the American social, cultural, and political landscape, however, the abolition movement was perhaps the most transformative reform element to emerge from the Early American Republic.

Chapter 11   The Soul of the Republic

1. Radical Quakers Appeal to Frances Wright, December 24, 1828[1]

Amidst the enthusiasm of the Second Great Awakening, radical ideas about worship and faith popped up to challenge the more orthodox hierarchies of American Christianity. Among a growing number of radical critics of organized religion, Frances Wright was one of the most notorious public speakers and writers of the Early Republic. Originally from England, Wright became embroiled in a number of reformist movements such as her plan to create a biracial, cooperative community in Nashoba, Tennessee in 1826. Following the failure of that venture, Wright and the utopian theorist Robert Dale Owen organized a "free thought" movement in New York that sponsored lectures on controversial topics such as free love and abolitionism and published a journal entitled the Free Enquirer. *In this letter published in that newspaper, a group of radical Quakers from Wilmington, Delaware, ask Wright to come and speak in their area.*

Esteemed Friend – We wish some of you would come and see what kind of people live in Wilmington; some of the women are particularly desiring of thy company. There is "a little flock" of us here who "fear not," and live in hope we shall yet posses the "kingdom." We all believe in a "saving faith,"

---

[1]   *The Free Enquirer* (New York), December 24, 1828.

faith in the spirit of free enquiry; that which is spoken of in the holy scriptures, to "prove all things and hold fast that which is good." We go to orthodox meeting, quaker meeting, or heretic meeting, as the spirit moves us; and there are many that watch over us and seem to expect that we will soon run into some great moral depravity, and wonder how it happens that we should all continue to be honest and peaceable citizens. We were attacked publicly, last summer, by the wolves; they had sheeps' clothing on, as they had in olden times; and during the conflict, all the orthodoxy in our little borough kept up a great "wailing and gnashing of teeth." They put up all their scarecrows, (as we used to call them in the country) one after another – infidelism, deism, and atheism; and then their isms were followed by the artillery of the church; she thundered her ana-themas of eternal perdition, and tried to rain down fire and brimstone on us out of heaven, as if we had been a second edition of Sodom and Gomorrah: finally, they concluded they would starve us, and separate us from all the world by preventing commercial intercourse; but, as we told them *we would live on sawdust pudding before we would abandon such a cause*, they gradually grew cool; and having no reasons to advance, the presbyterians quitted the field about a week ago. The methodists are now getting their fires lighted up, and are going to be at us in about a week; but, as they carry so much steam, we expect they will soon burst their boiler; however, let it terminate as it may, all parties now agree that the presbyterians have met with a complete defeat: we have, therefore, great rejoicing in our border, and some of the people begin to think a little better of us. We are nearly all members of the sect called quakers, but free as air, and ready to hear any doctrine, true or false, each one doing what he "believes to be right in his own eyes."

Give my compliments to the editors of the Free Enquirer, and of the Correspondent. I think they are not always right, but *they are certainly friends to the truth, who fearlessly advocate free discussion*. We will all get right if we hold to those principles: knowledge is the savior of man, and, sooner or later, will this savior divide "the foxes" from "the geese." The cry is gone forth to "separate the clean from the unclean," to place the priests (or goats, as Jesus of old called them) on the left hand, and the sheep on the right. Jesus, I suppose, must have meant the priests were the goats, for there were no people he disliked so much as the priests; and the goats, in this sentence, occupy the lowest place in his estimation. Some liberals think there was no such man as Jesus, but I have no mind to lose so good a heretic, as he appears to have been. Strip the account of the flummery of mystery and miracle, and there is nothing improbable in the relation.

2. Rev. Charles Finney on Changing One's Own Heart, 1836[2]

Charles Grandison Finney was one of the leading figures of the Second Great Awakening. Originally trained to be an attorney, Finney had a conversion experience at an upstate New York revival and decided to devote his life to saving souls. He led a series of revivals across western New York in which he delivered mesmerizing sermons that emphasized the possibility of salvation for everyone, leaving in his wake the "Burned Over" district. Although he eventually settled into the Methodist faith, Finney began his career as a Presbyterian. In 1836 he moved to the immense Broadway Tabernacle in lower Manhattan, which sat 2,400 worshippers. This sermon, entitled "Sinners Bound to Change Their Own Hearts," was one of Finney's most popular. Finney, like many preachers of the Second Great Awakening, highlighted the role of the individual in seeking faith and salvation. This particular sermon stresses the individual's choice to serve God and uses everyday language in order to get this point across to readers. Although we might find this tactic common in today's sermons, this accessible approach was a big part of Finney's popularity with American Christians of the Early Republic.

... A change of heart, then, consists in changing the controlling preference of the mind in regard to the *end* of pursuit. The selfish heart is a preference of self-interest to the glory of God and the interests of his kingdom. A new heart consists in a preference of the glory of God and the interests of his kingdom to one's own happiness. In other words, it is a change from selfishness to benevolence, from having a supreme regard to one's own interest to an absorbing and controlling choice of the happiness and glory of God and his kingdom.

It is a change in the choice of a *Supreme Ruler*. The conduct of impenitent sinners demonstrates that they prefer Satan as the ruler of the world, they obey his laws, electioneer for him, and are zealous for his interest, even to martyrdom. They carry their attachment to him and his government so far as to sacrifice both body and soul to promote his interest and establish his dominion. A new heart is the choice of JEHOVAH as the supreme ruler; a deep-seated and abiding preference of his laws, and government, and character, and person, as the supreme Legislator and Governor of the universe ...

Suppose a human sovereign should establish a government and propose as the great end of pursuit, to produce the greatest amount of happiness possible

---

[2] Charles G. Finney, *Sermons on Important Subjects* (New York: John S. Taylor, 1836), pp. 9–10, 13–15, 36–8.

within his kingdom. He enacts wise and benevolent laws, calculated to promote this object to which he conforms all his own conduct; in the administration of which, he employs all his wisdom and energies, and requires all his subjects to sympathize with him; to aim at the same object; to be governed by the same principles; to aim supremely and constantly at the same end; the promotion of the highest interests of the community. Suppose these laws to be framed, that universal obedience would necessarily result in universal happiness. Now suppose that one individual, after a season of obedience and devotion to the interest of government and the glory of his sovereign, should be induced to withdraw his influence and energies from promoting the public good, and set up for himself; suppose him to say, I will no longer be governed by the principles of good will to the community, and find my own happiness in promoting the public interest; but will aim at promoting my own happiness and glory, in my own way, and let the sovereign and the subjects take care of themselves. "Charity begins at home." Now suppose him thus to set up for himself; to propose his own happiness and aggrandizement as the supreme object of his pursuit, and should not hesitate to trample upon the laws and encroach upon the rights, both of his sovereign and the subjects, wherever those laws or rights lay in the way of the accomplishment of his designs. It is easy to see, that he has become a rebel; has changed his *heart*, and consequently his conduct; has set up an interest not only separate from but opposed to the interest of his rightful sovereign. He has changed his heart from good to bad; from being an obedient servant he has become a rebel; from obeying his sovereign, he has set up an independent sovereignty; from trying to influence all men to obey the government, from seeking supremely the prosperity and the glory of his sovereign, he becomes himself a little sovereign; and as Absalom caught the men of Israel and kissed them, and thus stole away their hearts; so he now endeavors to engross the affections, to enlist the sympathies, to command the respect and obedience of all around him. Now what would constitute a change of heart in this man towards his sovereign? I answer, for him to go back, to change his mind in regard to the supreme object of pursuit; – to prefer the glory of his sovereign and the good of the public to his own separate interest would constitute a change of heart.

Now this is the case with the sinner; God has established a government, and proposed by the exhibition of his own character, to produce the greatest practicable amount of happiness in the universe. He has enacted laws wisely calculated to promote this object, to which he confirms all his own conduct, and to which he requires all his subjects perfectly and undeviatingly to conform theirs ...

It has been common for those who believe that sinners are *unable* to change their own heart, when sinners have inquired what they should do to be saved, to substitute another requirement for that contained in the text, and instead of commanding them to make them a new heart, have told them to pray that God would change their heart. They have used language like the following: "You much remember that you are dependent on God for a new heart. Do not attempt to do any thing in your own strength – attend to your Bible, use the means of grace, call upon God to change your heart, and wait patiently for the answer." ...

Sinner! instead of waiting and praying for God to change you[r] heart, you should at once summon up your powers, put forth the effort, and change the governing preference of your mind. But here some one may ask, Can the carnal mind, which is enmity against God, change itself? I have already said that this text in the original reads, "The minding of the flesh is enmity against God." This minding of the flesh, then, is a choice or a preference to gratify the flesh. Now it is indeed absurd to say, that a choice can change itself; but it is not absurd to say, that the agent who exercises this choice, can change it. The sinner that minds the flesh, can change his mind, and mind God. ...

3. Zilpha Elaw Remembers Preaching in the North and South, 1846[3]

The prescriptions of race could not contain the zeal unleashed by the Second Great Awakening. For men and women of color, the religious enthusiasm that accompanied evangelical Protestantism carried a special message of deliverance. For those enslaved in the South, revivals encouraged long-term hope and, in some cases, the inspiration to resist their state of bondage. For African-Americans in the North, religious organizations offered a marginalized community a rallying point for various self-improvement movements as well as energizing anti-slavery ideas. Religious revivals drew both audiences without regard for race or gender, making them an egalitarian element in an otherwise rigidly segregated American society. Zilpha Elaw was an African-American woman who experienced the religious enthusiasm of the Second Great Awakening firsthand. A member of the Methodist Episcopal

---

[3]   Zilpha Elaw, *Memoirs of the Life, Religious Experience, Ministerial Travels and Labors of Mrs. Zilpha Elaw*, in William L. Andrews, ed., *Sisters of the Spirit: Three Black Women's Autobiographies of the Nineteenth Century* (Bloomington: Indiana University Press, 1986), pp. 85–8, 90–1.

Church, Elaw felt the stirrings of religious fervor at an early age, had them reinforced after attending a week-long revival in 1817, and eventually became a preacher of international renown. In this excerpt from her autobiography, Elaw remembers how she became an evangelist following her husband's death in 1823 and recalls a harrowing visit to the Slave South in 1828.

... After my dear husband was buried, and I had become a little settled, instead of submitting myself in all things to be led by the Spirit, I rather leaned to my own understanding, and procured a situation of servitude for my little girl, and another for myself, judging these the best means I could adopt for the liquidation of my debts; and I remained in service until my health was so impaired that I was compelled to relinquish it; nor did the blessing of my heavenly Father appear to prosper this course; for I was constantly obliged to be under medical treatment, and yet grew worse and worse. I therefore left my situation, and went back to my house, which I had still reserved in case I should want it. I then opened a school, and the Lord blessed the effort, and increased the number of my pupils, so that I soon had a nice little school; many of the [S]ociety of [F]riends came and visited it, and assisted me with books and other necessaries for it. They were also much pleased with the improvement of the children; and when any strangers came to visit Burlington, they introduced them to me; and it was gratifying to many of them to see a female of colour teaching the coloured children, whom the white people refused to admit into their seminaries and who had been suffered formerly to run about the streets for want of a teacher. The pride of a white skin is a bauble of great value with many in some parts of the United States, who readily sacrifice their intelligence to their prejudices, and possess more knowledge than wisdom. The Almighty accounts not the black races of man either in the order of nature or spiritual capacity as inferior to white; for He bestows his Holy Spirit on, and dwells in them as readily as in persons of whiter complexion: the Ethiopian eunuch was adopted as a son and heir of God; and when Ethiopia shall stretch forth her hands unto him [Ps. 68:31], their submission and worship will be graciously accepted. This prejudice was far less prevalent in that part of the country where I resided in my infancy; for when a child, I was not prohibited from any school on account of the colour of my skin. Oh! that men would outgrow their nursery prejudices and learn that "God hath made of one blood all the nations of men that dwell upon all the face on the earth" (Acts xvii. 26).

But my mind was not long at rest in this situation; for the remembrance of the commission which I had received from the Lord very strongly impressed me; and as the Lord had said, "Thou must preach the gospel, and thou must travel far and wide," so He was about to bring it to pass, but I knew not in what manner . . .

I started off for the southern territories of the United States, where slavery is established and enforced by law. When I arrived in the slave states, Satan much worried and distressed my soul with the fear of being arrested and sold for a slave, which their laws would have warranted, on account of my complexion and features. On one occasion, in particular, I had been preaching to a coloured congregation, and had exhorted them impressively to [ac] quit themselves as men approved of God, and to maintain and witness a good profession of their faith before the world &c. I had no sooner sat down, than Satan suggested to me with such force, that the slave-holders would speedily capture me, as filled me with fear and terror. I was then in a small town in one of the slave states; and the news of a coloured female preaching to the slaves had already been spread widely through the neighborhood; the novelty of the thing had produced an immense excitement and the people were collecting from every quarter, to gaze at the unexampled prodigy of a coloured female preacher. I was sitting in a very conspicuous situation near the door, and I observed, with very painful emotions, the crowd outside, pointing with their fingers at me, and saying, "that's her," "that's her;" for Satan strongly set before me the prospect of an immediate arrest and consignment by sale to some slave owner. Being very much alarmed, I removed from my seat to a retired part of the room, where, become more collected, I inquired within myself, "from whence cometh all this fear?" My faith then rallied and my confidence in the Lord returned, and I said, "get thee behind me Satan, for my Jesus hath made me free." My fears instantly forsook me, and I vacated my retired corner, and come forth before all the people again; and the presence and power of the Lord became greatly manifested in the assembly during the remainder of the service. At the earnest request of the friends, I consented to preach there again on the following Lord's-day morning, which I accordingly did. Some of the white brethren in connexion with the Methodist Society were present on that occasion; at the conclusion thereof, they introduced themselves to me, and wished me to preach for them in the afternoon; to which I agreed; and they obtained permission of the authorities to open and use the courthouse; and therein I obtained a very large auditory; and God gave forth proofs that my ministry was from Him, in giving me many seals to it on that day; thus was I relieved from my fearful forebodings, and pursued my course with increased energy, rejoicing in the prosperity and success with which the Almighty crowned my efforts . . .

Chapter 12   Improvement of Body and Soul

1. Boston Physicians on Temperance, 1832[1]

Americans of the Early Republic consumed quite a bit of liquor, wine, and beer. Alcoholic beverages seemed ubiquitous at home, at work, and at play, as adult Americans drank 7.1 gallons of alcohol per capita by the 1830s. Although early "temperance" advocates called for a curtailment in the consumption of whiskey, rum, and other hard liquors, a new wave of anti-alcohol activists followed the Reverend Lyman Beecher's 1825 call to abolish drunkenness from any source. Beecher helped form the American Society for the Promotion of Temperance (ASPT) and at the time of the following call for temperance, the ASPT claimed a membership of over 170,000. One of the distinguishing characteristics of this new form of temperance reform was its emphasis upon the ill effects of alcohol on social order and an individual's health. Previous attacks on drunkenness focused largely on the moral consequences of intemperance. As the following call from 75 Boston physicians demonstrates, health professionals, as well as ministers, could enlist in the campaign to reduce the consumption of alcohol.

THE DECLARATION OF SEVENTY-FIVE Physicians of Boston. *THEY* declare that "ardent spirit, as a drink, is *never* useful for men in health," and furnish the annexed certificate, to be seen and read of all men. This is their deliberate opinion, given after mature reflection, and with a full knowledge of the effects of ardent spirit upon the human system. They make

[1]   *The Declaration of Seventy-Five Physicians of Boston* (Boston, MA: Ford & Damrell, 1832).

no exception to this rule. All men, they declare, would be better, in all situations, without this stimulant. Every man, then, who is in health, by transgressing, violates the laws of life, and not only wastes his property, but he impairs his constitution, and takes one step towards a premature grave. Physicians know this better than any other class of men, and to them, under God, is our country greatly indebted, for the rapid progress of the temperance reformation. And to their praise it should be known, that almost without exception, in every part of our land, they have come forward, with a disinterestedness worthy of all imitation, and have thrown the weight of their character and influence into the scale of temperance. Having long seen and felt the difficulties which the use of ardent spirit presented to the healing art, they have denounced it as "a most subtle and dangerous *poison*," alike unnecessary, and injurious, to men in health, rendering them no assistance in cold or heat, giving no power to endure fatigue, or recruit an exhausted frame. Such testimony should forever settle the question, "Does drinking ardent spirit do any good?" – And it does settle it, where appetite or interest have not blinded the minds, or where gross ignorance does not prevail.

About fifty millions of dollars, it is estimated, are annually expended in this country, for this poisonous liquid, which is not only unnecessary, but the direct cause of nine tenths of all the pauperism, crime, wretchedness and woe, which degrade and afflict our fellow-men. Almost every paper records murders committed under the influence of ardent spirit, while the untold, hidden woes which it inflicts, will never be revealed in this world. Shall law-makers sanction the traffic, which causes all this calamity and waste of property and life? This question is submitted to the people of the United States of America, – who, in this land, are the only sovereigns. Read the opinion, and consider it well; then fix it upon the wall of every dwelling, shop, manufactory, steamboat, tavern, and place of assembly – the grog-shop not excepted – and recollect that it is most disinterested, for ardent spirit causes a large part of all the sickness and accidents which befal mankind; and if it is banished the change must materially diminish the practice and income of medical men.

They speak *what they do know*, and if all other temperance men are "insane and fanatics," they are in their sober senses, and were so when they signed the annexed opinion, which they freely gave, for the benefit of their friends, patrons and countrymen. Let us hear it, and let it sink deeply into all our minds, and influence our lives and conduct.

The Board of Directors of the Boston Society for the Promotion of Temperance, appointed a Committee, to obtain from the Physicians of Boston a united expression of their opinion in regard to the effects of ardent spirit.

The following paper was drawn up, by one of the faculty, and presented to every regular Physician who could be found in the city. It was signed by *seventy-five*, being all but about five of the regular practitioners of medicine then residing in Boston; and is as follows:

"The subscribers, Physicians of Boston, having been requested by the Directors of the Boston Society for the Promotion of Temperance, to express their opinion in regard to the effects of ardent spirits, hereby *declare* it to be their opinion that *men in health are* NEVER *benefited by the use of ardent spirits,* – that, on the contrary, the use of them is a frequent cause of *disease* and *death*, and often renders such diseases as arise from other causes more difficult of cure, and more fatal in their termination."
Boston, February, 1832 ...

2. Mathew Carey Advocates Reform for Seamstresses, 1833[2]

Antebellum reform movements often focused on the physical and spiritual needs of Americans; some reformers argued that economic reform in the wake of industrialization was just as important. As the market for ready-made clothing continued to expand, many urban women became enmeshed in the "outwork" system devised to lower tailoring costs. In this method of manufacturing clothes, agents would distribute work to seamstresses and pay them a piece rate for every article sewn. As piece rates dropped, these seamstresses found themselves caught in what would be renamed the "sweating" system by the 1840s. Other working women in the garment trade labored in a factory-like setting, but with similarly low wages and dismal futures. Mathew Carey, a prominent publisher and reformer in Philadelphia, highlighted the plight of working women in a pamphlet entitled An Appeal to the Wealthy of the Land. *Carey used statistics to hammer his point home, but also referred to the severe moral implications of poverty among Philadelphia's seamstresses.*

Let us now turn to the appalling case of seamstresses, employed on coarse work, and to that of spoolers: and here "I will a tale unfold, to harrow up the soul" of all those endowed with feelings of humanity.

[2] Mathew Carey, *Appeal to the Wealthy of the Land, Ladies as Well as Gentlemen, on the Character, Conduct, Situation and Prospects of Those Whose Sole Dependence for Subsistence is on the Labour of Their Hands* (Philadelphia: L. Johnson, 1833), pp. 13–15, 33–4.

Coarse shirts and duck pantaloons are frequently made for 8 and 10 cents. The highest rate in the United States, with two highly honorable exceptions, which I shall notice presently, is 12½ cents. Women free from the incumbrance of children, in perfect health, and with constant, uninterrupted employment, cannot, by the testimony of ladies of the first respectability, who have fully scrutinized the affair, make more than nine shirts per week, working from twelve to fifteen hours a day, and possessing considerable expertness.

The Boston Society for the employment of seamstresses, of which I know not the exact title, pays, as I am credibly informed, but *ten cents for those shirts*, thus limiting the ill-fated women to 90 cents per week, if fully employed, which is seldom the case. Rent of rooms in Boston is higher than here: but suppose it the same, there remain for food, drink, clothes, fuel, soap, candles &c. 40 cents per week, or less than 6 cents per day!

Those incumbered with children, or in indifferent health, or inexpert, cannot make more than six or seven. They are, moreover, as I have already stated, very partially employed. But laying aside all the various disadvantages and drawbacks, and placing the circumstances in the most favourable point of light, let us consider the case of a woman in perfect health, without children, and with uninterrupted employment; and see the result of her painful labours, and how little attention is paid to the awful denunciation against those that "*grind the faces of the poor.*" Allowing nine shirts per week, at 12½ cents, and constant, uninterrupted employment, let us view the appalling result.

9 shirts per week = 1.12½	Per annum, $58 50
Rent at 50 cents,	26 00
Shoes and clothes, suppose,	10 00
Fuel per week, say 15 cents,	7 80
Soap, candles &c., 8 cents,	4 16
Remain for food and drink 20 cents per week,	
or about 2¾ cents per day!!!	10 54

But suppose the woman to have one or two children; to work for ten cents, which is not below the usual average; to be a part of her time unemployed, say one day in each week; and to make, of course, six, but say seven shirts.

7 shirts, or 70 cents per week, is, per annum,	$36 40
Rents, fuel, soap, candles &c. as before	$47 96
Deficit,	11 56

Here is not declamation; no pathetic appeal; no solemn invocation, to arouse the dormant feelings of humanity. It is all a plain statement of harrowing facts, that defy the severest scrutiny. It exhibits a state of suffering which, I had almost said, cries to heaven for vengeance.

In speaking of the effect on some of the unfortunate seamstresses, to drive them to licentious courses, I ought to use the strongest language the subject would admit of, in order to make a deep impression on the reader, somewhat commensurate with the magnitude of the evil, and the enormity of the oppression under which they groan. A due consideration of their actual situation, and the gloomy prospects before them, would lead *a priori*, to anticipate such a deplorable and fatal result. Beset on one side by poverty and wretchedness, with scanty and poor fare, miserable lodgings, clothing inferior in quality and often inadequate in quantity, without the most distant hope of amelioration of condition, by a course of honest and unremitting industry; and on the other side, tempted by the allurements of present enjoyment, comfortable apartments, fine dress, with a round of pleasures: all these held out by vice and crime to entice them from the paths of virtue, is it not the trial almost too severe for poor human nature? Let those who pass a heavy censure on them, and are ready exultingly to cry out, with the Pharisee in the gospel, "Thank God, we are not like one of these," ponder well what might have been their conduct in similar circumstances ...

IT is frequently asked – what remedy can be found for the enormous and cruel oppression experienced by females employed as seamstresses on coarse work, spoolers, etc.? While these classes are so much more numerous than demand for their services requires, a complete remedy for the evil is, I am afraid, impracticable. I venture, to suggest a few palliatives.

1. Public opinion, a powerful instrument, ought to be brought to bear on the subject. All honourable members of society, male and female, ought to unite in denouncing those who "grind the faces of the poor," by taking female labour without a compensation at least adequate for the support of human existence. The pulpit ought to unite in this crusade against a crying injustice, productive of such distressing circumstances.

2. Let the employments of females be multiplied as much as possible. They are admirably calculated for various occupations from which they are at present in a great degree excluded, more especially shop-keeping in retail stores.

3. The poorer class ought to have exclusively the business of whitewashing and other low employments, now in a great degree monopolized by men.

4. Let the Provident Societies, intended to furnish employment for women in winter, be munificently supported; and let those Societies give fair and liberal wages, following the laudable example of the Impartial Humane Society of Baltimore, and the Female Hospitable Society of Philadelphia.

5. Let the ladies have some poor women, who are half-starved, making coarse shirts at 6, 8 and 10 cents each, taught fine needle-work, mantua-making, millinery, clear starching, quilting, &c. There is always a great want of women in these branches.

6. Let schools be opened for instructing poor women in cooking. Good cooks are always scarce.

7. Schools for young ladies, and infant schools, ought, with few exceptions, to be taught by females, who should be regularly educated for these important branches, which are peculiarly calculated for their sex, and which would afford excellent occupation for the daughters of reduced families.

8. Ladies who can afford it, ought to give out their sewing and washing, and pay fair prices. Let them display their economy in any other department than in one which has a tendency to distress and pauperize deserving persons of their own sex.

9. In the towns in the interior of the state, and in those in the western states, there is generally a want of females as domestics, seamstresses, &c. &c.; and in factories, as spoolers, spinners, and weavers. It would be a most meritorious appropriation of a part of the superfluous wealth of the rich, to provide for sending some of the superabundant poor females of our cities to those places.

10. To crown the whole, let ladies who lead the fashion, take up the cause of the poor women, *con amore*. It is a holy cause. They may, with moderate exertions, render it fashionable to endeavor to rescue from unmerited and cruel sufferings, oppressed, forlorn, and neglected classes, as precious, I emphatically repeat, in the eyes of Heaven, as the most exalted and high-minded among themselves.

Other palliatives might be devised, were public attention directed to the subject in any degree proportioned to its importance . . .

3. Sylvester Graham Denounces "The Appetites," 1837[3]

In 1830, Sylvester Graham made a small name for himself as a lecturer for the Pennsylvania Society for Discouraging the Use of Ardent Spirits. A few years later, however, Graham was working in New York City amidst the terrible

---

[3] "The Appetites," *The Graham Journal of Health and Longevity. Devoted to the Practical Illustration of the Science of Human Life, as Taught by Sylvester Graham and Others* (Boston), October 10, 1837.

*cholera epidemic. He began to advocate more than temperance in regard to
alcohol; instead he argued that the diarrhea and vomiting prevalent in cholera
patients was likely the result of various "overindulgences." More specifically,
Graham targeted poor diet, personal hygiene, and excessive sexual activity
as corrosive elements on human health. A "Grahamite" would therefore
advocate regular bathing, loose-fitting clothing, a diet revolving around
coarsely ground grains and vegetables, and a strict regulation of sexual activity
to avoid the "venereal indulgence" that plagued most adults.* The Graham
Journal of Health and Longevity *advertised this lifestyle with contributions
from physicians, moralists, and Sylvester Graham himself. In the following
editorial, Graham explains his approach to curbing human "appetites" that
might seem natural, but nonetheless require mastery in order to achieve
a healthy body and spirit.*

THE APPETITES
UNRESTRAINED IN HEALTH, AND THE VITAL
POWERS WASTED.

Intent as all men are on present enjoyment, they are little inclined to practice
present self-denial for the sake of a future good which they consider in any
possible degree contingent, and will only consent to bear the cross when
compelled by necessity, or when they find it the only means of shunning
imminent destruction, or of escaping from intolerable evils. Hence, so long
as mankind are favored with even a moderate degree of health, they rush
into the eagerly desired excitements of their various pursuits, and pleasures,
and indulgences, and nothing seems to them more visionary and ridiculous,
than precepts, and regulations, and admonitions, concerning the preservation of health. While they possess health, they will not believe that they are
in any danger of losing it – or if they are, nothing in their habits or practices
can have any effect, either in destroying or preserving it; nor can they be
convinced of the universal delusion, that if they enjoy health, they have
within themselves the constant demonstration, that their habits and practices
are conformable to the laws of health, at least in their own constitutions.
They will not, therefore, consent to be benefited contrarily to what they
regard as necessary to their present enjoyment, either by the experience or
by the learning of others.

The consequence is, as a general fact, that while in health, mankind
prodigally waste the resources of their constitutions as if the energies of
life were inexhaustible; and when, by the violence or by the continuance
of their excesses, they have brought on acute or chronic disease, which
interrupts their pursuits and destroys their comforts, they fly to the

physician – not to learn from him by what violations of the laws of life and health they have drawn the evil upon themselves, and by what means they can in future avoid the same and similar difficulties; but considering themselves as unfortunate beings, visited with afflictions which they have in no manner been concerned in causing, they require the exercise of the physician's skill in the application of remedies by which their sufferings may be alleviated and their disease removed; and in doing this, the more the practice of the physician conforms to the appetites of the patient, the greater his popularity, and the more cheerfully and generously is he rewarded.

When the Savior was on earth, and by the exercise of divine power, removed the multifarious evils of gluttony and drunkenness and lewd sensuality, without laying any restraints on the appetites of the multitudes which he healed, his popularity caused the very heavens to ring with the shouts of hosanna which were offered to his name. But when he began to teach men how to keep the evil spirits out of themselves, and how to avoid disease of every kind, by denying their appetites and crucifying their lusts, and obeying the laws which are constitutionally established in the nature of man, the cry of universal and furious indignation was – away with him! away with him!

Some external forms of things have changed since that time, but human nature has, in all respects, remained the same to this present moment; and the physician of this day has to deal with the same appetites and passions which at one moment lauded to heaven, and at the next, consigned to an ignominious death, the infinitely holy and benevolent Jesus. As a prescriber of remedies and a curer of disease, he may be esteemed, and honored, and rewarded by his fellow creatures; but in the present state of society, were he to attempt to enforce those rules of life by which disease may be avoided and health preserved, he would soon find himself surrounded by the cry – away with him! – and poverty and neglect, or persecution, would be the reward of his labors.

And what to a truly enlightened and philanthropic mind would be still more trying than even neglect, and poverty, and persecution, he would be doomed to see his deluded fellow creatures flocking in countless multitudes after every vile imposter, and becoming the infatuated dupes of every species of wicked and murderous quackery.

Every thing, therefore, in the structure and operations of society, tends to confine the practicing physician to the department of therapeutics, and makes him a mere curer of disease; and the consequence is, that excepting the few who are particularly favored by their situations as public teachers, the medical fraternity, even of the present day, have little inducement or opportunity to apply themselves to the study of science of human life, with that devotedness, and zeal, and perseverance, which the profoundness and intricacy of the subject require; while on the other hand, almost everything by which men can be corrupted is continually presented to induce them to become the mere panders of human ignorance, and depravity, and lust; and if they do not sink their noble profession to the level of the vilest empiricism, it is owing to their own moral sensibility, and philanthropy, and love of virtue, and magnanimity, rather than to the discriminating encouragement which they receive from society, to pursue an elevated scientific professional career.

Chapter 13   Anti-Slavery to Abolition

1. African-American Leaders Reject Colonization Schemes, 1831[1]

*Although it remained popular among conservative anti-slavery circles,
the American Colonization Society's (ACS) plan to repatriate former slaves
to Africa was not well received among many northern African-Americans.
The Society's acceptance of slaveholders as members, moreover, caused more
radical abolitionists to break from their ranks by the early 1830s. Only about
12,000 African-Americans migrated to ACS's colony, eventually named
Liberia, over the next half-century. In this address, three prominent
African-Americans from Wilmington, Delaware explain their opposition
to the idea of colonization.*

We the undersigned, in conformity to the wishes of our brethren, beg leave
to present to the public in a calm and unprejudiced manner, our decided and
unequivocal disapprobation of the American Colonization Society, and its
auxiliaries, in relation to the free people of color in the United States.
Convinced as we are, that the operations of this Society have been unchristian and anti-republican in principle, and at variance with our best interests
as a people, we had reason to believe that the precepts of religion, the

[1] "Address by Abraham D. Shadd, Peter Spencer, and William S. Thomas, 12 July 1831,"
Document 5 in C. Peter Ripley, ed., *The Black Abolitionist Papers*, Vol. III: *The United States,
1830–1846* (Chapel Hill: The University of North Carolina Press, 1991), pp. 102–3, 105–6.

dictates of justice and humanity, would have prevented any considerable portion of the community from lending their aid to a plan which we fear was designed to deprive us of rights that the Declaration of Independence declares are "unalienable rights" of all men. We were content to remain silent, believing that the justice and patriotism of a magnanimous people would prevent the annals of our native and beloved country from receiving so deep a stain. But observing the growing strength and influence of that institution, and being well aware that the generality of the public are unacquainted with our views on this important subject, we feel it a duty we owe to ourselves, our children and posterity, to enter our protest against a device so fraught with evil to us. That many sincere friends to our race are engaged in what they conceive to be a philanthropic and benevolent enterprise, we do not hesitate to admit; but that they are deceived, and are acting in a manner calculated most seriously to injure the free people of color, we are equally sensible.

We are natives of the United States; our ancestors were brought to this country by means over which they had no control; we have our attachments to the soil, and we feel that we have rights in common with other Americans; and although deprived through prejudice from entering into the full enjoyment of those rights, we anticipate a period, when in despite of the more than ordinary prejudice which has been the result of this unchristian scheme, "Ethiopia shall stretch forth her hands to God." But that this formidable Society has become a barrier to our improvement, must be apparent to every individual who will but reflect on the course to be pursued by the emissaries of this unhallowed project, many of whom, under the name of ministers of the gospel, use their influence to turn public sentiment to our disadvantage by stigmatizing our morals, misrepresenting our characters, and endeavoring to show what they are pleased to call the sound policy of perpetuating our civil and political disabilities for the avowed purpose of indirectly forcing us to emigrate to the western coast of Africa. That Africa is neither our nation nor home, a due respect to the good sense of the community forbids us to attempt to prove; that our language, habits, manners, morals and religion are all different from those of Africans, is a fact too notorious to admit of the controversy. Why then are we called upon to go and settle in a country where we must necessarily be and remain a distinct people, having no common interest with the numerous inhabitants of that vast and extensive country? Experience has proved beyond a doubt, that the climate is such as not to suit the constitutions of the inhabitants of this country; the fevers and various diseases incident to that tropical clime, are such as in most cases to bid defiance to the force of medicine ...

The present period is one of deep and increasing interest to the free people of color, relieved from the miseries of slavery and its concomitant evils, with the vast and (to us) unexplored field of literature and science before us, surrounded by many friends whose sympathies and charities need not the Atlantic between us and them, before they can consent to assist in elevating our brethren to the standing of men. We therefore particularly invite their attention to the subject of education and improvement; sensible that it is much better calculated to remove prejudice, and exalt our moral character, than any system of colonization that has been or can be introduced; and in which we believe we shall have the cooperation of the wisest and most philanthropic individuals of which the nation can boast. The utility of learning and its salutary effects on the minds and morals of a people, cannot have escaped the notice of any rational individual situated in a country like this, where in order successfully to prosecute any mechanical or other business, education is indispensable. Our highest moral ambition, at present, should be to acquire for our children a liberal education, give them mechanical trades, and thus fit and prepare them for useful and respectable citizens; and leave the evangelizing of Africa, and the establishing of a republic at Liberia, to those who conceive themselves able to demonstrate the practicability of its accomplishment by means of a people, numbers of whom are more ignorant than even the natives of that country themselves.

In conclusion, we feel it a pleasing duty ever to cherish a grateful respect for those benevolent and truly philanthropic individuals, who have advocated, and still are advocating our rights in our native country. Their indefatigable zeal in the cause of the oppressed will never be forgotten by us, and unborn millions will bless their names in the day when the all-wise Creator, in whom we trust, shall have bidden oppression to cease.

ABRAHAM D. SHADD
PETER SPENCER
WM. S. THOMAS

2. Declaration of Sentiments of the American Anti-Slavery Society, 1833[2]

The white abolitionist William Lloyd Garrison also rejected the gradualist doctrines of colonization and helped build a new anti-slavery movement. As editor of Boston's The Liberator, *Garrison argued that slaves should be emancipated immediately without compensation to slaveholders. He and*

---

[2] *Declaration of Sentiments of the American Antislavery Society. Adopted at the Formation of Said Society, in Philadelphia, on the 4th Day of December 1833.* (New York: William Dorr, 1833).

many other abolitionists spurned formal political action, but nonetheless
planned to organize and agitate for their cause. The American Anti-Slavery
Society (AAS), formed in 1833 at a meeting of 62 abolitionists in Philadelphia,
became the national organization dedicated to this relatively new doctrine
of "immediatism." The AAS opened membership to black abolitionists and
enlisted the help of women, both radical concepts for the Early Republic.
In this "Declaration of Sentiments," the AAS describes its abolitionist
principles and lays out an ambitious plan of action.

DECLARATION

The Convention assembled in the City of Philadelphia to organize
a National Anti-Slavery Society, promptly seize the opportunity to promulgate the following DECLARATION OF SENTIMENTS, as cherished
by them in relation to the enslavement of one-sixth portion of the American
people.

More than fifty-seven years have elapsed since a band of patriots convened in this place, to devise measures for the deliverance of this country
from a foreign yoke. The cornerstone upon which they founded the TEMPLE
OF FREEDOM was broadly this – "that all men are created equal; and they
are endowed by their Creator with certain inalienable rights; that among
these are life, LIBERTY, and the pursuit of happiness." At the sound of their
trumpet-call, three millions of people rose up as from the sleep of death, and
rushed to the strife of blood; deeming it more glorious to die instantly as
freemen, than desirable to live one hour as slaves. They were few in number –
poor in resources; but the honest conviction that TRUTH, JUSTICE, and
RIGHT were on their side, made them invincible.

We have met together for the achievement of an enterprise, without which
that of our fathers is incomplete; and which, for its magnitude, solemnity,
and probable results upon the destiny of the world, as far transcends theirs
as moral truth does physical force.

In purity of motive, in earnestness of zeal, in decision of purpose, in
intrepidity of action, in steadfastness of faith, in sincerity of spirit, we
would not be inferior to them.

Their principles led them to wage war against their oppressors, and to
spill human blood like water in order to be free. *Ours* forbid the doing of
evil that good may come, and lead us to reject, and to entreat the oppressed
to reject, the use of all carnal weapons for the deliverance from bondage;
relying solely upon those which are spiritual, and mighty through God to
the pulling down of strongholds.

Their measures were physical resistance – the marshalling in arms – the hostile array – the mortal encounter. *Ours* shall be such only as the opposition of moral purity to moral corruption – the destruction of error by the potency of truth – the overthrow of prejudice by the power of love – and the abolition of slavery by the spirit of repentance.

Their grievances, great as they were, were trifling in comparison with the wrongs and sufferings of those for whom we plead. Our fathers were never slaves – never bought and sold like cattle – never shut out from the light of knowledge and reason – never subjected to the lash of brutal task-masters.

But for those for whose emancipation we are striving – constituting, at the present time, at least one-sixth part of our countrymen – are recognized by the law, and treated by their fellow-beings, as marketable commodities, as goods and chattels, as brute beasts; are plundered daily of the fruits of their toil without redress; really enjoying no constitutional nor legal protection from licentious and murderous outrages upon their persons, are ruthlessly torn asunder – the tender babe from the arms of its frantic mother – the heart-broken wife from her weeping husband – at the caprice or pleasure of irresponsible tyrants. For the crime of having a dark complexion, they suffer the pangs of hunger, the infliction of stripes, and the ignominy of brutal servitude. They are kept in heathenish darkness by laws expressly enacted to make their instruction a criminal offense.

These are the prominent circumstances in the condition of more than two millions of our people, the proof of which may be found in thousands of indisputable facts, and in the laws of the slaveholding States.

Hence we maintain, – that in view of the civil and religious privileges of this nation, the guilt of its oppression is unequalled by any other on the face of the earth; and, therefore,

That it is bound to repent instantly, to undo the heavy burden, to break every yoke, and to let the oppressed go free.

We further maintain – that no man has a right to enslave or imbrute his brother – to hold or acknowledge him, for one moment, as a piece of merchandize – to keep back his hire by fraud – or to brutalize his mind by denying him the means of intellectual, social, and moral improvement.

The right to liberty is inalienable. To invade it is to usurp the prerogative of Jehovah. Every man has a right to his own body – the products of his own labor – to the protection of law, and to the common advantages of society. It is piracy to buy or steal a native African, and subject him to servitude. Surely the sin is as great to enslave an AMERICAN as an AFRICAN.

Therefore we believe and affirm – That there is no difference *in principle*, between the African slave-trade and American slavery.

That every American citizen who retains a human being in involuntary bondage as his property is, according to Scripture (Ex. xxi. 16) a MAN STEALER:

That the slaves ought instantly to be set free, and brought under the protection of law:

That if they lived from the time of Pharaoh down to the present period, and had been entailed through successive generations, their right to be free could never have been alienated, but their claims would have constantly risen in solemnity.

That all those laws which are now in force, admitting the right of slavery, are therefore before God utterly null and void; being an audacious usurpation of the Divine prerogative, a daring infringement on the law of nature, a base overthrow of the very foundations of the social compact, a complete extinction of all the relations, endearments, and obligations of man kind, and a presumptuous transgression of all the holy commandments – and that therefore they ought instantly to be abrogated.

We further believe and affirm – That all persons of color who possess the qualifications which are demanded of others, ought to be admitted forthwith to the enjoyment of the same privileges, and the exercise of the same prerogatives, as others; and that the paths of preferment, of wealth, and of intelligence, should be opened as widely to them as to persons of a white complexion.

We maintain that no compensation should be given to the planters emancipating the slaves;

Because it would be a surrender of the great fundamental principle that man cannot hold property in man;

Because SLAVERY IS A CRIME, AND THEREFORE IS NOT AN ARTICLE TO BE SOLD:

Because the holders of slaves are not the just proprietors of what they claim; freeing the slaves is not depriving them of property, but restoring it to its rightful owners; it is not wronging the master, but righting the slave – restoring him to himself . . .

We regard as delusive, cruel, and dangerous, any scheme of expatriation, which pretends to aid, either directly or indirectly, in the emancipation of the slaves, or to be a substitute for the immediate and total abolition of Slavery.

We fully and unanimously recognize the sovereignty of each State, to legislate exclusively on the subject of Slavery which is tolerated within its limits; we concede that Congress under the present national compact, has no right to interfere with any of the slave States, in relation to this momentous subject:

But we maintain that Congress has a right, and is solemnly bound, to suppress the domestic slave-trade between the several States, and to abolish Slavery in those portions of our territory which the Constitution has placed under its exclusive jurisdiction . . .

We shall organize Anti-Slavery Societies, if possible, in every city, town, and village, in our land.

We shall send forth agents to lift up the voice of remonstrance, of warning, of entreaty, and rebuke.

We shall circulate, unsparingly and extensively, anti-slavery tracts and periodicals.

We shall enlist the pulpit and the press in the cause of the suffering and the dumb.

We shall aim at a purification of the churches from all participation in the guilt of Slavery.

We shall encourage the labor of freemen rather than that of slaves, by giving a preference to their productions: and

We shall spare no exertions nor means to bring the whole nation to speedy repentance.

Our trust for victory is solely in God. We may be personally defeated, but our principles never. TRUTH, JUSTICE, REASON, HUMANITY, must and will gloriously triumph. Already a host is coming up to the help of the Lord, against the mighty, and the prospect before us is full of encouragement.

Submitting this DECLARATION to the candid examination of the people of this country, and of the friends of liberty throughout the world, we hereby affix our signatures to it; pledging ourselves that, under the guidance and by the help of Almighty God, we will do all that in us lies, consistently with this Declaration of our principles, to overthrow the most execrable system of Slavery that has ever been witnessed upon earth – to deliver our land from its deadliest curse – to wipe out the foulest stain which rests upon our national escutcheon – and to secure to the colored population of the United States all the rights and privileges which belong to them as men, and as Americans – come what may to our persons, our interests, or our reputation – whether we live to witness the triumph of LIBERTY, JUSTICE, and HUMANITY, or perish untimely as martyrs in this great, benevolent, and holy cause.

Done at Philadelphia, the 6th day of December, AD 1833.

3. Maria Stewart Speaks at the African Masonic Hall, February 27, 1833[3]

In 1831, a recently widowed free African-American, Maria Stewart, met with William Lloyd Garrison at the offices of The Liberator. *It was the beginning of a brief, but remarkable, career as an abolitionist. Stewart contributed*

---

[3]   *The Liberator* (Boston), April 27, 1833; May 4, 1833.

essays to the Liberator's *"Ladies Department" and emerged as an articulate voice in the cause of immediatism. Although influenced by David Walker's radical* Appeal, *Stewart integrated religious imagery and a message of moral improvement into her anti-slavery message. In September of 1832, she became one of the first women to address a mixed audience of men and women. At that speech in Boston, she denounced colonization. The following spring, Stewart addressed a crowd at the African Masonic Hall to explain her anti-slavery position as well as her frustration with the plight of the North's free African-American community.*

African rights and liberty is a subject that ought to fire the breast of every free man of color in these United States, and excite in his bosom a lively, deep, decided and heart-felt interest. When I cast my eyes on the long list of illustrious names that are enrolled on the bright annals of fame among the whites, I turn my eyes within, and ask my thoughts, "Where are the names of *our* illustrious ones?" It must certainly have been for the want of energy on the part of the free people of color, that they have been long willing to bear the yoke of oppression. It must have been the want of ambition and force that has given the whites occasion to say, that our natural abilities are not as good, and our capacities by nature inferior to theirs. They boldly assert, that, did we possess a natural independence of soul, and feel a love for liberty within our breasts, some one of our sable race, long before this, would have testified it, notwithstanding the disadvantages under which we labor. We have made ourselves appear altogether unqualified to speak in our own defence, and are therefore looked upon as objects of pity and commiseration. We have been imposed upon, insulted and derided on every side; and now, if we complain, it is considered as the height of impertinence. We have suffered ourselves to be considered as Bastards, cowards, mean, faint-hearted wretches; and on this account, (not because of our complexion) many despise us, and would gladly spurn us from their presence.

These things have fired my soul with a holy indignation, and compelled me thus to come forward; and endeavor to turn their attention to knowledge and improvement; for knowledge is power. I would ask, is it blindness of mind, or a stupidity of soul, or the want of education, that has caused our men who are 60 to 70 years of age, never to let their voices be heard, or nor their hands be raised in behalf of their color? Or has it been for the fear of offending the whites? If it has, O ye fearful ones, throw off your fearfulness, and come forth in the name of the Lord, and in the strength of the God of Justice, and make yourselves useful and active members in society; for they admire a noble and patriotic spirit in others; and should they not admire it in us? If you are men, convince them that you possess the spirit of men; and as your day, so shall your strength be. Have the sons of Africa no souls? feel they no ambitious desires? shall the chains of ignorance forever confine them? shall the insipid appellation of "clever negroes," or "good creatures," any longer content them? Where can we find among ourselves the man of science, or a philosopher, or an able statesman, or a counsellor at law? Show me our fearless and brave, our noble and gallant ones. Where are our lecturers on natural history, and our critics in useful knowledge? There may be a few such men among us, but they are rare. It is true, our fathers bled and died in the revolutionary war, and others fought bravely under the command of Jackson, in defence of liberty. But where is the man that has distinguished himself in these modern days by acting wholly in the defence of African rights and liberty? There was one, although he sleeps, his memory lives.

I am sensible that there are many highly intelligent gentlemen of color in those United States, in the force of whose arguments, doubtless, I should discover my inferiority; but if they are blest with wit and talent, friends and fortune, why have they not made themselves men of eminence, by striving to take all the reproach that is cast upon the people of color, and in endeavoring to alleviate the woes of their brethren in bondage? Talk, without effort, is nothing; you are abundantly capable, gentlemen, of making yourselves men of distinction; and this gross neglect, on your part, causes my blood to boil within me. Here is the grand cause which hinders the rise and progress of the people of color. It is their want of laudable ambition and requisite courage.

Individuals have been distinguished according to their genius and talents, ever since the first formation of man, and will continue to be while the world stands. The different grades rise to honor and respectability as their merits may deserve. History informs us that we sprung from one of the most learned nations of the whole earth; from the seat, if not the parent of science; yes, poor, despised Africa was once the resort of sages and legislators of other nations, was esteemed the school for learning, and the most illustrious men in Greece flocked thither for instruction. But it was our gross sins and abominations that provoked the Almighty to frown thus heavily upon us, and give our glory unto others. Sin and prodigality have caused the downfall of nations, kings and emperors; and were it not that God in wrath remembers mercy; we might indeed despair; but a promise is left us; "Ethiopia shall again stretch forth her hands unto God."

But it is of no use for us to boast that we sprung from this learned and enlightened nation, for this day a thick mist of moral gloom hangs over millions of our race. Our condition as a people has been low for hundreds of years, and it will continue to be so, unless, by true piety and virtue, we strive to regain that which we have lost. White Americans, by their prudence, economy and exertions, have sprung up and become one of the most flourishing nations in the world, distinguished for their knowledge of the arts and sciences, for their polite literature. While our minds are vacant, and starving for want of knowledge, theirs are filled to overflowing. Most of our color have been taught to stand in fear of the white man, from their earliest infancy, to work as soon as they could walk, and call "master," before they scarce could lisp the name of *mother*. Continual fear and laborious servitude have in some degree lessened in us that natural force and energy which belong to man; or else, in defiance of opposition, our men, before this, would have nobly and boldly contended for their rights. But give the man of color an equal opportunity with the white from the cradle to manhood, and from manhood to the grave, and you would discover the dignified statesman, the man of science, and the philosopher. But there is no such opportunity for the sons of Africa, and I fear that our powerful ones are fully determined that there never shall be. For bid, ye Powers on high, that it should any longer be said that our men possess no force. O ye sons of Africa, when will your voices be heard in our legislative halls, in defiance of your enemies, contending for equal rights and liberty? How can you, when you reflect from what you have fallen, refrain from crying mightily unto God, to turn away from us the fierceness of his anger, and remember our transgressions against us no more forever. But a God of infinite purity will not regard the prayers of those who hold religion in one hand, and prejudice, sin and pollution in the other; he will not regard the prayers of self-righteousness and hypocrisy. Is it possible, I exclaim, that for the want of knowledge, we have labored for hundreds of years to support others, and been content to receive what they chose to give us in return? Cast your eyes about, look as far as you can see; all, all is owned by the lordly white, except here and there a lowly dwelling which the man of color, midst deprivations, fraud and opposition, has been scarce able to procure. Like king Solomon, who put neither nail nor hammer to the temple, yet received the praise; so also have the white Americans gained themselves a name, like the names of the great men that are in the earth, while in reality we have been their principal foundation and support. We have pursued the shadow, they have obtained the substance; we have performed the labor, they have received the profits; we have planted the vines, they have eaten the fruits of them.

I would implore our men, and especially our rising youth, to flee from the gambling board and the dance-hall; for we are poor, and have no money to throw away. I do not consider dancing as criminal in itself, but it is astonishing to me that our young men are so blind to their own interest and the future welfare of their children, as to spend their hard earnings for this frivolous amusement; for it has been carried on among us to such an unbecoming extent, that it has became absolutely disgusting. "Faithful are the wounds of a friend, but the kisses of an enemy are deceitful." Had those men among us, who have had an opportunity, turned their attention as assiduously to mental and moral improvement as they have to gambling and dancing, I might have remained quietly at home, and they stood contending in my place. These polite accomplishments will never enroll your names on the bright annals of tune, who admire the belle void of intellectual knowledge, or applaud the dandy that talks largely on politics, without striving to assist his fellow in the revolution, when the nerves and muscles of every other man forced him into the field of action. You have a right to rejoice, and to let your hearts cheer you in the days of your youth; yet remember that for all these things, God will bring you into judgment. Then, O ye sons of Africa, turn your mind from these perishable objects, and contend for the cause of God and the rights of man. Form yourselves into temperance societies. There are temperate men among you; then why will you any longer neglect to strive, by your example, to suppress vice in all its abhorrent forms? You have been told repeatedly of the glorious results arising from temperance, and can you bear to see the whites arising in honor and respectability, without endeavoring to grasp after that honor and respectability also?

But I forbear. Let our money, instead of being thrown away as heretofore, be appropriated for schools and seminaries of learning for our children and youth. We ought to follow the example of the whites in this respect. Nothing would raise our respectability, add to our peace and happiness, and reflect so much honor upon us, as to be ourselves the promoters of temperance, and the supporters, as far as we are able, of useful and scientific knowledge. The rays of light and knowledge have been hid from our view; we have been taught to consider ourselves as scarce superior to the brute creation; and have performed the most laborious part of American drudgery. Had we as a people received, one half the early advantages the whites have received, I would defy the government of these United States to deprive us any longer of our rights.

I am informed that the agent of the Colonization Society has recently formed an association of young men, for the purpose of influencing those of us to go to Liberia who may feel disposed. The colonizationists are blind to their own interest, for should the nations of the earth make war with America, they would find their forces much weakened by our absence; or should we remain here, can our "brave soldiers," and "fellow-citizens," as they were termed in time of calamity, condescend to defend the rights of the whites, and be again deprived of their own, or sent to Liberia in return?

Or, if the colonizationists are real friends to Africa, let them expend the money which they collect, in erecting a college to educate her injured sons in this land of gospel light and liberty; for it would be most thankfully received on our part, and convince us of the truth of their professions, and save time, expense and anxiety. Let them place before us noble objects, worthy of pursuit, and see if we prove ourselves to be those unambitious negroes they term us. But ah! methinks their hearts are so frozen towards us, they had rather their money should be sunk in the ocean than to administer it to our relief; and I fear, if they dared, like Pharaoh, king of Egypt, they would order every male child among us to be drowned. But the most high God is still as able to subdue the lofty pride of these white Americans, as He was the heart of that ancient rebel. They say, though we are looked upon as things, yet we sprang from a scientific people. Had our men the requisite force and energy, they would soon convince them by their efforts both in public and private, that they were men, or things in the shape of men. Well may the colonizationists laugh us to scorn for our negligence; well may they cry, "Shame to the sons of Africa." As the burden of the Israelites was too great for Moses to bear, so also is our burden too great for our noble advocate to bear. You must feel interested, my brethren, in what he under-takes, and hold up his hands by your good works, or in spite of himself, his soul will become discouraged, and his heart will die within him; for he has, as it were, the strong bulls of Bashan to contend with.

It is of no use for us to wait any longer for a generation of well educated men to arise. We have slumbered and slept too long already; the day is far spent; the night of death approaches; and you have sound sense and good judgement sufficient to begin with, if you feel disposed to make a right use of it. Let every man of color throughout the United States, who possesses the spirit and principles of a man, sign a petition to Congress, to abolish slavery in the District of Columbia, and grant you the rights and privileges of common free citizens; for if you had had faith as a grain of mustard seed, long before this the mountains of prejudice might have been removed. We are all sensible that the Anti-Slavery Society has taken hold of the arm of our whole population, in order to raise them out of the mire. Now all we have to do is, by a spirit of virtuous ambition to strive to raise ourselves; and I am happy to have it in my power thus publicly to say, that the colored inhabitants of this city, in some respects, are beginning to improve. Had the free people of color in these United States nobly and boldly contended for their rights, and showed a natural genius and talent, although not so brilliant as some; had they help up, encouraged and patronized each other, nothing could have hindered us from being a thriving and flourishing people. There has been a fault among us. The reason why our distinguished men have not made themselves more influential is, because they fear that the strong current of opposition through which they must pass, would cause their downfall and prove their overthrew. And what gives rise to this opposition? Envy. And what has it amounted to? Nothing. And who are the cause of it? Our whited sepulchers, who want to be great, and don't know how; who love to be called of men "Rabbi, Rabbi," who put on false sanctity, and humble themselves to their brethren, for the sake of acquiring the highest place in the synagogue, and the uppermost seats at the feast. You, dearly beloved, who are the genuine followers of our Lord Jesus Christ, the salt of the earth and the light of the world, are not so culpable. As I told you, in the very first of my writing, I tell you again, I am but as a drop in the bucket – as one particle of the small dust of the earth. God will surely raise up those among us who will plead the cause of virtue, and the pure principles of morality, more eloquently than I am able to do.

It appears to me that America has become like the great city of Babylon, for she has boasted in her heart, – I sit a queen, and am no widow, and shall see no sorrow? She is indeed a seller of slaves and the souls of men; she has made the Africans drunk with the wine of her fornication; she has put them completely beneath her feet, and she means to keep them there; her right hand supports the reins of government, and her left hand the wheel of power, and she is determined not to let go her grasp. But many powerful sons and daughters of Africa will shortly arise, who will put down vice and immorality among us, and declare by Him that sitteth upon the throne, that they will have their rights; and if refused, I am afraid they will spread horror and devastation around. I believe that the oppression of injured Africa has come up before the Majesty of Heaven; and when our cries shall have reached the ears of the Most High, it will be a tremendous day for the people of this land; for strong is the arm of the Lord God Almighty.

Life has almost lost its charms for me; death has lost its sting and the grave its terrors; and at times I have a strong desire to depart and dwell with Christ, which is far better. Let me entreat my white brethren to awake and save our sons from dissipation, and our daughters from ruin. Lend the hand of assistance to feeble merit, plead the cause of virtue among our sable race; so shall our curses upon you be turned into blessings; and though you should endeavor to drive us from these shores, still we will cling to you the more firmly; nor will we attempt to rise above you: we will presume to be called your equals only.

The unfriendly whites first drove the native American from his much loved home. Then they stole our fathers from their peaceful and quiet dwellings, and brought them hither, and made bond-men and bond-women of them and their little ones; they have obliged our brethren to labor, kept them in utter ignorance, nourished them in vice, and raised them in degradation; and now that we have enriched their soil, and filled their coffers, they say that we are not capable of becoming like white men, and that we never can rise to respectability in this country. They would drive us to a strange land. But before I go, the bayonet shall pierce me through. African rights and liberty is a subject that ought to fire the breast of every free man of color in these United States, and excite in his bosom a lively, deep, decided and heart-felt interest.

Discussion Questions

1. Do the religious sentiments expressed in these documents seem particular to the Early Republic? Do they offer hints as to why this period saw such active revivalism? What elements from other documents might explain the resurgence in religious enthusiasm?
2. Can we lump together the various perspectives in Part V into a single unified "reform" movement? Is it important to do so? Why or why not?
3. Would you expect the various reforms advocated in Part V to be closely linked with the descriptions of everyday life found in Part IV? How might the changes in the American economy and urban life contribute to the spirit of reform? Are the two developments inseparable? Or do you think you could consider them in isolation?
4. In a document later in this volume, Henry Clay argues that abolitionism undermines American political parties. Is there evidence of why this is the case in these documents from the abolitionists themselves? Do they mention politics at all? Does it naturally follow that their movement would move from religious and moral reform circles into American politics?
5. Do you see traces of the logic and persuasive rhetoric used in these Early Republic reformers in today's self-improvement or philanthropic movements? Would folks like Sylvester Graham make any headway in modern American society? Why or why not?

Part VI   Jackson's America

Introduction to Part VI

Many American historians label the period from 1815 to 1848 the "Age of Jackson." Although he only served the customary two terms as president, the shadow Andrew Jackson cast over those three decades was quite large. As the self-appointed representative of the American "common man," Jackson claimed to represent his interests in Washington. This attitude translated into electoral success for Jackson and his Democratic Party during the 1830s, but Americans quickly discovered that the idea of the "people" was limited by race and gender. Free African-Americans, Native Americans, and other minorities did not figure into Jackson's idea of the "common man," and women of all races encountered the proscriptive limits of domesticity. So, on the one hand, this period saw an unprecedented opening of the political system. The Second American Party System of Whigs and Democrats mobilized voters to show up at the polls in record numbers. Using the partisan press to knit together local, state, and national communities of like-minded voters, party operatives marshaled resources on behalf of their candidates and laid the foundation for an American system of mass politics that still resonates today. But, on the other hand, it is important to keep in mind that even as Jacksonian politics signaled the triumph of the "common man," Jacksonian America remained strictly segregated along racial, cultural, and gender lines.

Chapter 14   The Rise of the "Common Man"

1. The Inauguration of Andrew Jackson, March 4, 1829[1]

Andrew Jackson won 56 percent of the popular vote in the presidential election of 1828, but his candidacy meant more for American politics than these numbers would suggest. The first real mass political campaign in the United States portrayed Andrew Jackson as the foremost representative of the "common man." The political ascendancy of "Old Hickory," therefore, signaled an end to the older, deferential style of campaigning and ushered in a new and brash form of party politics. On the occasion of Jackson's Inaugural on March 4, 1829, thousands of observers flocked to the capital to see their champion firsthand, creating a political spectacle of unprecedented dimensions. Jackson delivered the following address while still mourning the death of his wife, Rachel, only a few months earlier. Nonetheless, the political spectacle surrounding the arrival of the new president caught the attention of several Washington insiders. Among them was Margaret Bayard Smith, a well-connected political insider who recorded this celebration of the "common man" for posterity. This section reproduces Smith's description of the celebrations of that day followed by the text of Andrew Jackson's official inaugural address.

---

[1]   Margaret Bayard Smith, *The First Forty Years of Washington Society, Portrayed by the Family Letters of Mrs. Samuel Harrison Smith (Margaret Bayard), From the Collection of Her Grandson, J. Henley Smith*, ed. Gaillard Hunt (New York: Charles Scribner's Sons, 1906), pp. 290–7; *Saturday Evening Post* (Philadelphia), March 14, 1829.

... I left the rest of this sheet for an account of the inauguration. It was not a thing of detail of a succession of small incidents. No, it was one grand whole, an imposing and majestic spectacle and to a reflective mind one of moral sublimity. Thousands and thousands of people, without distinction of rank, collected in an immense mass round the Capitol, silent, orderly and tranquil, with their eyes fixed on the front of that edifice, waiting the appearance of the President in the portico. The door from the Rotunda opens, preceded by the marshals, surrounded by the Judges of the Supreme Court, the old man with his grey locks, that crown of glory, advances, bows to the people, who greet him with a shout that rends the air, the Cannons, from the heights above Alexandria and Fort Warburton proclaim the oath he has taken and all the hills reverberate the sound. It was grand, – it was sublime! An almost breathless silence succeeded and the multitude was still, – listening to catch the sound of his voice, tho' it was so low, as to be heard only by those nearest to him. After reading his speech, the oath was administered to him by the Chief Justice. The Marshal presented the Bible. The President took it from his hands, pressed his lips to it, laid it reverently down, then bowed again to the people – Yes, to the people in all their majesty. And had the spectacle closed here, even Europeans must have acknowledged that a free people, collected in their might, silent and tranquil, restrained solely by a moral power, without a shadow around of military force, was majesty, rising to sublimity, and far surpassing the majesty of Kings and Princes, surrounded with armies and glittering in gold. But I will not anticipate, but will give you an account of the inauguration in mere detail ...

We stood on the South steps of the terrace; when the appointed hour came saw the General and his company advancing up the Avenue, slow, very slow, so impeded was his march by the crowds thronging around him. Even from a distance, he could be discerned from those who accompanied him, for he only was uncovered, (the Servant in presence of his Sovereign, the People). The south side of the Capitol hill was literally alive with the multitude, who stood ready to receive the hero, and the multitude who attended him. "There there, that is he," exclaimed different voices. "Which?" asked others. "He with the white head," was the reply. "Ah," exclaimed others, "there is the old man and his gray hair, there is the old veteran, there is Jackson." ...

At the moment the General entered the Portico and advanced to the table, the shout that rent the air, still resounds in my ears. When the speech was over, and the President made his parting bow, the barrier that had separated the people from him was broken down and they rushed up the steps all eager to shake hands with him. It was with difficulty that he made his way through the Capitol and down the hill to the gateway that opens on the avenue. Here for a moment he was stopped. The living mass was impenetrable. After a while a passage was opened, and he mounted his horse which had been provided for his return (for he had walked to the Capitol) then such a cortege as followed him! Country men, farmers, gentlemen, mounted and dismounted, boys, women and children, black and white. Carriages, wagons and carts all pursuing him to the President's house, – this I only heard of for our party went out at the opposite side of the square and went to Col. Benton's lodgings, to visit Mrs. Benton and Mrs. Gilmore. Here was a perfect levee, at least a hundred ladies and gentlemen, all happy and rejoicing, – wine and cake was handed in profusion ...

We continued promenading here, until near three, returned home unable to stand and threw ourselves on the sopha. Some one came and informed us the crowd before the President's house, was so far lessen'd, that they thought we might enter. This time we effected our purpose. But what a scene we did witness! The *Majesty of the People* had disappeared, and a rabble, a mob, of boys, negros, women, children, scrambling, fighting, romping. What a pity what a pity! No arrangements had been made, no police officers placed on duty and the whole house had been inundated by the rabble mob. We came too late. The President, after having been *literally* nearly pressed to death and almost suffocated and torn to pieces by the people in their eagerness to shake hands with Old Hickory, had retreated through the back way or south front and had escaped to his lodgings at Gadsby's. Cut glass and china to the amount of several thousand dollars had been broken in the struggle to get the refreshments, punch and other articles had been carried out in tubs and buckets, but had it been in hogsheads it would have been insufficient, ice-creams, and cake and lemonade, for 20,000 people, for it is said that number were there, tho' I think the estimate exaggerated. Ladies fainted, men were seen with bloody noses and such a scene of confusion took place as is impossible to describe, – those who got in could not get out by the door again, but had to scramble out the windows. At one time, the President who had retreated and retreated until he was pressed against the wall, could only be secured by a number of gentlemen forming round him and making a kind of barrier of their own bodies, and the pressure was so great that Col. Bomford who was one said that at one time he was afraid they should have been pushed down, or on the President. It was then the windows were thrown open, and the torrent found an outlet, which otherwise might have proved fatal.

This concourse had not been anticipated and therefore not provided against. Ladies and gentlemen, only had been expected at this Levee, not the people en masse. But it was the People's day, and the People's President and the People would rule. God grant that one day or other, the People, do not put down all rule and rulers. I fear, enlightened Freemen as they are, they will be found, as they have been found in all ages and countries where they get the Power in their hands, that of all tyrants, they are the most ferocious, cruel and despotic. The noisy and disorderly rabble in the President's House brought to mind descriptions I had read, of the mobs in the Tuileries and at Versailles, I expect to hear the carpets and furniture are ruined, the streets were muddy, and these guests all went thither on foot.

The rest of the day, overcome with fatigue I lay upon the sopha ...

First Inaugural Address of President Andrew Jackson

Fellow-Citizens:

About to undertake the arduous duties that I have been appointed to perform by the choice of a free people, I avail myself of this customary and solemn occasion to express the gratitude which their confidence inspires and to acknowledge the accountability which my situation enjoins. While the magnitude of their interests convinces me that no thanks can be adequate to the honor they have conferred, it admonishes me that the best return I can make is the zealous dedication of my humble abilities to their service and their good.

As the instrument of the Federal Constitution it will devolve on me for a stated period to execute the laws of the United States, to superintend their foreign and their confederate relations, to manage their revenue, to command their forces, and, by communications to the Legislature, to watch over and to promote their interests generally. And the principles of action by which I shall endeavor to accomplish this circle of duties it is now proper for me briefly to explain.

In administering the laws of Congress I shall keep steadily in view the limitations as well as the extent of the Executive power, trusting thereby to discharge the functions of my office without transcending its authority. With foreign nations it will be my study to preserve peace and to cultivate friendship on fair and honorable terms, and in the adjustment of any differences that may exist or arise to exhibit the forbearance becoming a powerful nation rather than the sensibility belonging to a gallant people.

In such measures as I may be called on to pursue in regard to the rights of the separate States I hope to be animated by a proper respect for those sovereign members of our Union, taking care not to confound the powers they have reserved to themselves with those they have granted to the Confederacy.

The management of the public revenue – that searching operation in all governments – is among the most delicate and important trusts in ours, and it will, of course, demand no inconsiderable share of my official solicitude. Under every aspect in which it can be considered it would appear that advantage must result from the observance of a strict and faithful economy. This I shall aim at the more anxiously both because it will facilitate the extinguishment of the national debt, the unnecessary duration of which is incompatible with real independence, and because it will counteract that tendency to public and private profligacy which a profuse expenditure of money by the Government is but too apt to engender. Powerful auxiliaries to the attainment of this desirable end are to be found in the regulations provided by the wisdom of Congress for the specific appropriation of public money and the prompt accountability of public officers.

With regard to a proper selection of the subjects of impost with a view to revenue, it would seem to me that the spirit of equity, caution and compromise in which the Constitution was formed requires that the great interests of agriculture, commerce, and manufactures should be equally favored, and that perhaps the only exception to this rule should consist in the peculiar encouragement of any products of either of them that may be found essential to our national independence.

Internal improvement and the diffusion of knowledge, so far as they can be promoted by the constitutional acts of the Federal Government, are of high importance.

Considering standing armies as dangerous to free governments in time of peace, I shall not seek to enlarge our present establishment, nor disregard that salutary lesson of political experience which teaches that the military should be held subordinate to the civil power. The gradual increase of our Navy, whose flag has displayed in distant climes our skill in navigation and our fame in arms; the preservation of our forts, arsenals, and dockyards, and the introduction of progressive improvements in the discipline and science of both branches of our military service are so plainly prescribed by prudence that I should be excused for omitting their mention sooner than for enlarging on their importance. But the bulwark of our defense is the national militia, which in the present state of our intelligence and population must render us invincible. As long as our Government is administered for the good of the people, and is regulated by their will; as long as it secures to us the rights of person and of property, liberty of conscience and of the press, it will be worth defending; and so long as it is worth defending a patriotic militia will cover it with an impenetrable aegis. Partial injuries and occasional mortifications we may be subjected to, but a million of armed freemen, possessed of the means of war, can never be conquered by a foreign foe. To any just system, therefore, calculated to strengthen this natural safeguard of the country I shall cheerfully lend all the aid in my power.

It will be my sincere and constant desire to observe toward the Indian tribes within our limits a just and liberal policy, and to give that humane and considerate attention to their rights and their wants which is consistent with the habits of our Government and the feelings of our people.

The recent demonstration of public sentiment inscribes on the list of Executive duties, in characters too legible to be overlooked, the task of reform, which will require particularly the correction of those abuses that have brought the patronage of the Federal Government into conflict with the freedom of elections, and the counteraction of those causes which have disturbed the rightful course of appointment and have placed or continued power in unfaithful or incompetent hands.

In the performance of a task thus generally delineated I shall endeavor to select men whose diligence and talents will insure in their respective stations able and faithful cooperation, depending for the advancement of the public service more on the integrity and zeal of the public officers than on their numbers.

A diffidence, perhaps too just, in my own qualifications will teach me to look with reverence to the examples of public virtue left by my illustrious predecessors, and with veneration to the lights that flow from the mind that founded and the mind that reformed our system. The same diffidence induces me to hope for instruction and aid from the coordinate branches of the Government, and for the indulgence and support of my fellow-citizens generally. And a firm reliance on the goodness of that Power whose providence mercifully protected our national infancy, and has since upheld our liberties in various vicissitudes, encourages me to offer up my ardent supplications that He will continue to make our beloved country the object of His divine care and gracious benediction.

2. David Walker Describes the Condition of Free African-Americans, 1829[2]

David Walker was born a free African-American in North Carolina, but by the 1820s he was living and working in Boston, Massachusetts. In 1829 he published a pamphlet, commonly called An Appeal to the Coloured Citizens of the World, *which contained a scathing indictment of slavery and called upon African-Americans to resist the institution, with violence if necessary.*

[2] David Walker, *Appeal to the Coloured Citizens of the World*, ed. Peter Hinks (University Park, PA: Penn State Press, 2000), pp. 30–3.

Although Walker wrote the Appeal *for circulation among enslaved African-Americans in the South, it is an important document that linked the cause of free northern blacks to the issue of slavery and made him a leading abolitionist writer. Walker died in 1830, probably from an illness, but before long his* Appeal *became one of the most controversial pamphlets in antebellum America. In this brief excerpt, Walker describes how the existence of American slavery affects the status of African-Americans regardless of their status or location. In an era in which politicians championed the image of the "common man," David Walker reminds us of the ways in which that representation often excluded free African-Americans.*

... Men of colour, who are also of sense, for you particularly is my APPEAL designed. Our more ignorant brethren are not able to penetrate its value. I call upon you therefore to cast your eyes upon the wretchedness of your brethren, and to do your utmost to enlighten them – *go to work and enlighten your brethren!* – Let the Lord see you doing what you can to rescue them and yourselves from degradation. Do any of you say that you and your family are free and happy, and what have you to do with the wretched slaves and other people? So can I say, for I enjoy as much freedom as any of you, if I am not quite as well off as the best of you. Look into our freedom and happiness, and see of what kind they are composed!! They are of the very lowest kind – they are the very *dregs*! – they are the most servile and abject kind, that ever a people was in possession of! If any of you wish to know how FREE you are, let one of you start and go through the southern and western States of this country, and unless you travel as a slave to a white man (a servant is a *slave* to the man whom he serves) or have your free papers, (which if you are not careful they will get from you) if they do not take you up and put you in jail, and if you cannot give good evidence of your freedom, sell you into eternal slavery, I am not a living man: or any man of colour, immaterial who he is, or where he came from, if he is not the fourth from the negro race!! (as we are called) the white Christians of America will serve him the same they will sink him into wretchedness and degradation for ever while he lives. And yet some of you have the hardihood to say that you are free and happy! May God have mercy on your freedom and happiness!! I met a coloured man in the street a short time since, with a string of boots on his shoulders; we fell into conversation, and in course of which, I said to him, what a miserable set of people we are! He asked, why? – Said I, we are so subjected under the whites, that we cannot obtain the comforts of life, but by cleaning their boots and shoes, old clothes, waiting on them, shaving them &c. Said he, (with the boots on his shoulders) "I am completely happy!!! I never want to live any better or happier than when I can get a plenty of boots and shoes to clean!!!" Oh! How can those who are actuated by avarice only, but think, that our Creator made us to be an inheritance to them fore ever, when they see that our greatest glory is centered in such mean and low objects? Understand me, brethren, I do not mean to speak against the occupations by which we acquire enough and sometimes scarcely that, to render ourselves and families comfortable through life. I am subjected to the same inconvenience, as you all. – My objections are, to our *glorying* and being *happy* in such low employments; for if we are men, we ought to be thankful to the Lord for the past, and for the future. Be looking forward with thankful hearts to higher attainments than *wielding the razor* and *cleaning boots and shoes.* The man whose aspirations are not *above*, and even *below* these, is indeed, ignorant and wretched enough. I advanced it therefore to you, not as a *problematical*, but as an unshaken and for ever immovable *fact*, that your full glory and happiness, as well as all other coloured people under Heaven, shall never be fully consummated, but with the *entire emancipation of your enslaved brethren all over the world.* You may therefore, go to work and do what you can to rescue, or join in with tyrants to oppress them and yourselves, until the Lord shall come upon you all like a thief in the night. For I believe it is the will of the Lord that our greatest happiness shall consist in working for the salvation of our whole body. When this is accomplished a burst of glory will shine upon you, which will indeed astonish you and the world. Do any of you say this never will be done? I assure you that God will accomplish it – if nothing else will answer, he will hurl tyrants and devils into *atoms* and make way for his people. But O my brethren! I say unto you again, you must go to work and prepare the way of the Lord.

There is great work for you to do, as trifling as some of you may think of it. You have to prove to the Americans and the world that we are MEN, and not *brutes*, as we have been represented, and by millions treated. Remember, to let the aim of your labors among your brethren, and particularly the youths, be the dissemination of education and religion. It is lamentable, that many of our children go to school, from four until they are eight or ten, and sometimes fifteen years of age, and leave school knowing but a little more about the grammar of their language than a horse does about handling a musket – and not a few of them are really so ignorant, that they are unable to answer a person correctly, general questions in geography, and to hear them read, would only be to disgust a man who has a taste for reading; which, to do well, as trifling as it may appear to some, (to the ignorant in particular) is a great part of learning. Some few of them, may make out to scribble tolerably well, over a half sheet of paper, which I believe has hitherto been a powerful obstacle in our way, to keep us from acquiring knowledge. An ignorant father, who knows no more than what nature has taught him, together with what little he acquires by the senses of hearing and seeing, finding his son able to write a neat hand, sets it down for granted that he has as good learning as any body; the young, ignorant gump, hearing his father or mother, who perhaps may be ten times more ignorant, in point of literature, than himself, extolling his learning, struts about, in the full assurance, that his attainments in literature are sufficient to take him through the world, when, in fact, he has scarcely any learning at all!!!! ...

3. Sarah Grimké Defends the Rights of Women, 1837[3]

Angelina and Sarah Grimké were the daughters of a slaveholding judge and planter in South Carolina. Despite their upbringing the Grimké sisters became prominent abolitionist speakers in the 1830s, drawing huge "promiscuous" (mixed men and women) crowds to their lectures. When Angelina spoke at Boston's State House to present anti-slavery petitions signed by 20,000 Massachusetts women in 1838, she was the first American woman to ever formally address a legislature. As effective speakers in the cause of abolition, the Grimké sisters also pushed conventional notions as to the proper place of women in American society. More specifically, they challenged gender proscriptions that called upon women to be passive, non-political, and submissive to men. In this letter to a fellow abolitionist, Sarah responds to a letter from the General Association of Congregational Ministers of Massachusetts that denounced female reformers and public speakers. So, for the Grimké sisters and other women, the rise of the "common man" in the United States need not stop along gender lines in order to truly realize the nation's democratic potential.

Haverhill, 7th Mo. 1837
Dear Friend,
When I last addressed thee, I had not seen the pastoral Letter of the General Association. It has since fallen into my hands, and I must digress from my intention of exhibiting the condition of women in different parts of the

[3] Sarah Grimké, ed., *Letters on the Equality of the Sexes and the Condition of Woman. Addressed to Mary S. Parker, President of the Boston Female Anti-Slavery Society* (Boston, MA: Isaac Knapp, 1838), pp. 14–21.

world, in order to make some remarks on this extraordinary document. I am persuaded that when the minds of men and women become emancipated from the thralldom of superstition and "traditions of men," the sentiments contained in the Pastoral Letter will be recurred to with as much astonishment as the opinions of Cotton Mather and other distinguished men of his day, upon the subject of witchcraft; nor will it be deemed less wonderful, that a body of divines would gravely assemble and endeavor to prove that woman has no right to "open her mouth for the dumb," than it now is that judges would have sat on the trials of witches, and solemnly condemned nineteen persons and one dog to death for witchcraft.

But to the letter. It says, "We invite your attention to the dangers which at present seem to threaten the FEMALE CHARACTER with wide-spread and permanent injury." I rejoice that they have called the attention of my sex to this subject, because I believe if woman investigates it, she will soon discover that danger is impending, though from a totally different source from which the Association apprehends, – danger from those who, having long held the reins of *usurped* authority, are unwilling to permit us to fill that sphere which God created us to move in, and who have entered into league to crush the immortal mind of woman. I rejoice, because I am persuaded that the rights of woman, like the rights of slaves, need only be examined to be understood and asserted, even by some of those, who are now endeavoring to smother the irrepressible desire for mental and spiritual freedom which glows in the breast of many, who hardly dare to speak their sentiments . . .

The Lord Jesus defines the duties of his followers in his Sermon on the Mount. He lays down grand principles by which they should be governed, without any references to sex or conditions. – "Ye are the light of the world. A city that is set on a hill cannot be hid. Neither do men light a candle and put it under a bushel, but on a candlestick, and it giveth light unto all that are in the house. Let your light so shine before men, that they may see your good works, and glorify your Father which is in Heaven" [Matt. 5:14–16]. I follow him through all his precepts, and find him giving the same directions to woman as to men, never even referring to the distinction now so strenuously insisted upon between masculine and feminine virtues: this is one of the anti-Christian "traditions of men" which are taught instead of the "commandments of God." Men and women were CREATED EQUAL; they are both moral and accountable beings, and whatever is *right* for man to do, is *right* for woman.

But the influence of woman, says the Association, is to be private and unobtrusive; her light is not to shine before man like that of her brethren; but she is passively to let the lords of the creation, as they call themselves, put the bushel over it, lest peradventure it might appear that the world has been benefited by the rays of *her* candle. So that her quenched light, according to their judgment, will be of more use than if it were set on the candlestick. "Her influence is the source of mighty power." This has ever been the flattering language of man since he laid aside the whip as a means to keep woman in subjection. He spares the body; but the war he has waged against her mind, her heart, and her soul, has been no less destructive to her as a moral being. How monstrous, how anti-Christian, is the doctrine that woman is to be dependent on man! Where, in all the sacred Scriptures, is this taught? Alas! she has too well learned the lesson, which MAN has labored to teach her. She has surrendered her dearest RIGHTS, and has been satisfied with the privileges which man has assumed to grant her; she has been amused with the show of power, whilst man has absorbed all the reality into himself. He has adorned the creature whom God gave him as a companion, with baubles and gewgaws, turned her attention to personal attractions, offered incense to her vanity, and made her the instrument of his selfish gratification, a plaything to please his eye and amuse his hours of leisure. "Rule by obedience and by submission sway," or in other words, study to be a hypocrite, pretend to submit, but gain your point, has been the code of household morality which woman has been taught. The poet has sung, in sickly strains, the loveliness of woman's dependence upon man, and now we find it reechoed by those who profess to teach the religion of the Bible. God says, "Cease ye from man whose breath is in his nostrils, for wherein is he to be accounted of?" Man says, depend upon me. God says, "HE will teach us of his ways." Man says, believe it not, I am to be your teacher. This doctrine of dependence upon man is utterly at variance with the doctrine of the Bible. In that book I find nothing like the softness of woman, nor the sternness of man: both are equally commanded to bring forth the fruits of the Spirit, love, meekness, gentleness, &c.

But we are told, "the power of woman is in her dependence, flowing from a consciousness of that weakness which God has given her for her protection." If physical weakness is alluded to, I cheerfully concede the superiority; if brute force is what my brethren are claiming, I am willing to let them have all the honor they desire; but if they mean to intimate, that mental or moral weakness belongs to woman, more than to man, I utterly disclaim the charge. Our powers of mind have been crushed, as far as man could do it, our sense of morality has been impaired by his interpretation of our duties; but no where does God say that he made any distinction between us, as moral and intelligent beings ...

The General Association say, that "when woman assumes the place and tone of man as a public performer, our care and protection of her seem unnecessary; we put ourselves in self-defense against her, and her character becomes unnatural." Here again the unscriptural notion is held up, that there is a distinction between the duties of men and women as moral beings; that what is virtue in man, is vice in woman; and women who dare to obey the command of Jehovah, "Cry aloud, spare not, lift up thy voice like a trumpet, and show my people their transgression" [Isa. 58:1], are threatened with having the protection of the brethren withdrawn. If this is all they do, we shall not even know the time when our chastisement is inflicted; our trust is in the Lord Jehovah, and in him is everlasting strength. The motto of woman, when she is engaged in the great work of public reformation should be, – "The Lord is my light and my salvation; whom shall I fear? The Lord is the strength of my life; of whom shall I be afraid?" [Ps. 27:1]. She must feel, if she feels rightly, that she is fulfilling one of the important duties laid upon her as an accountable being, and that her character, instead of being "unnatural," is in exact accordance with the will of Him to whom, and to no other, she is responsible for the talents and the gifts confided to her. As to the pretty simile, introduced into the "Pastoral Letter," "If the vine whose strength and beauty is to lean upon the trellis work, and half conceal its clusters, thinks to assume the independence and the overshadowing nature of the elm," &c. I shall only remark that it might well suit the poet's fancy, who sings to me utterly inconsistent with the dignity of a Christian body, to endeavor to draw such an anti-scriptural distinction between men and women. Ah! how many of my sex feel in the dominion, thus unrighteously exercised over them, under the gentle appellation of *protection*, that what they have leaned upon has proved a broken reed at best, and oft a spear.

Thine in the bonds of womanhood,
Sarah M. Grimké

Chapter 15   Native Americans and the Common Man

1. Andrew Jackson Attempts to Justify Indian Removal to Congress, 1830[1]

The Removal Act was one of the most controversial pieces of legislation of the Jackson Administration. It authorized the creation of territories west of the Mississippi River for the relocation of eastern Native Americans, outlined the process by which this transfer of land would occur, and provided $500,000 to carry out the entire program. Inherent in this legislation was the idea that Native Americans must be removed from areas of white settlement because coexistence was impossible. A bare-knuckle debate in Congress followed, buttressed by the appearance of petitions, memorials, and letters weighing in on both sides of the issue. While Jackson and his followers argued that Native Americans needed to be relocated for their own protection, opponents of the Removal Act argued that its provisions were arbitrary, its logic unjust, and its philosophy un-Christian. The Senate eventually passed the bill 28 to 19 in April of 1830 and it only squeaked through the House, 102 to 97, a month later. In December of that same year, President Jackson attempted to rationalize the program to a skeptical Congress.

... It gives me pleasure to announce to Congress that the benevolent policy of the Government, steadily pursued for nearly thirty years, in relation to the removal of the Indians beyond the white settlements is approaching to a happy consummation. Two important tribes have accepted the provision

---

[1]   *US Senate Journal*, 21st Cong., 2nd Sess. (Washington: Duff Green, 1830), pp. 22–5.

made for their removal at the last session of Congress, and it is believed that their example will induce the remaining tribes also to seek the same obvious advantages.

The consequences of a speedy removal will be important to the United States, to individual States, and to the Indians themselves. The pecuniary advantages which it promises to the Government are the least of its recommendations. It puts an end to all possible danger of collision between the authorities of the General and State Governments on account of the Indians. It will place a dense and civilized population in large tracts of country now occupied by a few savage hunters. By opening the whole territory between Tennessee on the north and Louisiana on the south to the settlement of the whites it will incalculably strengthen the southwestern frontier and render the adjacent States strong enough to repel future invasions without remote aid. It will relieve the whole State of Mississippi and the western part of Alabama of Indian occupancy, and enable those States to advance rapidly in population, wealth, and power. It will separate the Indians from immediate contact with settlements of whites; free them from the power of the States; enable them to pursue happiness in their own way and under their own rude institutions; will retard the progress of decay, which is lessening their numbers, and perhaps cause them gradually, under the protection of the Government and through the influence of good counsels, to cast off their savage habits and become an interesting, civilized, and Christian community. These consequences, some of them so certain, and the rest so probable, make the complete execution of the plan sanctioned by Congress at their last session an object of much solicitude.

Toward the aborigines of the country no one can indulge a more friendly feeling than myself, or would go further in attempting to reclaim them from their wandering habits, and make them a happy, prosperous people. I have endeavored to impress upon them my own solemn convictions of the duties and powers of the General Government in relation to the State authorities . . .

Humanity has often wept over the fate of the aborigines of this country; and philanthropy has been long busily employed in devising means to avert it. But its progress has never for a moment been arrested; and, one by one, have many powerful tribes disappeared from the earth. To follow to the tomb the last of his race, and to tread on the graves of extinct nations, excite melancholy reflections. But true philanthropy reconciles the mind to these vicissitudes, as it does to the extinction of one generation to make room for another. In the monuments and fortresses of an unknown people, spread over the extensive regions of the west, we behold the memorials of a once powerful race, which was exterminated, or has disappeared, to make room for the existing savage tribes. Nor is there any thing in this, which, upon a comprehensive view of the general interests of the human race, is to be regretted. Philanthropy could not wish to see this continent restored to the condition in which it was found by our forefathers. What good man would prefer a country covered with forests and ranged by a few thousand savages to our extensive Republic, studded with cities, towns, and prosperous farms embellished with all the improvements which art can devise or industry execute, occupied by more than 12,000,000 happy people, and filled with all the blessings of liberty, civilization and religion!

The present policy of the Government is but a continuation of the same progressive change by a milder process. The tribes which occupied the countries now constituting the Eastern States were annihilated or have melted away to make room for the whites. The waves of population and civilization are rolling to the westward, and we now propose to acquire the countries occupied by the red men of the South and West by a fair exchange, and, at the expense of the United States, to send them to land where their existence may be prolonged and perhaps made perpetual. Doubtless it will be painful to leave the graves of their fathers; but what do they more than our ancestors did or than our children are now doing? To better their condition in an unknown land our forefathers left all that was dear in earthly objects. Our children by thousands yearly leave the land of their birth to seek new homes in distant regions. Does humanity weep at these painful separations from everything, animate and inanimate, with which the young heart has become entwined? Far from it. It is rather a source of joy that our country affords scope where our young population may range unconstrained in body or in mind, developing the power and facilities of man in their highest perfection. These remove hundreds and almost thousands of miles at their own expense, purchase the lands they occupy, and support themselves at their new homes from the moment of their arrival. Can it be cruel in this Government when, by events which it can not control, the Indian is made discontented in his ancient home to purchase his lands, to give him a new and extensive territory, to pay the expense of his removal, and support him a year in his new abode? How many thousands of our own people would gladly embrace the opportunity of removing to the West on such conditions! If the offers made to the Indians were extended to them, they would be hailed with gratitude and joy.

And is it supposed that the wandering savage has a stronger attachment to his home than the settled, civilized Christian? Is it more afflicting to him to leave the graves of his fathers than it is to our brothers and children? Rightly considered, the policy of the General Government toward the red man is not only liberal, but generous. He is unwilling to submit to the laws of the States and mingle with their population. To save him from this alternative, or perhaps utter annihilation, the General Government kindly offers him a new home, and proposes to pay the whole expense of his removal and settlement ...

2. John Ross Explains the Position of the Cherokee Nation, 1834[2]

John Ross was an influential leader within the Cherokee Nation at its time of greatest crisis. Ross had fought with Andrew Jackson against the pro-British Creeks during the War of 1812. A decade later Ross lived on a large plantation in western Georgia, owned African-American slaves, and was among the principal architects of the American-inspired Cherokee Constitution. In all respects, save for his Cherokee heritage, John Ross was indistinguishable from white Georgians of wealth and prestige.
But when gold was discovered on Indian land in 1828, white prospectors inundated the Cherokee Nation. The resulting tension between Native American landowners and white trespassers encouraged Georgia's legislature to claim their authority to land guaranteed to the Cherokee by treaty. Despite the violation of federal law and the Supreme Court's backing of Cherokee treaty rights, the state-level confiscation of Native American land continued. Although some Cherokees chose to migrate to their mandated federal lands west of the Mississippi, John Ross and the majority of Cherokee fought removal through the courts and with appeals to leading American politicians. In this 1834 letter to President Jackson, Ross and other Cherokee leaders maintain their rights as spelled out in various federal treaties and outline their opposition to the State of Georgia's continued confiscation of their lands.

Washington, Browns Hotel, 12th March 1834

Honored Sir:

The relations of peace and friendship so happily and so long established between the white and the red man by your illustrious predecessors and our beloved chieftains, induces us, as representatives of the Cherokee nation, to address you in the language of our departed sires, and in the character of

[2] Gary E. Moulton, ed., *The Papers of Chief John Ross, Vol. 1: 1807–1839* (Norman: University of Oklahoma Press, 1985), pp. 277–9. © 1985 by University of Oklahoma Press. Reprinted with permission from the University of Oklahoma Press.

children – call you Father. The appellation in its original sense carries with it simplicity, and the force of filial regard. By treaty the Cherokee nation for divers important considerations acknowledge the Cherokee people to be under the protection of these *United States* and *of no other sovereign whosoever* and stipulated that they *will not hold any treaty with any foreign power*, with individual State, or individuals of any State. And the United States, in return, gave *assurances* of protection, good neighborhood and the solemn guarantee for the remainder of their lands not ceded, forever. From this alliance the redman very naturally was induced to look upon the Chief Magistrate of this great nation as the guardian of his rights. Hence the emphatic and endearing appellation "Father" was bestowed on him. Under the fostering care and patronage of this government the arts of civilization and christianization were successfully introduced into our nations; and from the growing intercourse of the good neighborhood between the Cherokees and the citizens of bordering states, the progress of improvement soon spread its happy influence over the whole country – thereby exhibiting clearly by practical demonstration the force and effects of surrounding circumstances. It is not our purpose in this address, to go into an argument on the question of the relations which the Cherokee nation sustain towards the United States, nor to discuss the merits of our rights under them, as have been recognized and established by existing treaties. The records of the several Departments of this Government, as we humbly conceive, amply testify to, and proclaim them. It is enough for us to know, and say to you frankly, Father – your Cherokee children are in deep distress owing to the unnatural and very oppressive acts extended by the illegal hand of their white brethren of Georgia, and other bordering states. By those enacted by Georgia the property, the liberty, the freedom and life of the Cherokee are placed in jeopardy because they are left at the mercy of the white robber and assassin to be taken with impunity. No redress of wrongs can the Cherokee receive from the Georgia courts, unless the foul deed be perpetrated in the sight of a white person, who may possess sufficient independence and honesty to testify to the facts, in behalf of the injured person. In a word, Georgia has not only surveyed and lotteried off all the Cherokee lands among her citizens, within the chartered limits of that state, but she has gone on in her legislation to act on the principle that the Cherokees are intruders upon her soil, and are liable to be expelled therefrom at her discretion. For such is the fact exhibited by the late act we laid before you – and the effects of that law have already been witnessed and felt by some of the Cherokees. Thus it is seen that solemn treaty engagements, made under the Constitution of the United States, by those departed sages who once sat in the exalted chair you now fill, with the

Cherokee nation, have been assailed and are about to be destroyed by a power from a quarter least to have been expected. Our territory within the limits of the other adjoining states are also likely to be overrun by intruders from the several states, as there are already numerous trespassers on Cherokee lands in those sections of the country. Each state being a party bound by the constitution of the Union, must equally be so in relation to the treaties made under its provisions. The power of making treaties having been conceded by the states to the general Government, the Cherokee nation established its alliance with the United States alone, and have ever since faithfully observed and never departed therefrom.

It is reasonable to suppose had Georgia not conceded this power to the General Government and the Cherokees had preserved the right of treating with whatsoever power they pleased, treaties at that early day might have been entered into by the Cherokee nation with Georgia upon as favorable principles as those made with the United States. However, be this as it may, the Cherokees can now only hang their hopes on the magnanimity and good faith of the United States. And in order to relieve our suffering people from their present distressed situation we feel it to be our duty to bring the subject immediately before your serious consideration in such a matter, as in our judgment the principles of honor and justice will sanction. The great body of the Cherokee people having refused & will never voluntarily consent to remove west of the Mississippi. And with the view of harmonizing the good feeling of all the interested parties & to put an end to the perplexing difficulties which have so unhappily brought distress upon our people, we most respectfully call your particular attention to the following point. Should the Cherokee nation agree to cede to the United States for the use of Georgia a portion of its territory, will the President agree to have the laws and treaties executed and enforced for the effectual protection of the Cherokee nation on the remainder of their territory.

And should you be disposed to enter into an arrangement on this basis, you will please to signify it as early as practicable. To avoid misunderstanding and waste of your time by a personal interview, we have deemed it most proper to communicate these sentiments in writing. And we should be gratified, if possible, to receive your reply from under your own signature. With great respect we have the honor to be, Sir yr. obt. Hble. Servts.

Jno Ross Hair Conrad (X)
Danl. McCoy John Tinson
R. Taylor

3. A Description of Native American Removal in Tennessee, January 24, 1835[3]

Although some members of Congress fought to preserve the claims of nations like the Cherokees, Creeks, and Choctaws, individual states continued to pass legislation extending their jurisdiction over lands recognized as Native American by federal treaties. Although the Indian Removal Act was a piece of federal legislation, state governments played a major role in the confiscation and redistribution of Native American land within their own boundaries. In this 1835 letter Samuel G. Smith, Tennessee's Secretary of State, describes the relations between whites and Cherokees in Eastern Tennessee to Representative James K. Polk. Tennessee had passed legislation claiming sovereignty over Cherokee lands in 1833, and Smith was sent to reconcile several conflicting claims on land ownership.

Cheroke Agency Jany 24 1835

Dear Sir

A few weeks since I apprised you of a visit in contemplation to reconcile the difference between the Cherokes and border settlers within the chartered limits of the State of Tennessee. I have spent a week in this nation bordering on the frontier. There is evidently much unfriendly feeling between the Whites & Indians, but I am satisfied that this matter can be adjusted so far as to guard against hostilities or acts of violence.

The Whites have been poring in this country since the passage of the law by the Legislature of Tennessee extending the jurisdiction over this country. The population at present within that boundary is estimated at four thousand and rapidly increasing by emigration.

The policy of Georgia, North Carolina, and Alabama is pressing the whole Indians population over into the limits of Tennessee which causes the difficulties.

The land known as Cheroke country within the three former states may now be considered as settled and literally in the occupation of the whites.

The subject is unusually agitated and may probably become a subject of discussion that when the Indian title is extinguished that part of the land in Tennessee is the property of the State and designed for the promotion

[3]   Herbert Weaver and Kermit L. Hall, eds., *Correspondence of James K. Polk*, Vol. III: *1835–1836* (Nashville: Vanderbilt University Press, 1975), pp. 64–5.

of education – that the Indians now crowding in & settling will ask for reservations in a treaty. If such an impression should be made in Tennessee they will take decisive steps against the Indians.

My own opinion is that the principal men of the Nation are seriously engaged in the consideration of the subject of a treaty & that necessity will bring them to the determination to sell. They are holding private [*illegible*] the object of which is not disclosed but since I cam among them several who were intently opposed to selling say they are willing and that they believe it for the best but they ask unreasonable terms. The time is fast approaching when the common Indians constituting the great body of the Nation which must [*illegible*] where they are. The country will be filled up with the whites and it is now folly to think of removing them. Taking all those in the four states and undertake to remove them would be like depopulating a whole State.

I am about to make an excursion through the nation of about twenty days when I shall set out for home. I shall then be able to form some opinion upon this subject. I will then give you the opinion I form. Excuse this hasty & imperfect note.

I will write in reply to your letter in a day or two.

Sam G. Smith

Chapter 16   The Second American
Party System

1. A Violent Election Season in New York City, 1834[1]

*By the time of Andrew Jackson's second presidential term, his political
opponents derisively referred to him as "King Andrew." It makes sense, then,
that when this opposition crystallized into a formal political party in 1834,
Jackson's enemies invoked the anti-monarchist faction from British politics,
the "Whigs," to name themselves. For the next two decades, the Democrats
and Whigs battled for political supremacy at all levels of American electoral
politics. Elections became enthusiastic demonstrations of partisan affiliation,
as party activists rushed to "turn out the vote" for their favored candidates.
This selection from Philip Hone's diary captures the hustle and bustle of
New York City during an election season. As the former mayor of New York
City and president of the Delaware and Hudson Canal Company, Hone was
most comfortable with the Whig Party's emphasis upon economic growth and
order, and was a constant critic of the "mobocracy" that many Whigs saw
inherent in the Democratic Party's followers.*

Tuesday, April 8. – The election for mayor and charter officers commenced
this day with a degree of spirit and zeal in both parties never before
witnessed ... The number of votes will be very great, probably thirty-five
thousand; the Whig Party, whose candidate for mayor is Mr. Verplanck, are
active, zealous, and confident of success. A great meeting was held yesterday

---

[1]   Allan Nevins, ed., *The Diary of Philip Hone, 1828–1851. Volume 1* (New York: Dodd,
Mead, & Company, 1927), pp. 121–5.

at four o'clock at the Exchange, at which Benjamin Strong presided ...
Several resolutions were passed, one of which recommends to the merchants
and traders to omit their usual attendance at the Exchange, to close their
stores and places of business at noon on each of the three days of election, in
order to devote their undivided attention to the great business of reform at the
polls. This last suggestion has been in part observed; many stores are closed
to-day, and several have notices on their doors that the inmates have gone
to the polls to vote for Verplanck. A very large meeting was also held last
evening of adopted citizens at Masonic Hall to approve the course of
Dr. MacNevin in joining our party. After the meeting adjourned they went to
his house and cheered him, and he addressed them, wishing the party success.
They came also before my door and gave me some hearty huzzas, but I was
unfortunately absent, having gone to the theater with my girls and Miss Kane.
My wife was alarmed at the row, as I had a visit of another kind a few evenings
since from a party of retainers of Tammany Hall, and she was not able in her
fright to distinguish between the shouts of enemies and the cheers of friends.

Wednesday, April 9. – *Election*. There were several riots yesterday in the
Sixth Ward, which have been repeated this morning. Respectable persons
were beaten and trampled in the mud. Joseph Strong, the former alderman
of the ward, is charged with having instigated and encouraged the rioters.
The mayor and sheriff were called upon and interfered promptly and
vigorously, and order was restored. Similar disturbances took place at the
same polls this morning, and many persons were seriously hurt.

Thursday, April 10. – Last day of the election; dreadful riots between the
Irish and the Americans have again disturbed the public peace. I happened
to be a witness of the disgraceful scene which commenced the warfare.
On leaving the hospital at noon, Mr. Goodhue and I, observing the mini-
ature frigate which our people have drawn through the streets during the
election standing before the Masonic Hall, we went over and ascended to
the large room, where several persons of the Whig Party were assembled,
all perfectly quiet, as were the crowd in the streets, when suddenly the alarm
was given, and a band of Irishmen of the lowest class came out of Duane
Street from the Sixth Ward poll, armed with clubs, and commenced a savage
attack upon all about the ship and the hall. There was much severe fighting
and many persons were wounded and knocked down. The Irishmen then
retired and the frigate was drawn away, but in a few minutes the mob
returned with a strong reinforcement, and the fight was renewed with the
most unrelenting barbarity. The mayor arrived with a strong body of watchmen, but they were attacked and overcome, and many of the watchmen
are severely wounded. Eight of them were carried to the hospital, where
I went to visit them ...

Friday, April 11. – Such an excitement! So wonderful is the result of this election that all New York has been kept in a state of alarm; immense crowds have been collected at Masonic and Tammany Halls, but the greatest concourse was in front of the Exchange. The street was a dense mass of people. Partial returns were coming in every few minutes, and so close has been the vote that the Whigs at the Exchange and the small party for Jackson in front of the office of the *Standard* opposite shouted alternately as the news was favorable to one or the other; and up to the last moment the result was doubtful, when, at the close of the canvass, the majority for Mr. Lawrence, the Jackson candidate, out of the immense number of votes, 35,141, was found to be 179. There is no doubt, however, that we have elected a majority of aldermen and assistants. The Common Council is reformed and we shall succeed in the great fall election. It is a signal triumph of good principles over violence, illegal voting, party discipline, and the influence of officeholders ...

Tuesday, April 15. – This was the day of the great fête at Castle Garden to celebrate the triumph gained by the Whig Party in the late charter election in this city, and it went off gloriously. Tens of thousands of freemen, full of zeal and patriotism, filled the area of the castle; every inch of ground was occupied. Tables were spread in a double row within the outer circumference; three pipes of wine and forty barrels of beer were placed in the center under an awning, and served out during the repast. Many speeches were made, regular and volunteer toasts were drunk, and the beautiful little frigate *Constitution*, which has borne so conspicuous a station in the late struggle, was placed upon the top of the building which forms the entrance to the garden, from which she fired a salute during the fête. All was enthusiasm and the shouts from time to time rent the air. But on a signal given the immense concourse broke up in good order and no excess or rioting marred the pleasure of the day. Six or eight thousand men formed a procession, and marched off the Battery preceded by a band of music ...

2. Henry Clay on Whig Strategy, November 3, 1838[2]

If the Whig Party had a single face, it would be that of Henry Clay.
This five-time presidential contender began his career as one of the pro-war
"War Hawks" during the Madison Administration, spurred on internal
improvements as a "National Republican" in the decade following the war,

[2]   Henry Clay to Francis Brooke, November 3, 1838, in Robert Seager, ed., *The Papers of Henry Clay, Vol. 9: The Whig Leader, January 1, 1837–December 31, 1843* (Lexington: University Press of Kentucky, 1988), pp. 245–6.

and became Andrew Jackson's greatest political rival as the leader of the
Whig Party during the 1830s and 1840s. Clay often played up his image of
a humble Kentuckian with the same "common man" origins as Jackson.
Throughout his career, however, he demonstrated a keen legal mind and a
strong support for the pro-banking and high tariff policies of his fellow Whigs.
As a resident of a "border state" when it came to slavery, Clay also advocated
compromise in regards to its future and extension into the western territories.
As this letter to a fellow politico demonstrates, Clay viewed the budding
abolitionist movement as as much of a threat to the Whig Party's future as
the machinations of the great Democratic strategist, Amos Kendall.

... I received your favor of the 18th ultimo, and, as it informed me of your intention to go to Richmond, I address this letter to that city. You think I have too good an opinion of mankind. I confess that I have, throughout life, striven to think well of them, but the last thirteen years have shaken my faith very much. I yet, however, believe the mass to be honest, although very liable to deception.

You are certainly right as to one of the two gentlemen mentioned, perhaps as to both, being unwilling to see me elected Chief Magistrate. I was great surprised at the course of "The [Boston] Atlas;" and although Mr. Webster disavows its authority to speak for him, in that particular, there are intelligent persons near him who believe that "The Atlas" presumed upon his concurrence. The issue of the elections, this fall, so far, have been very unfavorable to the Whig cause. From September of last year to September of this, the current ran deep and strong in our favor, and swept over every State, changing majorities against us, or at least, diminishing them. All at once, and without any apparent cause, the current reverses its direction. What has produced it? To give you a proof that I am not too confiding, I can not forbear expressing my suspicion that a profuse and corrupt use has been made of the public money. It is almost impossible otherwise to account satisfactorily for what we have witnessed. Amos Kendall was at Columbus the week before the election. How easy was it for him to give orders throughout the State, from that central point of Ohio, to carry the election at any cost. And how can he be brought to account, if he has given such orders?

Other circumstances will enable us to account for some of the results of these elections. In Ohio, the Abolitionists are alleged to have gone against us, almost to a man. Senator [Thomas] Morris, you know, is one of them, and that, put together with the unfortunate case of the Methodist preacher, delivered up by Governor [Joseph] Vance upon the demand of the Governor of Kentucky [James Clark], turned them against us. Perhaps they were previously inclined toward Mr. Van Buren.

If New York goes against us, as is to be apprehended after what has occurred, our cause will look bad. You will know the event by the time this letter reaches you. It is to be apprehended, because, whether changes have been produced in other States by voluntary impulse of the people, or by corrupt means, the same cause, whatever it may be, is likely to exert itself in New York.

The introduction of this new element of Abolitionism into our elections can not fail to excite, with all reflecting men, the deepest solicitude. It is, I believe, the first time it has been done. Although their numbers are not very great, they are sufficiently numerous, in several States, to turn the scale. I have now before me a letter from the Secretary [James G. Birney] of the American Anti-Slavery Society, in New York, in which he says: "I should consider (as in all candor I acknowledge that I would) the election of any slaveholder to the Presidency a great calamity to the country."

The danger is that the contagion may spread until it reaches all the free States; and if it ever comes to be acted on as a rule among them, to proscribe slaveholders, they have the numbers to enforce it. Union and concert with them will throw the whole Government into their hands, and when they have once possession, the principle by which they have acquired it will urge them on to other and further encroachments. They will begin by prohibiting the slave trade, as it is called, among the slave States, and by abolishing it in the District of Columbia, and the end will be —

My own position, touching slavery, at the present time, is singular enough. The Abolitionists are denouncing me as a slaveholder, and slaveholders as an Abolitionist, while they both unite on Mr. Van Buren.

I should be extremely happy to visit Richmond and see you and the many other friends I have there, but I can not do it while I remain a *quasi* candidate for the Presidency. A candidate in fact I can not say, and have not said to any human being I would be. I am strongly inclined to promulgate that I will not be, under any circumstances. How would it do? The principal objection which I perceive, is, that they would say that I saw the grapes were sour. But then, what need I care for any thing they may say? ...

3. New Hampshire Papers Debate the "Log Cabin" Campaign, 1840[3]

Newspapers served as the lifeblood of American party politics during the Early Republic. Many small towns had two, even three, newspapers with

[3] *New-Hampshire Sentinel* (Keene), February 12, 1840; *New Hampshire Patriot and State Gazette* (Concord), June 8, 1840.

open partisan affiliations. Editors therefore acted more as loyal devotees to the Democratic or Whig cause than they did independent arbiters of political issues. As a result, elections in the Second American Party System relied upon the printed media to disseminate ideas, positions, and stereotypes. During the heated presidential contest of 1840, newspapers played a critical role. Democrats ran Martin Van Buren, a wily New Yorker with a long political career; Whigs supported the famous war hero General William Henry Harrison. In these brief selections from two newspapers from New Hampshire – a state with no little political import today – the role of the partisan press in circulating stereotypes about the opponent while dispelling those of their own candidates come across in short bursts of political rhetoric.

– From the *New-Hampshire Sentinel* (Keene), February 12, 1840

ARISTOCRACY. – The darling theme of the loco focos is and has been the *aristocracy of the Whigs – the rich against the poor*; and similar cant phrases, to catch the ears of the groundlings, and to prejudice the poorer, but honest portions of the community against the Whig party and their principles. But in illustration of the *truth* of such assertions, the great Whig party, through their representatives, the brilliant and honored of the land, have selected, in General Convention, WILLIAM HENRY HARRISON, the old solider and poor farmer, as their candidate for presidency! And who do the loco focos present to run against this candidate? Martin Van Buren, a court dandy, a ruffle-shirt-aristocrat, riding in his coach-and-six – aping the luxurious nobility of Europe, and rolling like an eastern monarch, in glittering wealth, amassed, as some say, from the hard-earnings of the poor! Look, ye, "democrats," upon the picture and cease prating about aristocracy!

– From the *New Hampshire Patriot and State Gazette* (Concord), June 8, 1840

THE "PRINCIPLES" OF THE WHIGS.

The Keene Sentinel speaks of Gen. Harrison as a "man with ability and determination to carry out the *principles* of the Whigs." The question has a thousand times been asked *what are the principles of the Whigs?* and the only answer we have seen is that given by Gen. Harrison's keepers, *"that the national whig convention deemed IMPOLITIC to publish any general declaration of the PRINCIPLES of the great opposition party,"* and that *"the General make no further declaration of HIS PRINCIPLES for the public eye."* The inference from all this is, that the whigs have some principles, of some sort, but that they are such as they are *ashamed* to avow. Why should it be deemed *impolitic* to avow principles which are right? or why attempt to cheat the people by *concealing* principles which are odious? If the British whigs wish for a *National Bank – a tariff – a system of internal improvements – an assumption of the State debts by the general government,* – why not openly and boldly avow it, and place the issue on these questions? Why attempt to cheat the people into the support of a black cockade federalist, by a *hurrah for hard cider,* and when they have placed him at the head of the government, force upon the country all these odious measures which the people have time and again repudiated? The cheat is too palpable to be successful. The people will not be satisfied to go with a party, who either have no principles at all, or if any, such as are too odious to be tolerated. If Mr. Prentiss will state *what* the *"whig principles"* are, which Gen. Harrison will carry out, he will do what no whig politician has attempted to do, and what it is much doubted any whig politician *can* do, for the simple reason, that the British whigs have no principles to avow. If the whigs have really any principles, and Mr. Prentiss knows what they are, he has now an opportunity to immortalize his name and his paper by being the first to proclaim them.

Discussion Questions

1. Consider the enthusiasm exhibited by Jackson's followers in the first document in Part VI, followed by the frustration expressed by David Walker and Sarah Grimké. How would you use these contrasting accounts to gauge American "public opinion" during Jacksonian America?
2. Do the documents concerning Indian removal in Part VI suggest that US–Native American relations were based on racial ideology? Or do you think that cultural differences were paramount in this relationship?
3. Do the documents in Part VI describe an optimistic or pessimistic nation? Do you get a sense of where most Americans felt their country was headed? How would you say that these documents relate to the concept of the "common man" in the Early Republic? Does Andrew Jackson's inaugural address suggest that he is championing the "common man"? How about Margaret Bayard Smith's description of his inaugural celebration?
4. What was the driving force behind the party system of Whigs and Democrats? Do you get a sense of the two parties from the documents in Part VI? How do they compare with today's political parties?
5. Imagine that you're charged with titling a textbook on this period and the editors have told you that "Jacksonian America" or the "Age of Jackson" is unacceptable. What title would you provide that would reflect all of the voices in Part VI? Do these documents give you a sense of how the era should be remembered by historians or the American public?

Part VII   The American Continent

Introduction to Part VII

Most citizens of the Early American Republic lived within a few hundred miles of the Atlantic Ocean and never laid eyes on the Mississippi River or the vast lands beyond its banks. An increasing number of Anglo-Americans, however, began to regard the West as a future home. Of course, this land was not uninhabited. Native American nations as diverse as those of Europe and Asia still lived in the territory west of the Mississippi, even as the United States laid claim to much of the continent following the 1803 Louisiana Purchase. To the southwest, moreover, the Republic of Mexico held vast amounts of land coveted by the United States. By the early 1840s, Americans were present in the Oregon Territory to the northwest and California on the west coast; and the national debate over whether to annex the newly created Republic of Texas was in full swing. President James K. Polk's foreign policy insured that the United States eventually absorbed these territories, either by treaty or by force. The resulting War with Mexico was as much a smashing military success as the War of 1812 was a military failure. But unlike the earlier contest, in which the nation saw an upsurge in patriotism and confidence, the end of the War with Mexico left the American nation with a political conundrum: what to do about the future of slavery in newly acquired territories? The answer would consume the political landscape of the 1850s, but suffice to say here that it suggests that the American West offered both great opportunities and great dangers for citizen and country alike.

Chapter 17   The Mississippi and Beyond

1. Narcissa Whitman Describes Missionary Life in Oregon, 1836[1]

The Oregon Territory was a political entity created by a series of treaties between Russia, Great Britain, and the United States. By the 1820s, few Europeans lived in the area, so claims of ownership seemed fairly irrelevant to the Cayuse, Nez Perce, Chinook, and other Native Americans living in the area. These peoples soon became the target of American missionaries, as Narcissa Whitman and her husband Marcus traveled to Oregon in 1836 on behalf of the American Board of Commissioners for Foreign Missions and set up a small mission in Waiilatput, outside of modern-day Walla Walla. Narcissa's letters to her family, excerpted below, are a good example of the attitude that many missionaries held towards Native Americans, as well as the loneliness that accompanied such work. The Whitmans would not be the only Americans in the area for long. In 1842, the first wagon train of American settlers arrived via the "Oregon Trail" and, within a few years, thousands of white migrants flowed into the region. The Whitman Mission became a prominent stop along the Oregon Trail and thus an important key to white settlement of Oregon. This transition did not come without friction, as in 1847 members of the Cayuse Nation attacked the Whitman Mission and killed Marcus and Narcissa.

---

[1] Clifford Merrill Drury, ed., *Where Wagons Could Go: Narcissa Whitman and Eliza Spalding* (Lincoln: University of Nebraska Press, 1997), pp. 121–4, 126–7.

DEC 26th Where are we now? & and who are we that we should be thus blessed of the Lord. I can scarcely realize that we are thus comfortably fixed & keeping house so soon after our marriage when considering what was then before us. We arrived here on the tenth distance twenty five miles from W[alla] W[alla] found a house reared & the lean too enclosed, a good chimney & fire place & the floor laid. No windows or door except blankets. My heart truly leaped for joy as I alighted from my horse entered and seated myself before a pleasant fire (for it was now night). It occurred to me that my dear Parents had made a similar beginning & perhaps more difficult one than ours ...

... Wieletpoo Jan 2 1837. Universal fast day. Through the kind Providence of God we are permitted to celebrate this day in heathen lands. It has been one of peculiar interest to us, so widely separated from kindred souls, alone, in the thick darkness of heathenism. We have just finished a seperate room for ourselves with a stove in it, lent by Mr P for our use this winter. Thus I am spending my winter as comfortably as heart could wish, & have suffered less from excessive cold than in many winters previous & that the winter is nearly over. After a season of worship during which I felt great depressure of spirits, we visited the lodges. All seemed well pleased as I had not been to any of them before.

We are on the lands of the Old Chief Umtippe who with a lodge or two are now absent for a few days hunting deer. But a few of the Cayuses winter here. They appear to seperate in small companies, make caches of provision in the fall & remain for the winter, & besides they are not well united. The young Chief Towerlee is of another family & is more properly the ruling chief. He is Uncle to the Young Cayuse Halket now at Red River Mission whom we expect to return this fall & to whom the chieftainship belongs by inheritance. The Old Chief Umtippe has been a savage creature in his day. His heart is still the same, full of all manner of hypocrisy deceit and guile. He is a mortal beggar as all Indians are. If you ask a favour of him, sometimes it is granted or not just as he feels, if granted it must be well paid for. A few days ago he took it into his head to require pay for teaching us the language & forbid his people from coming & talking with us for fear we should learn a few words of them. The Cayuses as well as the Nez Perces are very strict in attending to their worship which they have regularly every morning at day break & eve at twilight and once on the Sab. They sing & repeat a form of prayers very devoutly after which the Chief gives them a talk. The tunes & prayer were taught them by a Roman Catholic trader. Indeed their worship was commenced by him. As soon as we became settled we established a meeting among them on the Sab in our own house. Did not think it best to interfere with their worship especially evenings, when we spend considerable time in teaching them to sing. About 12 or 14 boys come regularly every night & are delighted with it.

SAB JAN 29 Our meeting today with the Indians was more interesting than usual. I find that as we succeed in their language in communicating the truth to them so as to obtain a knowledge of their views & feelings, my heart becomes more & more interested in them. They appear to have a partial knowledge of the leading truths of the Bible; of sin, so far as it extends to outward actions, but know [no] knowledge of the heart.

FEB 1st Husband has gone to Walla W to day & is not expected to return until tomorrow eve, & I am alone for the first time to sustain the family alter, in the midst of a room full of native youth & boys, who have come in to sing as usual. After worship several gathered close arround me as if anxious I should tell them some thing about the Bible. I had been reading the 12 chap of Acts, & with Richards help endeavored to give them an account of Peters imprisonment &c, as well as I could. O that I had full possession of their language so that I could converse with them freely . . .

MARCH 30th Again I can speak of the goodness & mercy of the Lord to us in an especial manner. On the evening of my birthday March 14th we received the gift of a little Daughter a treasure invaluable. During the winter my health was very good, so as to be able to do my work. About a week before her birth I was afflicted with an inflammatory rash which confined me mostly to my room. After repeated bleeding it abated very considerably. I was sick but about two hours. She was born half past eight, so early in the evening that we all had time to get considerable rest that night . . .

Thus you see Beloved Sisters how the missionary does in heathen lands. No Mother, No Sister, to relieve me of a single care, only an affectionate Husband, who was a Physition & nurse exceeds all I ever knew. He was excessively pressed with care and labour during the whole time of my confinement. Besides the attention I required of him, he had my washing & the cooking to do for the family. (Mrs. P had two children with her & on account of her ill health she could not give much assistance). During the same week we were thronged with company for the whole camp of Indians had arrived. . . . It was a great mercy that I have been able to take the whole care of my babe & that she is so well & quiet. The Little Stranger is visited daily by the Chiefs & principal men in camp & the women throng the house continually waiting an opportunity to see her. Her whole appearance is so new to them. Her complexion her size & dress & all excite a deal of wonder for they never raise a child here except they are lash tight to a board & the girls heads undergo the flatening process . . . She is plump & large, hold her head up finely & looks about considerably. She weighs ten pounds. Tee-low-kike, a friendly Indian, called to see her the next day after she was born; Said she was a Cayuse Te-mi (Cayuse girl) because she was born on Cayuse wai-tis (Cayuse land). He told us her arrival was expected by all the peoples of the country. The Nez Perces, Cayuses & Walla Wallapoos Indians & now she had arrived it would soon be heard of by them all, & we must write to our land & tell our Parents & friends of it. The whole tribe are highly pleased because we allow her to be called a Cayuse Girl. We have beautiful weather this month. March here is as pleasant as May is in New York.

2. George Catlin Describes the Mandan Buffalo Dance, 1841[2]

Although many white Americans traveled to the lands west of the Mississippi River to displace Native Americans, some sought to observe their unique culture. George Catlin was among the most prolific of these students of Native American life. He originally studied law, but as a young man he dropped this pursuit to become an artist. By the late 1820s, Catlin had established himself as one of Washington DC's leading portrait artists. He then decided to combine his interest in Native Americans with his artistic expertise. From 1829 to 1838, Catlin painted over 600 portraits of Native American leaders for public display. His aims could perhaps be seen as perpetuating the "noble savage" stereotype of Native Americans, but Catlin continued to travel across the American West and South writing narratives and sketching Native Americans in their homelands. This excerpt of his observations of the Mandan Nation, who lived in the Missouri River Valley in modern-day North Dakota, comes from his 1841 book entitled Letters and Notes on the Manners, Customs, and Condition of the North American Indians.

The Mandans, like all other tribes, lead lives of idleness and leisure; and of course, devote a great deal of time to their sports and amusements, of which they have a great variety. Of these, dancing is one of the principal, and may be seen in a variety of forms: such as the buffalo dance, the boasting dance, the begging dance, the scalp dance, and a dozen other kinds of dances, all of which have their peculiar characters and meanings or objects.

These exercises are exceedingly grotesque in their appearance, and to the eye of a traveler who knows not their meaning or importance, they are an uncouth and frightful display of starts, and jumps, and yelps, and jarring gutturals, which are sometimes truly terrifying. But when one gives them

---

[2]   George Catlin, *Letters and Notes on the Manners, Customs, and Condition of the North American Indians*, Vol. 1 (London: Tosswill and Myers, 1841), pp. 126–8.

a little attention, and has been lucky enough to be initiated into their mysterious meaning, they become a subject of the most intense and exciting interest. Every dance has its peculiar step, and every step has its meaning; every dance also has its peculiar song, and that is so intricate and mysterious oftentimes, that not one in ten of the young men who are dancing and singing it, know the meaning of the song which they are chanting over. None but the medicine-men are allowed to understand them; and even they are generally only initiated into these secret arcane, on the payment of a liberal stipend for their tuition, which requires much application and study. There is evidently a set song and sentiment for every dance, for the songs are perfectly measured, and sung in exact time with the beat of a drum; and always with an uniform and invariable set of sounds and expressions, which clearly indicate certain sentiments, which are expressed by the voice, though sometimes not given in any known language whatever . . .

My ears have been almost continually ringing since I came here, with the din of yelping and beating of the drums; but I have for several days past been peculiarly engrossed, and my senses almost confounded with the stamping, and grunting, and bellowing of the *buffalo* dance, which closed a few days since at sunrise (thank Heaven), and which I must needs describe to you.

Buffaloes, it is known, are a sort of roaming creatures, congregating occasionally in huge masses, and strolling away about the country from east to west, or from north to south, or just where their whims or strange fancies may lead them; and the Mandans are sometimes, by this means, most unceremoniously left without any thing to eat; and being a small tribe, and unwilling to risk their lives by going far from home in the face of their more powerful enemies, are oftentimes left almost in a state of starvation. In any emergency of this kind, every man musters and brings out of his lodge his mask (the skin of a buffalo's head with the horns on), which he is obligated to keep in readiness for this occasion; and then commences the buffalo dance, of which I have above spoken, which is held for the purpose of making "buffalo come" (as they term it), of inducing the buffalo herds to change the direction of their wanderings, and bend their course towards the Mandan village, and graze about on the beautiful hills and bluffs in its vicinity, where the Mandans can shoot them down and cook them as they want them for food.

For the most part of the year, the young warriors and hunters, by riding out a mile or two from the village, can kill meat in abundance; and sometimes large herds of these animals can be seen grazing in full view of the village. There are other seasons also when the young men have ranged about the country as far as they are willing to risk their lives, on account of their enemies, without finding meat. This sad intelligence is brought back to the chiefs and doctors, who sit in solemn council, and consult on the most expedient measures to be taken, until they are sure to decide upon the old and only expedient which "never has failed."

The chief issues his order to his runners or criers, who proclaim it through the village – and in a few minutes the dance begins. The place where this strange operation is carried on is in the public area in the centre of the village, and in front of the great medicine, or mystery lodge. About ten or fifteen Mandans at a time join in the dance, each one with the skin of the buffalo's head (or mask) with the horns on, placed over his head, and in his hand his favourite bow or lance, with which he is used to slay the buffalo.

I mentioned that this dance always had the desired effect, that it never fails, nor can it, for it cannot be stopped (but is going incessantly day and night) until "buffalo come." Drums are beating and rattles are shaken, and songs and yells incessantly are shouted, and lookers-on stand ready with masks on their heads, and weapons in hand, to take the place of each one as he becomes fatigued, and jumps out of the ring.

During this time of general excitement, spies or "*lookers*" are kept on the hills in the neighborhood of the village, who, when they discover buffaloes in sight, give appropriate signal, by "throwing their robes," which is instantly seen in the village, and understood by the whole tribe. At this joyful intelligence there is a shout of thanks to the Great Spirit, and more especially to the mystery-man, and the dancers who *have been the immediate cause of their success*! There is then a brisk preparation for the chase – a grand hunt takes place. The choicest pieces of the victims are sacrificed to the Great Spirit, and then a surfeit and a carouse.

These dances have sometimes been continued in this village two and three weeks without stopping an instant, until the joyful moment when buffaloes made their appearance. So they *never* fail; and they think they have been the means of bringing them in.

Every man in the Mandan village (as I have before said) is obliged by a village regulation, to keep the mask of a buffalo, hanging on a post at the head of his bed, which he can use on his head whenever he is called upon by the chiefs, to dance for the coming of the buffaloes. The mask is put over the head, and generally has a strip of the skin hanging to it, of the whole length of the animal, with the tail attached to it, which, passing down over the back of the dancer, is dragging on the ground. When one becomes fatigued of the exercise, he signifies it by bending quite forward, and sinking his body towards the ground; when another draws a bow upon him and hits him with a blunt arrow, and he falls like a buffalo – is seized by the bye-standers, who drag him out of the ring by the heels, brandishing their knives about him; and having gone through the motions of skinning and cutting him up, they let him off, and his place is at once supplied by another, who dances into the ring with his mask on; and by this taking of places, the scene is easily kept up night and day, until the desired effect has been produced, that of "making buffalo come." ...

3. Notchininga's Map of the Upper Mississippi, 1837[3]

Native American concepts of geography, as the following map demonstrates, could be quite different from Anglo-American notions. This map of the Iowa Nation in the Upper Mississippi Valley was presented to American officials by Notchininga at a meeting in Washington in October of 1837. As one of the high-ranking leaders of the Iowas, Notchininga used the map as a way to justify their land claims against other Native Americans displaced by American removal policies as well as white settlers. The Mississippi and Missouri rivers are the diagonal and vertical lines, respectively, on the map. Villages appear as circles, and the dotted lines show the Iowan migratory routes. Although Anglo-American misinterpretations of semi-sedentary populations asserted that they forfeited any permanent claims to land ownership, this map suggests that migration routes could be quite permanent fixtures on the Native American landscape.

---

[3]   Mark Warhus, *Another America. Native American Maps and the History of Our Land* (New York: St. Martin's Press, 1997), p. 38.

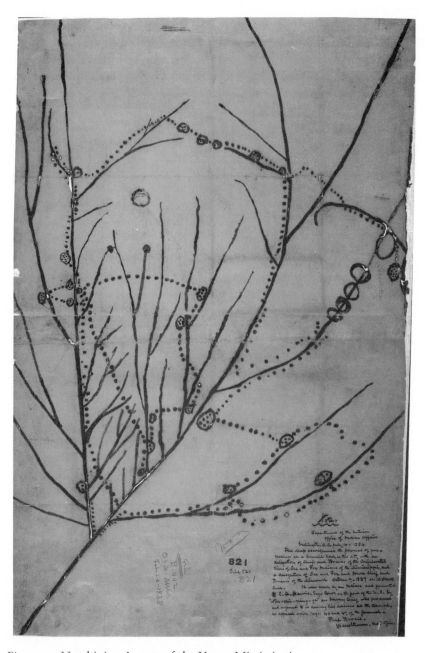

Figure 4 Notchininga's map of the Upper Mississippi.
Source: National Archives and Records Administration, Cartographic and Architectural Branch, Washington, DC.

Chapter 18   The Era of Manifest Destiny

1. Sam Houston's Inaugural Address for the Republic of Texas, 1836[1]

In order to shield its more populous interior from the powerful Comanche and Apache nations, the Republic of Mexico allowed 20,000 setters from the United States to inhabit its northeast province of Texas during the 1820s. These Texans retained their native language, religion, and other institutions, such as slavery, despite the laws governing their residency in Catholic, Spanish-speaking, and anti-slavery Mexico. By 1835, the rise of President Antonio López de Santa Anna triggered an armed revolt among Anglo and Tejano residents of Texas, who sought to sever their ties with Mexico and form an independent republic of their own. At the head of their army was a former protégé of Andrew Jackson and Tennessee politician, Samuel Houston. At the Battle of San Jacinto, Houston's army soundly defeated the Mexican Army, captured President Santa Anna, and secured independence for Texas. In that same year, 1836, Sam Houston became the first President of the Republic of Texas. In his inaugural address, Houston not only refers to the past battle with Mexico, but also to the future with the Republic's large neighbor to the northeast, the United States of America.

---

[1] *Telegraph and Texas Register* (Columbia, TX), November 9, 1836.

MR. SPEAKER AND GENTLEMEN:

Deeply impressed with a sense of responsibility devolving on me, I cannot, in justice to myself, repress the emotion of my heart, or restrain the feelings which my sense of obligation to my fellow-citizens has inspired. Their suffrage was gratuitously bestowed. Preferred to others, possibly superior in merit to myself, called to the most important station among mankind by the voice of a free people, it is utterly impossible not to feel impressed with the deepest sensations of delicacy in my present position before the world. It is not here alone, but our present attitude before all nations has rendered my position, and that of my country, one of peculiar interest.

A spot of earth almost unknown to the geography of the age, destitute of all available resources, comparatively few in numbers, we modestly remonstrated against oppression, and, when invaded by a numerous host, we dared to proclaim our Independence and to strike for freedom on the breast of the oppressors. As yet, our course is onward. We are only in the onset of the campaign of Liberty. Futurity has locked up the destiny which awaits our people.

Who can contemplate a situation so imposing in the physical and moral world? None! no not one. The relations among ourselves are peculiarly delicate and important; for no matter what zeal or fidelity I may possess in the discharge of my official duties, if I do not obtain co-operation and an honest support from the co-ordinate departments of the government, wreck and ruin must be the inevitable consequences of my administration.

If, then, in the discharge of my duty, my competency should fail in the attainment of the great objects in view, it would become your sacred duty to correct my errors and sustain me by your superior wisdom. This much I anticipate, – this much I demand. I am perfectly aware of the difficulties that surround me, and the convulsive throes through which our country must pass. I have never been emulous of the civic wreath, when merited, it crowns a happy destiny. A country situated like ours is environed in difficulties, its administration is fraught with perplexities. Had it been my destiny, I would infinitely have preferred the toils, privations and perils, of a solider, to the duties of my present station. Nothing but zeal, stimulated by the holy spirit of patriotism, and guided by philosophy and wisdom, can give that impetus to our energies necessary to surmount the difficulties with which our political path is obstructed.

By the aid of your intelligence, I trust all impediments in our advancement will be removed; that all wounds in the body politic will be healed, and the Constitution of the Republic will derive strength and vigor equal to all opposing energies. I shall confidently anticipate the establishment of

Constitutional liberty. In the attainment of this object, we must regard our relative situation to other countries.

A subject of no small importance is the situation of an extensive frontier, bordered by Indians, and open to their depredations. – Treaties of peace and amity, and the maintenance of good faith with the Indians, present themselves to my mind as the most rational grounds on which to obtain their friendship. Let us abstain on our part from aggressions, establish commerce with the different tribes, supply their useful and necessary wants, maintain even-handed justice with them, and natural reason will teach them the utility of our friendship.

Admonished by the past, we can not, in justice, disregard our national enemies; vigilance will apprise us of their approach, a disciplined and valiant army will insure their discomfiture. Without discrimination and system, how unavailing would all the resources of an old and overflowing treasury prove to us. It would be as unprofitable to us in our present situation as the rich diamond locked in the bosom of the adamant.

We cannot hope that the bosom of our beautiful prairies will soon by visited by the balmy breezes of peace. We may again look for the day when their verdure will be converted into dyes of crimson. We must keep all our energies alive, our army organized, disciplined and increased agreeably to our present necessities. With these preparations we can meet and vanquish despotic thousands. This is the attitude we at present must regard as our own. We are battling for human liberty; reason and firmness must characterize our acts.

The course our enemies have pursued has been opposed to every principle of civilized warfare – bad faith, inhumanity, and devastation, marked their path of invasion. We were a little band, contending for liberty – they were thousands, well appointed, munitioned, and provisioned, seeking to rivet chains upon us, or extirpate us from the earth. Their cruelties have incurred the universal denunciation of Christendom. They will not pass from their nation during the present generation.

The contrast of our conduct is manifest: We were hunted down as the felon wolf, our little band driven from the fastness to fastness, exasperated to the last extreme, while the blood of our kindred and our friends, was invoking the vengeance of an offended God – was smoking to high heaven, we met the enemy and vanquished them. They fell in battle, or suppliantly kneeled and were spared. We offered up our vengeance at the shrine of humanity, while Christendom rejoiced at the act and viewed with delightful pride the ennobling sacrifice. The civilized world contemplated with proud emotions conduct which reflected so much glory on the Anglo-Saxon race. The moral effect has done more towards our liberation, than the defeat of the army of veterans. When our cause has been presented to our friends in the land of our origin, they have embraced it with their warmest sympathies. They have rendered us manly and efficient aid. They have rallied to our standard, they have fought side by side with our warriors. They have bled and their dust is mingling with our heroes ...

A circumstance of the highest import will claim the attention of the court at Washington. In our recent election the important subject of annexation to the United States of America was submitted to the consideration of the people. They have expressed their feelings and their wishes on that momentous question. They have with a unanimity unparalleled, declared that they will be reunited to the great Republican family of the North. The appeal is made by a willing people. Will our friends disregard it? They have already bestowed upon us their warmest sympathies. Their manly and generous feelings have been enlisted in our behalf. We ware cheered by the hope that they will receive us to a participancy of their civil, political, and religious rights, and hail us welcome into the great family of freemen. Our misfortunes have been their misfortunes; our sorrows, too, have been theirs, and their joy at our success has been irrepressible. ...

2. An Editor Endorses the Idea of "Manifest Destiny," 1845[2]

The idea of annexing Texas simmered in Congress for nearly a decade. Whereas Whigs tended toward the conservative approach to adding new territory, Democrats enthusiastically embraced the idea of annexation. During the election of 1844, the Texas issue assumed a prominent place in the national debate over expansionism. Some critics of annexation argued that it would disrupt the delicate balance between slave and free states preserved since the Missouri Compromise of 1820. The Democratic candidate, James K. Polk of Tennessee, adroitly wedded Texas annexation to the settlement of the Oregon controversy, thus providing American expansionism a northern and southern component. As the notion of extending the United States across the North American continent gained political purchase, some Americans believed that their nation had an obligation to spread the benefits of republican government, Christianity, and other elements of American culture across the continent and even beyond. The following essay by Democratic editor John L. O'Sullivan officially deals with the issue of adding Texas to the United States, but it also lays out a rationalization of American expansionism. O'Sullivan is credited with coining the phrase "manifest destiny," which became a rallying cry for expansionists of any political stripe.

[2]   John L. O' Sullivan, "Annexation," *The United States Magazine and Democratic Review* 17 (July/August 1845): 17.

ANNEXATION

IT is time now for opposition to the Annexation of Texas to cease, all further agitation of the waters of bitterness and strife, at least in connexion with this question, – even though it may perhaps be required of us as a necessary condition of the freedom of our institutions, that we must live on for ever in a state of unpausing struggle and excitement upon some subject of party division or other. But, in regard to Texas, enough has now been given to party. It is time for the common duty of Patriotism to the Country to succeed; – or if this claim will not be recognized, it is at least time for common sense to acquiesce with decent grace in the inevitable and the irrevocable.

Texas is now ours. Already, before these words are written, her Convention has undoubtedly ratified the acceptance, by her Congress, of our proffered invitation into the Union; and made the requisite changes in her already republican form of constitution to adapt it to its future federal relations. Her star and her stripe may already be said to have taken their place in the glorious blazon of our common nationality; and the sweep of our eagle's wing already includes within its circuit the wide extent of her fair and fertile land. She is no longer to us a mere geographical space – a certain combination of coast, plain, mountain, valley, forest and stream. She is no longer to us a mere country on the map. She comes within the dear and sacred designation of Our Country . . .

Why, were other reasoning wanting, in favor now of elevating this question of Texas into the Union, out of the lower region of our past party dissentions, up to its proper level of a high and broad nationality, it surely is to be found, found abundantly, in the manner in which other nations have undertaken to intrude themselves into it, between us and the proper parties to the case, in a spirit of hostile interference against us, for the avowed object of thwarting our policy and hampering our power, limiting our greatness and checking the fulfilment of our manifest destiny to overspread the continent allotted by Providence for the free development of our yearly multiplying millions. . . .

Nor is there any just foundation for the charge that Annexation is a great pro-slavery measure – calculated to increase and perpetuate that institution. Slavery had nothing to do with it. Opinions were and are greatly divided, both at the North and South, as to the influence to be exerted by it on Slavery and the Slave States. That it will tend to facilitate and hasten the disappearance of Slavery from all the northern tier of the present Slave States, cannot surely admit of serious question. The greater value in Texas of the slave labor now employed in those States, must soon produce the effect of draining off that labor southwardly, by the same unvarying law that bids water descend the slope that invites it. Every new Slave State in Texas will make at least one Free State from among those in which that institution now exists – to say nothing of those portions of Texas on which slavery cannot spring and grow – to say nothing of the far more rapid growth of new States in the free West and North-west, as these fine regions are overspread by the emigration fast flowing over them from Europe, as well as from the Northern and Eastern States of the Union as it exists. On the other hand, it is undeniably much gained for the cause of the eventual voluntary abolition of slavery, that it should have been thus drained off towards the only outlet which appeared to furnish much probability of the ultimate disappearance of the negro race from our borders. The Spanish-Indian-American populations of Mexico, Central America and South America, afford the only receptacle capable of absorbing the race whenever we shall be prepared to slough it off – to emancipate it from slavery, and (simultaneously necessary) to remove it from the midst of our own. Themselves already of mixed and confused blood, and free from the "prejudices" which among us so insuperably forbid the social amalgamation which can alone elevate the Negro race out of virtually servile degradation, even though legally free, the regions occupied by those populations must strongly attract the black race in that direction; and as soon as the destined hour of emancipation shall arrive, will relieve the question of one of its worst difficulties, if not absolutely the greatest ...

California will, probably, next fall away from the loose adhesion which, in such a country as Mexico, holds a remote province in a slight equivocal kind of dependence on the metropolis. Imbecile and distracted, Mexico never can exert any real governmental authority over such a country. The impotence of the one and the distance of the other, must make the relation one of virtual independence; unless, by stunting the province of all natural growth, and forbidding that immigration which can alone develope its capabilities and fulfil the purposes of its creation, tyranny may retain a military dominion, which is no government in the legitimate sense of the term. In the case of California this is not impossible. The Anglo-Saxon foot is already on its borders. Already the advance guard of the irresistible army of Anglo-Saxon emigration has begun to pour down upon it, armed with the plough and the rifle, and marking its trail with schools and colleges, courts and representative halls, mills and meeting-houses. A population will soon be in actual occupation of California, over which it will be idle for Mexico to dream of dominion. They will necessarily become independent. All this without the agency of our government – in the natural flow of events, the spontaneous working of principles, and the adaptation of the tendencies and wants of the human race to the elemental circumstances in the midst of which they find themselves placed. And they will have a right to independence – to self-government – to the possession of the homes conquered from the wilderness by their own labors and dangers, sufferings and sacrifices – a better and a truer right than the artificial title of sovereignty in Mexico, a thousand miles distant, inheriting from Spain a title good only against those who have none better. Their right to independence will be the natural right of self-government belonging to any community strong enough to maintain it – distinct in position, origin and character, and free from any mutual obligations of membership of a common political body, binding it to others by the duty of loyalty and compact of public faith. This will be their title to independence; and by this title, there can be no doubt that the population now fast streaming down upon California will both assert and maintain their independence. Whether they will then attach themselves to our Union or not, is not to be predicted with any certainty ...

Away, then, with all idle French talks of *balances of power* on the American Continent. There is no growth in Spanish America! Whatever progress of population there may be in the British Canadas, is only for their own early severance of their present colonial relation to the little island three thousand miles across the Atlantic; soon to be followed by Annexation, and destined to swell the still accumulating momentum of our progress. And whosoever may hold the balance, though they should cast into the opposite scale all the bayonets and cannon, not only of France and England, but of the Europe entire, how would it kick the beam against the simple, solid weight of the two hundred and fifty, or three hundred millions – and American millions – determined to gather beneath the flutter of the stripes and stars, in the fast hastening year of the Lord 1945!

3. Walter Colton on the Discovery of Gold in California, 1850[3]

In 1845, California was a sparsely settled province in the Republic of Mexico dotted by Catholic missions, military presidios, and herds of sheep, cattle, and horses. The following year, however, a small group of American residents declared California to be an independent republic. This "Bear Flag Revolt" was made possible by the backing of US forces nearby and American occupation of California ensued. Walter Colton arrived in Monterey, California soon after this regime change. In September of 1846, he was made alcade, *or chief magistrate, of the area. Although Colton began his term*

---

[3]   Walter Colton, *Three Years in California* (New York: A. S. Barnes, 1850), pp. 242–9, 253–4.

sorting out the kinds of small-scale disputes typical of a small ranching community, a singular event quickly and irrevocably altered the course of Monterey's – and all of California's – history. Nearby residents of Sutter's Mill found gold in 1848 and by the following year, thousands of Americans set out to California during the nation's first major "gold rush." As a result, the territory's non-Indian population swelled from about 14,000 at the time of Colton's arrival in Monterey, to near 100,000 at the time of California's admission to the Union in 1850, and a quarter of a million only two years later. The following series of entries from Colton's memoirs, entitled Three Years in California, *describe the initial excitement (and Colton's initial disgust) of the discovery of gold in California.*

MONDAY, MAY 29. Our town was startled out of its quiet dreams to-day, by the announcement that gold have been discovered on the American Fork. The men wondered and talked, and the women too; but neither believed. The sibyls were less skeptical they said the moon had, for several nights, appeared not more than a cable's length from the earth; that a white raven had been seen playing with an infant; and that an owl had rung the church bells ...

MONDAY, JUNE 5. Another report reached us this morning from the American Fork. The rumor ran, that several workmen, while excavating for a mill-race, had thrown up little shining scales of a yellow ore, that proved to be gold; that an old Sonorian, who had spent his life in gold mines, pronounced it the genuine thing. Still the public incredulity remained, save here and there a glimmer of faith, like the flash of a fire-fly at night. One good lady, however, declared that she had been dreaming of gold every night for several weeks, and that it had so frustrated her simple household economy, that she had relieved her conscience, by confessing to her priest –

"Absolve me, father, of that sinful dream."

TUESDAY, JUNE 6. Being troubled with the golden dream almost as much as the good lady, I determined to put an end to the suspense, and dispatched a messenger this morning to the American Fork. He will have to ride, going and returning, some four hundred miles, but his report will be reliable. We shall then know whether this gold is a fact or a fiction – a tangible reality on the earth, or a fanciful treasure at the base of some rainbow, retreating over hill and waterfall, to lure pursuit and disappoint hope ...

MONDAY, JUNE 12. A straggler came in to-day from the American Fork, bringing a piece of yellow ore weighing an ounce. The young dashed the dirt from their eyes, and the old from their spectacles. One brought a spyglass, another an iron ladle; some wanted to melt it, others to hammer it, and a few were satisfied with smelling it. All were full of tests; and many, who could not be gratified in making their experiments, declared it a humbug. One lady sent me a huge gold ring, in the hope of reaching the truth by comparison; while a gentleman placed the specimen on the top of his gold-headed cane and held it up, challenging the sharpest eyes to detect a difference. But doubts still hovered on the minds of the great mass. They could not conceive that such a treasure could have lain there so long undiscovered. The idea seemed to convict them of stupidity. There is nothing of which a man is more tenacious than his claims to sagacity. He sticks to them like an old bachelor to the idea of his personal attractions, or a toper to the strength of his temperance ability, whenever he shall wish to call it into play . . .

TUESDAY, JUNE 20. My messenger sent to the mines has returned with specimens of the gold; he dismounted in a sea of upturned faces. As he drew forth the yellow lumps from his pockets, and passed them around among the eager crowd, the doubts, which had lingered till now, fled. All admitted they were gold, except one old man, who still persisted they were some Yankee invention, got up to reconcile the people to the change of the flag. The excitement produced was intense; and many were soon busy in their hasty preparations for a departure to the mines. The family who had kept house for me caught the moving infection. Husband and wife were both packing up; the blacksmith dropped his hammer, the carpenter his plane, the mason his trowel, the farmer his sickle, the baker his loaf, and the tapster his bottle. All were off for the mines, some on horses, some on carts, and some on crutches, and one went in a litter. An American woman, who had recently established a boarding-house here, pulled up stakes, and was off before her lodgers had even time to pay their bills. Debtors ran, of course. I have only a community of women left, and a gang of prisoners, with here and there a soldier, who will give his captain the slip at the first chance. I don't blame the fellow a whit; seven dollars a month, while others are making two or three hundred a day! that is too much for human nature to stand.

SATURDAY, JULY 15. The gold fever has reached every servant in Monterey; none are to be trusted in their engagement beyond a week, and as for compulsion, it is like attempting to drive fish into a net with the ocean before them. Gen. Mason Lieut. Lanman, and myself, form a mess; we have a house and all the table furniture and culinary apparatus requisite; but our servants have run, one after another, till we are almost in despair: even Sambo, who we thought would stick by from laziness, if no other cause, ran last night; and this morning, for the fortieth time, we had to take to the kitchen, and cook our own breakfast. A general of the United States Army, the commander of a man-of-war, and the Alcade of Monterey, in a smoking kitchen, grinding coffee, toasting a herring, and pealing onions! These gold mines are going to upset all the domestic arrangements of society, turning the head to the tail, and the tail to the head. Well, it is a ill wind that blows nobody any good: the nabobs have had their time, and now comes that of the "niggers." We shall all live just as long, and be quite as fit to die.

TUESDAY, JULY 18. Another bag of gold from the mines, and another spasm in the community. It was brought down by a sailor from Yuba river, and contains a hundred and thirty-six ounces. It is the most beautiful gold that has appeared in the market; it looks like the yellow scales of the dolphin, passing through his rainbow hues at death. My carpenters, at work on the school-house, on seeing it, threw down their saws and planes, shouldered their picks, and are off for the Yuba. Three seamen ran from the Warren, forfeiting their four years' pay; and a whole platoon of soldiers from the fort left only their colors behind. One old woman declared she would never again break an egg or kill a chicken, without examining yolk and gizzard ...

TUESDAY, AUG. 28. The gold mines have upset all social and domestic arrangements in Monterey; the master has become his own servant, and the servant his own lord. The millionaire is obliged to groom his own horse, and roll his wheelbarrow; and the hidalgo – in whose veins flow the blood of all the Cortes – to clean his own boots! Here is lady L–, who has lived here seventeen years, the pride and ornament of the place, with a broomstick in her jewelled hand! And here is lady B– with her daughter – all the way from "old Virginia," where they graced society with their varied accomplishments – now floating between the parlor and kitchen, and as much at home in one as the other! And here is lady S–, whose cattle are on a thousand hills, lifting, like Rachel of old, her bucket of water from the deep well! And here is lady M.L–, whose honeymoon is still full of soft seraphic light, unhouseling a potatoe, and hunting the hen that laid the last egg. And here am I, who have been a man of some note in my day, loafing on the hospitality of the good citizens, and grateful for a meal, though in an Indian's wigwam. Why, is not this enough to make one wish the gold mines were in the earth's flaming centre, from which they sprung? Out on this yellow dust! it is worse than the cinders which buried Pompeii, for there, high and low shared the same fate! ...

Chapter 19   War with Mexico

1. President Polk's War Message, May 11, 1846[1]

Immediately following the annexation of Texas in 1845, tension between the United States and Mexico spilled into open conflict. The Polk Administration first attempted to negotiate a settlement that would result in the sale of California to the United States and a resolution of the contested Texas border. These efforts failed, and President Polk ordered troops under the command of General Zachary Taylor to the Rio Grande Valley. Since Mexico claimed that their northern boundary was the Nueces, not the Rio Grande, Mexican forces from nearby Matamoros attacked an American patrol in April of 1846. This prompted President James K. Polk to announce to Congress that a state of war existed between the two nations in the spring of 1846. The following message to Congress outlines Polk's position that a de facto war existed; no formal request for a declaration of war followed. After an abbreviated debate, Congress passed an acknowledgment of the war and funded its prosecution by a large margin, 174 to 14 in the House and 40 to 2 in the Senate. Dissenters complained that they had not been given enough time to debate the action and that affairs were emotional in the wake of Zachary Taylor's report from the field that, "Hostilities may now be considered as commenced."

Washington, May 11, 1846
To the Senate and House of Representatives:
   The existing state of the relations between the United States and Mexico renders it proper that I should bring the subject to the consideration

---

[1]   US Senate, *Message of the President of the United States*, Serial 476 S.doc.337, May 11, 1846.

of Congress. In my message at the commencement of your present session the state of these relations; the causes which led to the suspension of diplomatic intercourse between the two countries in March, 1845, and the long-continued and unredressed wrongs and injuries committed by the Mexican Government on citizens of the United States in their persons and property were briefly set forth.

As the facts and opinions which were then laid before you were carefully considered, I can not better express my present convictions of the condition of affairs up to that time than by referring you to that communication.

The strong desire to establish peace with Mexico on liberal and honorable terms, and the readiness of this Government to regulate and adjust our boundary and other causes of difference with that power on such fair and equitable principles as would lead to permanent relations of the most friendly nature, induced me in September last to seek the reopening of diplomatic relations between the two countries. Every measure adopted on our part had for its object the furtherance of these desired results. In communicating to Congress a succinct statement of the injuries which we had suffered from Mexico, and which have been accumulating during a period of more than twenty years, every expression that could tend to inflame the people of Mexico or defeat or delay a pacific result was carefully avoided. An envoy of the United States repaired to Mexico with full powers to adjust every existing difference. But though present on the Mexican soil by agreement between the two Governments, invested with full powers, and bearing evidence of the most friendly dispositions, his mission has been unavailing. The Mexican Government not only refused to receive him or listen to his propositions, but after a long-continued series of menaces have at last invaded our territory and shed the blood of our fellow-citizens on our own soil.

It now becomes my duty to state more in detail the origin, progress, and failure of that mission. In pursuance of the instructions given in September last, an inquiry was made on the 13th of October, 1845, in the most friendly terms, through our consul in Mexico, of the minister for foreign affairs, whether the Mexican Government would receive an envoy from the United States intrusted with full powers to adjust all the questions in dispute between the two Governments, with the assurance that should the answer be in the affirmative such an envoy would be immediately dispatched to Mexico. The Mexican minister on the 15th of October gave an affirmative answer to this inquiry, requesting at the same time that our naval force at Vera Cruz might be withdrawn, lest its continued presence might assume the appearance of menace and coercion pending the negotiations. This force was immediately withdrawn. On the 10th of November, 1845,

Mr. John Slidell, of Louisiana, was commissioned by me as envoy extraordinary and minister plenipotentiary of the United States to Mexico, and was intrusted with full powers to adjust both the questions of the Texas boundary and of indemnification to our citizens. The redress of the wrongs of our citizens naturally and inseparably blended itself with the question of boundary. The settlement of the one question in any correct view of the subject involves that of the other. I could not for a moment entertain the idea that the claims of our much-injured and long-suffering citizens, many of which had existed for more than twenty years, should be postponed or separated from the settlement of the boundary question.

Mr. Slidell arrived at Vera Cruz on the 30th of November, and was courteously received by the authorities of that city. But the Government of General Herrera was then tottering to its fall. The revolutionary party had seized upon the Texas question to effect or hasten its overthrow. Its determination to restore friendly relations with the United States, and to receive our minister to negotiate for the settlement of this question, was violently assailed, and was made the great theme of denunciation against it. The Government of General Herrera, there is good reason to believe, was sincerely desirous to receive our minister; but it yielded to the storm raised by its enemies, and on the 21st of December refused to accredit Mr. Slidell upon the most frivolous pretexts ...

Thus the Government of Mexico, though solemnly pledged by official acts in October last to receive and accredit an American envoy, violated their plighted faith and refused the offer of a peaceful adjustment of our difficulties. Not only was the offer rejected, but the indignity of its rejection was enhanced by the manifest breach of faith in refusing to admit the envoy who came because they had bound themselves to receive him. Nor can it be said that the offer was fruitless from the want of opportunity of discussing it; our envoy was present on their own soil. Nor can it be ascribed to a want of sufficient powers; our envoy had full powers to adjust every question of difference. Nor was there room for complaint that our propositions for settlement were unreasonable; permission was not even given our envoy to make any proposition whatever. Nor can it be objected that we, on our part, would not listen to any reasonable terms of their suggestion; the Mexican Government refused all negotiation, and have made no proposition of any kind. In my message at the commencement of the present session I informed you that upon the earnest appeal both of the Congress and convention of Texas I had ordered an efficient military force to take a position between the Nueces and the Del Norte. This had become necessary to meet a threatened invasion of Texas by the Mexican forces, for which extensive military preparations had been made. The invasion was threatened solely because

Texas had determined, in accordance with a solemn resolution of the Congress of the United States, to annex herself to our Union, and under these circumstances it was plainly our duty to extend our protection over her citizens and soil.

This force was concentrated at Corpus Christi, and remained there until after I had received such information from Mexico as rendered it probable, if not certain, that the Mexican Government would refuse to receive our envoy. Meantime Texas, by the final action of our Congress, had become an integral part of our Union. The Congress of Texas, by its act of December 19, 1836, had declared the Rio del Norte to be the boundary of that Republic. Its jurisdiction had been extended and exercised beyond the Nueces. The country between that river and the Del Norte had been represented in the Congress and in the convention of Texas, had thus taken part in the act of annexation itself, and is now included within one of our Congressional districts. Our own Congress had, moreover, with great unanimity, by the act approved December 31, 1845, recognized the country beyond the Nueces as a part of our territory by including it within our own revenue system, and a revenue officer to reside within that district has been appointed by and with the advice and consent of the Senate. It became, therefore, of urgent necessity to provide for the defense of that portion of our country. Accordingly, on the 13th of January last instructions were issued to the general in command of these troops to occupy the left bank of the Del Norte. This river, which is the southwestern boundary of the State of Texas, is an exposed frontier . . .

The Mexican forces at Matamoras assumed a belligerent attitude, and on the 12th of April General Ampudia, then in command, notified General Taylor to break up his camp within twenty-four hours and to retire beyond the Nueces River, and in the event of his failure to comply with these demands announced that arms, and arms alone, must decide the question. But no open act of hostility was committed until the 14th of April. On that day General Arista, who had succeeded to the command of the Mexican forces, communicated to General Taylor that he considered hostilities commenced and should prosecute them. A party of dragoons of 63 men and officers were on the same day dispatched from the American camp up the Rio del Norte, on its left bank, to ascertain whether the Mexican troops had crossed or were preparing to cross the river, became engaged with a large body of these troops, and after a short affair, in which some 16 were killed and wounded, appear to have been surrounded and compelled to surrender. The grievous wrongs perpetrated by Mexico upon our citizens throughout a long period of years remain unredressed, and solemn treaties pledging her public faith for this redress have been disregarded. A government either unable or unwilling to enforce the execution of such treaties fails to perform one of its plainest duties.

Our commerce with Mexico has been almost annihilated. It was formerly highly beneficial to both nations, but our merchants have been deterred from prosecuting it by the system of outrage and extortion which the Mexican authorities have pursued against them, whilst their appeals through their own Government for indemnity have been made in vain. Our forbearance has gone to such an extreme as to be mistaken in its character. Had we acted with vigor in repelling the insults and redressing the injuries inflicted by Mexico at the commencement, we should doubtless have escaped all the difficulties in which we are now involved.

Instead of this, however, we have been exerting our best efforts to propitiate her good will. Upon the pretext that Texas, a nation as independent as herself, thought proper to unite its destinies with our own she has affected to believe that we have severed her rightful territory, and in official proclamations and manifestoes has repeatedly threatened to make war upon us for the purpose of reconquering Texas. In the meantime we have tried every effort at reconciliation. The cup of forbearance had been exhausted even before the recent information from the frontier of the Del Norte. But now, after reiterated menaces, Mexico has passed the boundary of the United States, has invaded our territory and shed American blood upon the American soil. She has proclaimed that hostilities have commenced, and that the two nations are now at war ...
James K. Polk

2. An American Sergeant's Perspective on the War with Mexico, August 1847[2]

In early 1847, American forces occupied New Mexico and California and Zachary Taylor's soldiers defeated President Santa Anna's larger army at Buena Vista. With much of northern Mexico under American control, President Polk sought a definitive end to the war by authorizing a campaign against Mexico City. In March, an army of 8,900 American soldiers, mostly volunteers, under the command of General Winfield Scott landed at Veracruz and began to work their way inland. A month later, Scott's army routed Santa Anna's defense forces at Cerro Gordo. By August,

---

[2]   Allan Peskin, ed., *Volunteers: The Mexican War Journals of Private Richard Coulter and Sergeant Thomas Barclay, Company E, Second Pennsylvania Infantry* (Kent, OH: The Kent State University Press, 1991), pp. 142–3, 145–51.

the invading force swelled to 14,000 and engaged in fierce fighting at Contreras and Churubusco, just outside the capital city. Scott authorized a ceasefire while American and Mexican officials negotiated peace terms. The following journal entry describes the fighting in the suburbs of Mexico City from the perspective of a non-commissioned officer serving in Scott's army. The soldier, Sergeant Thomas Barclay, was a lawyer from western Pennsylvania who enlisted in a volunteer company called the Westmoreland Guards, attached to the 2nd Pennsylvania Infantry. Barclay survived the war and returned home in 1848.

August 19

Early start and soon arrived in San Agustin a small village deserted in a great measure by the inhabitants. Remained over an hour under arms in the plaza. In the meantime Pillow marched out, his Division to act as a strong covering force to the reconnoitering parties and also for the purpose of cutting roads. Quitman's Division moved into Pillow's Quarters. We pitched tents in the yard in front of the church and orders that no man leave. Pillow moving some 5 or 6 miles in a N.W. direction unexpectedly comes upon a large body of the enemy in a chosen position and protected by several pieces of heavy artillery. Twiggs' Division is hurried up to the support of Pillow and about 3 p.m. the cannonading opens. The light batteries of the flying artillery, hastily got into position, for a long time maintain a fire with the heavy advance of the enemy. From the steeple of the church at San Agustin the firing is plainly seen. The greatest excitement prevails among the volunteers. The long roll beats and in an instant the 2nd Regt. is formed. But as it is necessary to leave a force in reserve at San Agustin, the 2nd Penna. Vol. and the marines are left behind and the New York and South Carolina Volunteers comprising Shields' Brigade are ordered onwards. There was a feeling of gloom and despondency in our Regt. which is indescribable. At Cerro Gordo the Pennsylvanians were blamed for *waving* and all feel the necessity of wiping off the imputation of anything like backwardness. A volunteer Regt. like the Roman's wife should be above suspicion. Here is an opportunity and for some reason or another we must stay back. This evening was spent in watching the firing which continued until dark. The reports brought in are that no impression has been made upon the enemy and that our loss is considerable. The night sets up dark and gloomy and is in unison with our feelings. A heavy rain commences and pours down during the entire night. Sheltered by our tents we pity our brethren who are exposed to the storm. But gladly would we exchange situations and endure all the horrors of the — storm. They are in the path to honor. We are lying here idle in the honorable post of wagon guards. In today's fight it is discovered that the Dragoons cannot act on account of the roughness of the ground. The Mexican force is composed of over 6,000 men from the army of the North. They are under the command of Gen. Valencia ...

August 20

Last night during the rain and storm our troops were not idle. Covered by the darkness of the night plans were carried into execution which could not be done in day time and by daylight the different corps were in the desired positions. Making a joint attack in front which attracted the enemy's attention, Riley's Brigade made a furious onset in their rear. Covered by the nature of the ground, the enemy were ignorant of the advance of the Brigade, who suddenly rising from the ground as it were within a few hundred yards rear rushed furiously forward yelling and cheering. Completely panic struck, the enemy fled in all directions. But so skillfully was the American force posted that a great many were killed and many taken prisoners. Those that escaped were hotly pursued. A large force sent out by Santa Anna to the relief of Valencia and a heavy body of Lancers who were hovering around could give no assistance. The 2nd Penna. Regt. had early this morning been formed and moved towards the battle ground. All was joyous and full of hopes but after a march of about 2 miles information arrived that the work was already done and we were marched back disappointed to our quarters. The results of the Battle of Padierna or Contreras were great. This position was the key of all the enemy's fortifications on the western and s. western part of the City. Nor could any of their other works have been approached until this was carried. Altho their works were defended by 24 pieces of heavy artillery, 6,000 veteran troops and chiefly by the volcanic formation and roughness of the ground in their front and flanks, yet all the action lasted 17 minutes from the time Riley charged until all was over. A great many of the Mexicans were killed in their retreat. Ninety four officers and near 800 privates were taken prisoners, together with the artillery ammunition and a great number of small arms ... Part of the retreating Mexicans, hotly pursued by a small party of our troops, flying thru San Angel never stopped until they reached the City distant from Contreras over 12 miles. The chief body of them, however, fell back upon their fortifications at Churubusco where lay Santa Anna with the main army. About 1 p.m. the fight again commenced. Scott taking advantage of their panic advanced with Pillow, Twiggs' and Shields Brigade to Churubusco. Worth in the meantime drove the enemy from San Antonio and rapidly approached to form in the grand battle. From the roofs of San Agustin we were for a long time the anxious spectators of this conflict. For hours nothing was heard but the continuous roar of cannon and the

sharp rattle of musketry. All were in doubt. No one dreaded defeat but all mourned the long continued conflict which foretold the deaths of many of our brave men. About 4 p.m. an express arrived and announced that victory had again perched upon our —, that the enemy had lost all, their artillery, ammunition and defences and that the City now lay open to the advance of the army. Santa Anna has escaped. As usual he fled early. Among the many prisoners taken are some 40 deserters from our army, the notorious San Patricio Legion with the villainous Riley at their head. Their position was in a church and their resistance now desperate. Three times the Mexican troops in the Church hoisted the white flag and three times did these desperadoes tear it down, most of them knowing and all fearing that death would be their portion if taken fought until all was lost. It was their cursed fire which mowed down so many of our brave men and which prolonged the contest. The Dragoons hitherto from the nature of the ground prevented from participating in the battles, now were hurled upon the retreating foe and right freely did their sabres fall. The road from the City to the works at Churubusco was filled with wagons going and returning, loaded with ammunition, provisions, etc. A wagon which broke down near the City caused a delay which gave our Dragoons time to overtake and capture the whole train and many prisoners who were detained by the blockading of the road. So impetuous was the pursuit that a company of Dragoons advanced to the gates of the City whereupon the enemy opened a fire indiscriminately upon our men and their own masses. It was in this pursuit that Major [Frederick D.] Mills of the 15th Inf. was killed. Our loss in the Bloody Battle of Churubusco was very great numbering near 1,000 men killed and wounded. It was necessary to cover the charging columns were all exposed to a terrible fire of grape and musketry. Almost every Reg. in the army were engaged and all suffered severely, particularly Shields' Brigade. The brave Col. Butler fell at the head of his Regt. Lt. Col. [James P.] Dickinson was badly wounded as was Col. [Ward B.] Burnett of the N.Y. Vols. Over 100 men in each of these regiments were killed and wounded ...
August 21
This day is the anniversary of the entry of Cortes into the City of Mexico – 326 years ago. The bold and crafty Spaniard by arms and arts made an entrance into the magnificent City of the Montezumas. It would be a singular coincidence if the American army should enter today. The New York and South Carolina men return to San Agustin. Another batch of prisoners are brought in today. The officers are confined in the church in front of which our Regt. is encamped. Among the officers taken are Gen. Salas of Guerilla memory and Gen. Anaya, Ex-President of the Republic. The former was taken at Contreras, the latter at Churubusco.

The officers confined in the church appear very indifferent as to their fate. Many of them are young and none of them appear much to regard the death and slaughter of their friends or the downfall of their country.

August 23

As many of the houses have been deserted and their contents not removed several burglaries have been committed and guard duty is consequently pretty severe. This is always the case. The quiet and honorable solider suffers for the crimes and misconduct of the scoundrels who disgrace the army and nation. Nothing of any interest occuring ...

August 26

At Dress Parade today was read the Articles of an Armistice entered into between the American and Mexican Commissioners. The object of the Armistice is that the Commissioners of the two governments may meet and conclude a treaty of peace. No additional fortifications are to be thrown up and neither party to receive reinforcements. The Armistice to be ended by either party giving the other 48 hours notice. Gen. Scott could have entered the City on the evening of the 20th, but considering that the great object of the war, an honorable peace, might probably be better obtained from the foe before they were completely humiliated, he halted his victorious columns at the gates of the Capitol and agreed to the appointment of Commissioners. All are now fully impressed with the belief that a treaty of peace will be signed by the Commissioners. The rumors confirm and strengthen this belief. The treaty signed, the question arises whether we volunteers will be sent home immediately on the signature or be detained here until the ratification of the instrument by the Congress of the two nations. That we will be sent home forthwith is the general impression and many fear we will be marched back without seeing the City. This will be hard and many schemes are laid as to how we manage to see the City. Altho all are anxious to get home again, the unpleasant reflection forces itself upon our minds that if we return home *we* can claim but little glory in our Mexican campaign. It is true we have suffered sickness, endured hardships, but upon what battle field has the flag of Pennsylvania been unfurled? At Cerro Gordo it *waved*, not in victory, but *from the line*. At least so Gen. Pillow said and Col. Roberts was not the man to contradict him. At Vera Cruz we were not mentioned and in the two great battles which have been fought in the valley we have not been engaged. Notwithstanding this disagreeable view of our actions we are on tiptoe expectation of returning home and will tell our friends there that it is opportunity, fair opportunity which makes heroes and that we never have had a fair opportunity ...

3. Guillermo Prieto Describes the Occupation
of Mexico City, 1850[3]

Initial efforts to sign a permanent peace treaty between Mexico and the
United States stalled in the summer of 1847. In September, General Winfield
Scott renewed the military assault on Mexico City. When his forces entered
the city on September 14, rioting, looting and sporadic violence plagued the
city. General Scott declared martial law, but fighting persisted into October.
By that time, the only remaining battle was fought on the diplomatic front.
In exchange for $15 million and a settlement of its citizens' claims against
their government, Mexico agreed to the Rio Grande boundary and ceded
California and New Mexico to the United States. The Treaty of Guadalupe
Hidalgo, however, awaited finalization until February 2, 1848 and was ratified
by the US Senate a month later. The following account describes the first day
of American occupation of Mexico City and comes from the writer Guillermo
Prieto, an eyewitness to the fighting. Prieto wrote a series of essays describing
the war from a Mexican perspective, published in 1848 as Apuntes para la
historia de la Guerra entre México y los Estados-Unidos. *An American officer*
serving in the war, Colonel Albert C. Ramsey, was so taken with Prieto's
account that he translated it into English and published as The Other
Side: or Notes for the History of the War Between Mexico and the United
States *(1850).*

The inhabitants of Mexico, in spite of the defeats on the days before, had
slept in the belief that the troops even yet remaining would defend the
capital from street to street. This was in conformity with the solemn
promise of General Santa Anna: but the 14th of September dissipated it
under the yoke of foreign bayonets.

The Nationals, who had received the order to dissolve, were not in
general inclined to obey. In the corps of the Hidalgo they had a junta to
resolve upon what should be done: and the chiefs and officers deeming it
would be only a useless sacrifice of the young men forming this regiment to
oppose, agreed to comply with the command. Nevertheless, the fourth
company, situated in the convent of Santa Isabel, did not wish to do so till
early the next day, being now completely surrounded by the enemy. But
some Nationals withdrew their arms, and afterwards to place their colors
in safety.

---

[3]   Albert C. Ramsey, ed., *The Other Side: or Notes for the History of the War Between Mexico and the United States* (New York: John Wiley, 1850), pp. 374–8.

In the night of the 13th the division of General Quitman constructed a fortification in the garita of Belen, sustained by a twenty-four pounder, another of eighteen, and an eight inch howitzer. Early on the 14th certain messengers came from the Citadel with a white flag saying, that Santa Anna had abandoned the city.

They took possession of the Citadel and left a detachment in the garita. According to their official report they found 15 pieces of mounted cannon; and following on they sent a column, supported by a light battery, through the principal streets to the grand Plaza. Captain Roberts of the Rifles was directed by General Quitman to place the American standard upon the Palace ...

It was six in the morning when the column of General Quitman entered the city. Afterwards the troops penetrated, whom General Worth commanded, and through the day the remaining forces of the enemy. General Scott, on a large and beautiful horse, with a proud escort, made his entrance about nine in the morning.

The citizens of Mexico, who on the former days had given a greater example of indolence than patriotism, could not bear the appearance of the invaders who so haughtily took possession of the capital. People assembled and undertook to form circles: their anger rose at the haughtiness of the North Americans; and quick despising the danger, they desired to provoke a sanguinary conflict, and raised the cry for war. The conquerors, who now did not calculate on meeting resistance, saw themselves encountered in the plazas and streets with a rush that alarmed them.

We have heard a variety of stories as to the place where the first shot came from: and it is even difficult to discover which is most exact; but according to very many of them this fire was made from the store of Lopez.

Colonel Carbajal of the National Guard, in union with certain others, had formed the plan to fight the enemy on their entrance into the city. In this combination was the greater part in the neighborhood of the streets from the Alameda to the Santo del Agua. A citizen, named Esquivel, fired before the time of which we have spoken, and they, believing it was the signal for combat, opened the attack on the streets of the Hospital Real, and the San Juan.

The firing was at General Worth, who was on horseback at the corner of the store of Lopez, but without hitting him, but Colonel Garland was struck in the leg. The Americans penetrated through the streets to that point, bringing cannon, breaking down the doors, sacking houses, and committing a thousand other excesses. Those who spoke Spanish found out the first that had fired; and Colonel Carbajal, being denounced by two persons, incurred great danger of being shot.

Hereupon the strife now became general. In all the streets which the enemy occupied they fought with boldness and enthusiasm. A majority of the people who were engaged, were without fire-arms, with the exception of some who, more fortunate than others, had carbines and muskets. The others, to annoy the enemy, used stones and billets of wood, from whence it followed that the Americans made among the Mexicans a terrible havoc.

Some Nationals, who we have seen on the night before had to abandon their posts, sallied from their houses into the streets, carrying with them their arms to take part in the affray. They occupied certain high buildings and various churches, from whence they could damage the enemy. At the barriers of San Lázaro, San Pablo, la Palma, and El Carmen, men were seen to break out, decided to seek death in the defence of their liberty. Many who, in consequence of the distance, could not injure the enemy, with their arms hastily prepared, walked out to the middle of the streets, without any other object than to provoke them and to throw themselves on them, which they might do with good effect when the pieces of the Americans were discharged.

Many of the victims of this day watered with their blood the streets and plazas of the city. It is mournful to say that this generous exertion of the low people was, in general, censured with acrimony by the class privileged by fortune, who saw with indifference the humiliation of their country, if they could only preserve their interests and their comfort.

The desolating noise of musketry resounded all day, and the artillery, shaking the buildings to their foundations, spread despair and death. For whole hours the strife was prolonged, undertaken by a very small part of the people, without plan, without order, without assistance, or any element which could promise a good result. But it was a terrible conflict worthy to be remembered ...

The Ayuntamiendo published on the same day, the 14th, a proclamation explaining the evils resulting from this state of strife to the public tranquil-lity, which they insisted should be re-established. It is said the American general refused to concede to the municipal authorities all the guarantees for their natural and national rights while the fighting lasted, and that he had marched the army, and given orders to his troops, that the house in which they discovered the firing to be continued should be demolished by the artillery and its inhabitants killed.

The night was dark and awful. The suffering families remained within their houses constantly in dread that the Americans would come to break open their homes, and perpetrate the most shameful crimes upon their persons. The aged father trembled for his innocent daughter, and she in return for his life, while neither lamp nor light of any kind illuminated the fearful Mexico. Dead bodies lay scattered throughout the streets: many soldiers of the cavalry ran through the city, striking their swords against the walls, violating the doors of private houses and the stores of merchants, taking from the one the most precious goods and from the other eatables scarce among the inhabitants; for fear of going forth to purchase them, at the very few shops open during the day, induced the quiet people to remain without food.

It may be asserted that the greater part of the many inhabitants of Mexico passed the night in watching. Who could sleep with the thought of the country so recently outraged, and with the painful recollection of the numerous Mexicans who had perished on this and former days! Few families, in truth, were spared, who had not to lament some most beloved object ...

Discussion Questions

1. There are accounts in Part VII that describe Native Americans from an Anglo-American perspective. Do you think that these accounts are meant to be sympathetic? What do they reveal about the historical actors that created them? Are they fundamentally different from the sole Native American primary source presented?
2. How does Sam Houston's inaugural address compare with the previous ones that appear in this volume? In particular, do you think that Houston's and Washington's addresses express similar sentiments? Do you think that Houston's address suggests that he wants Texas to join the United States? Would he agree with John L. O' Sullivan's interpretation of the annexation issue? Why or why not?
3. Considering the variety of these sources, do you think that it is fair for historians to talk about a single "American West?" Do the documents in Part VII reinforce any stereotypes that still persist about the West?
4. If you had to write a two- or three-sentence description of the War with Mexico for a modern audience, and could only use the documents in this chapter as sources, what would your description say? Do you think that you can form clearer opinions about the war by reading the Mexican source also? Does this perspective change any of your preconceptions about the War with Mexico?
5. Do you have any inkling from these sources that the issue of slavery in the western territories of the United States would ever become a point of contention? What evidence leads you to your conclusion?

Epilogue: The President and the Ex-Slave

When Zachary Taylor became the twelfth President of the United States in 1849, the nation was almost unrecognizable from the one that George Washington led in 1789. From a population of 4 million Americans in Washington's time, the USA had grown to encompass 22 million people. The recent addition of the Mexican Cession, preceded by the acquisition of the Louisiana Purchase in 1803, Florida in 1819, and the finalization of the Oregon dispute with Great Britain in 1846, more than doubled the physical size of the nation. But although the 30 states of the union could claim a common legacy back to George Washington's Inaugural, their future together looked less certain. The issue of whether to extend slavery into newly acquired territories, more specifically, drove a wedge between the 15 free and 15 slave states. The Jacksonian political system of Whigs and Democrats tried to ignore this growing sectional divide and looked for some sort of compromise solution. But for those personally invested in the slavery debate – southern slave owners and northern anti-slavery advocates – ignoring the impending problem was impossible. The following two documents illustrate two approaches to the problem. The first one, Zachary Taylor's inaugural speech, seems in line with the past expectations of the presidency. The second document, a speech at the same time delivered by Frederick Douglass, offers a completely different interpretation of Taylor's election. Together, they hint at a real change in the demeanor of public debate in the United States in the 1850s.

1. Zachary Taylor's Inaugural Address, March 5, 1849[1]

At the time of Zachary Taylor's inauguration, the territory acquired in the War with Mexico – or more accurately the future of slavery in that land – had become a topic of great controversy. The hero of the Battle of Buena Vista, General Taylor was a wealthy slave owner with cotton plantations in Louisiana and Mississippi. But Taylor was hardly a firebrand. His mild identification with their party, popular standing, and lack of a coherent platform made him an ideal Whig Party candidate in 1848. As the second Whig to be elected president, Taylor avoided repeating his partisan predecessor William Henry Harrison's loquacious approach to the inauguration ceremony. Whereas Harrison took about two hours to deliver his 8,500-word address, Taylor took minutes to deliver this address of about 1,000 words. But Taylor shared a more ominous similarity with Harrison, as 16 months after he delivered this reserved and somewhat platitudinal address, Taylor died short of completing his term just as Harrison had a decade earlier.

Elected by the American people to the highest office known to our laws, I appear here to take the oath prescribed by the Constitution, and, in compliance with a time-honored custom, to address those who are now assembled.

The confidence and respect shown by my countrymen in calling me to be the Chief Magistrate of a Republic holding a high rank among the nations of the earth have inspired me with feelings of the most profound gratitude; but when I reflect that the acceptance of the office which their partiality has bestowed imposes the discharge of the most arduous duties and involves the weightiest obligations, I am conscious that the position which I have been called to fill, though sufficient to satisfy the loftiest ambition, is surrounded by fearful responsibilities. Happily, however, in the performance of my new duties I shall not be without able cooperation. The legislative and judicial branches of the Government present prominent examples of distinguished civil attainments and matured experience, and it shall be my endeavor to call to my assistance in the Executive Departments individuals whose talents, integrity, and purity of character will furnish ample guaranties for the faithful and honorable performance of the trusts to be committed to their charge. With such aids and an honest purpose to do whatever is right,

[1] *Home Journal* (New York), March 10, 1849.

I hope to execute diligently, impartially, and for the best interests of the country the manifold duties devolved upon me.

In the discharge of these duties my guide will be the Constitution, which I this day swear to "preserve, protect, and defend." For the interpretation of that instrument I shall look to the decisions of the judicial tribunals established by its authority and to the practice of the Government under the earlier Presidents, who had so large a share in its formation. To the example of those illustrious patriots I shall always defer with reverence, and especially to his example who was by so many titles "the Father of his Country."

To command the Army and Navy of the United States; with the advice and consent of the Senate, to make treaties and to appoint ambassadors and other officers; to give to Congress information of the state of the Union and recommend such measures as he shall judge to be necessary; and to take care that the laws shall be faithfully executed – these are the most important functions intrusted to the President by the Constitution, and it may be expected that I shall briefly indicate the principles which will control me in their execution.

Chosen by the body of the people under the assurance that my Administration would be devoted to the welfare of the whole country, and not to the support of any particular section or merely local interest, I this day renew the declarations I have heretofore made and proclaim my fixed determination to maintain to the extent of my ability the Government in its original purity and to adopt as the basis of my public policy those great republican doctrines which constitute the strength of our national existence. In reference to the Army and Navy, lately employed with so much distinction on active service, care shall be taken to insure the highest condition of efficiency, and in furtherance of that object the military and naval schools, sustained by the liberality of Congress, shall receive the special attention of the Executive.

As American freemen we can not but sympathize in all efforts to extend the blessings of civil and political liberty, but at the same time we are warned by the admonitions of history and the voice of our own beloved Washington to abstain from entangling alliances with foreign nations. In all disputes between conflicting governments it is our interest not less than our duty to remain strictly neutral, while our geographical position, the genius of our institutions and our people, the advancing spirit of civilization, and, above all, the dictates of religion direct us to the cultivation of peaceful and friendly relations with all other powers. It is to be hoped that no international question can now arise which a government confident in its own strength and resolved to protect its own just rights may not settle by wise negotiation; and it eminently becomes a government like our own, founded on the morality and intelligence of its citizens and upheld by their affections, to exhaust every resort of honorable diplomacy before appealing to arms. In the conduct of our foreign relations I shall conform to these views, as I believe them essential to the best interests and the true honor of the country.

The appointing power vested in the President imposes delicate and onerous duties. So far as it is possible to be informed, I shall make honesty, capacity, and fidelity indispensable prerequisites to the bestowal of office, and the absence of either of these qualities shall be deemed sufficient cause for removal.

It shall be my study to recommend such constitutional measures to Congress as may be necessary and proper to secure encouragement and protection to the great interests of agriculture, commerce, and manufactures, to improve our rivers and harbors, to provide for the speedy extinguishment of the public debt, to enforce a strict accountability on the part of all officers of the Government and the utmost economy in all public expenditures; but it is for the wisdom of Congress itself, in which all legislative powers are vested by the Constitution, to regulate these and other matters of domestic policy. I shall look with confidence to the enlightened patriotism of that body to adopt such measures of conciliation as may harmonize conflicting interests and tend to perpetuate that Union which should be the paramount object of our hopes and affections. In any action calculated to promote an object so near the heart of everyone who truly loves his country I will zealously unite with the coordinate branches of the Government.

In conclusion I congratulate you, my fellow-citizens, upon the high state of prosperity to which the goodness of Divine Providence has conducted our common country. Let us invoke a continuance of the same protecting care which has led us from small beginnings to the eminence we this day occupy, and let us seek to deserve that continuance by prudence and moderation in our councils, by well-directed attempts to assuage the bitterness which too often marks unavoidable differences of opinion, by the promulgation and practice of just and liberal principles, and by an enlarged patriotism, which shall acknowledge no limits but those of our own widespread Republic.

2. Frederick Douglass on "Morals and Men," May 8, 1849[2]

Although born and raised in slavery on Maryland's Eastern Shore, Frederick Douglass had become a prominent abolitionist speaker by the 1840s. As one of the most important African-American speakers in American history, his

[2]   John W. Blassingame, ed., *The Frederick Douglass Papers. Series One: Speeches, Debates, and Interviews*, Vol. 2: *1847–1854* (New Haven, CT: Yale University Press, 1982), pp. 170–4.

eloquence was only surpassed by his passion for anti-slavery causes.
He delivered this speech at the fifteenth annual meeting of the American
Anti-Slavery Society in New York City. His talk was cut short by a previous
speaker's verbosity, so Douglass had to make his point quickly to the restless
audience. Although brief, the lecture provides an insight into what Douglass
and others in the abolitionist community thought of the current direction of
the American nation; a direction that stands in sharp contrast to the platitudes
offered by Zachary Taylor a few weeks earlier.

... I suppose that meetings of this description will continue to be necessary as long as Slavery continues to exist. While it exists in our country its moral influence will continue to make it necessary for the advocates of Slavery to hold up the mirror before the Union, that it may see the real state of its morals. We have had here this morning an appalling picture of the low state of American morals and American religion, with respect to American Slavery. I do not know that I can make that state of morals look more dark, ore appalling and disgusting than it has already been made to appear. But I think I see in it a grosser and darker and more polluted state than either of those who have addressed you; and this fact is owing, not to my keener perception or my keener sensibilities, but to the fact that I am one of those who are continually exposed to the action of the low and demoralizing pro-slavery sentiments of this country. I am one of those who have not only smarted under the lash of the Southern tyrant; but I am continually smarting under the indignities, and insults, and outrages heaped upon the free, or nominally free, coloured people of the North. Placed in such circumstances, I may be expected to see and feel the state of American morals, American law, and American religion to be more revolting, more disgusting, and more in violation of the rights of man than others may ever be expected to feel it.

In the few remarks that I am to make I will call your attention to the state of American morals and religion, as illustrated in the character of our nation's great men. It was said by a wise man long ago, whose name I do not now remember, but whose saying I shall never forget, that no nation has yet been found better than its laws. That was the sentiment, though not the exact language. It may as well be added also, that no nation has yet produced a higher standard of morality than that embodied in the character of its great men. The stream cannot rise higher than its source. "A good tree cannot bring forth evil fruit, neither can corrupt tree bring forth good fruit." Within the character of the representation may be also seen reflected the true character of the constituency. The American people may be as accurately measured by the character of her great men, as the degree of temperature may be determined by the face of the thermometer. Our great men

I believe to be the fairest illustration of our real moral state. Now what are our great men? How have they distinguished themselves? In what respect do they command the admiration and regard of the American people? In a truly Christian community, that man alone will be the most popular who is engaged in works of benevolence, and is foremost in improving and elevating mankind around him. In a community of peace-lovers, that man only will be popular who is found engaged in peaceable pursuits, and spreading the blessings of peace around him. In a community where men love freedom, that man only will be popular who is sacredly and continually engaged in shedding the blessings of freedom upon mankind around him. Are we such a people? Let Zachary Taylor answer. For in what respect has he distinguished himself? By what means has he brought around him a train of circumstances which have carried him to the highest seat in the gift of the nation? He is not a peace man; he is not a man who is in favor of freedom. For the great and only thing which he has ever done that has made him popular in the estimation of the people has been, that he was the successful instrument in the hand of this blood-thirsty government in carrying on war for no higher purpose than to establish Slavery where it had been before abolished, and that by a semi-civilized nation. It is the worst element in the character of the American people that is uppermost. It was said that Gen. Taylor was the only man in America that could be President of the United States. The man who said it, the party which believed and adopted the idea, showed their sagacity, showed their keen appreciation of the moral sense of this nation. They knew that all the pretension of the people of this country concerning their love of freedom, their love of God, their love of humanity, and their love of just rulers meant nothing whatever. They knew that the pulpit and the church of this country was ready to be swayed in support of any man, no matter how base, no matter how diabolical the record of his deeds; and they judged rightly, as the result has shown ...

Bibliography

Part I: Building the United States

Allgor, Catherine (2000) *Parlor Politics: In Which the Ladies of Washington Help Build a City and a Government*. Charlottesville: University Press of Virginia.

Cornell, Saul (1999) *The Other Founders: Anti-Federalism and the Dissenting Tradition in America, 1788–1828*. Chapel Hill, NC: published for the Omohundro Institute of Early American History and Culture, Williamsburg, Virginia, by the University of North Carolina Press.

Elkins, Stanley M. and McKitrick, Eric (1993) *The Age of Federalism: The Early American Republic, 1788–1800*. New York: Oxford University Press.

Ellis, Joseph J. (2000) *Founding Brothers: The Revolutionary Generation*. New York: Alfred A. Knopf.

Ferling, John (2004) *Adams vs. Jefferson: The Tumultuous Election of 1800*. New York: Oxford University Press.

Freeman, Joanne B. (2001) *Affairs of Honor: National Politics in the New Republic*. New Haven, CT: Yale University Press.

Furstenberg, François (2006) *In the Name of the Father: Washington's Legacy, Slavery, and the Making of a Nation*. New York: Penguin Press.

Newman, Simon P. (2000) *Parades and Politics of the Street: Festive Culture in the Early American Republic*. Philadelphia: University of Pennsylvania Press.

Pasley, Jeffrey L. (2001) *"The Tyranny of Printers:" Newspaper Politics in the Early American Republic*. Charlottesville: University Press of Virginia.

Waldstreicher, David (1997) *In the Midst of Perpetual Fetes: The Making of American Nationalism, 1776–1820*. Chapel Hill, NC: published for the Omohundro Institute of American History and Culture, Williamsburg by the University of North Carolina Press.

Part II: Clashes East and West

Borneman, Walter R. (2005) *1812: The War that Forged a Nation*. New York: HarperCollins Publishers.

Buel, Richard Jr. (2005) *America on the Brink: How the Political Struggle over the War of 1812 Almost Destroyed the Young Republic*. Basingstoke: Palgrave Macmillan.

Cusick, James G. (2003) *The Other War of 1812: The Patriot War and the American Invasion of Spanish East Florida*. Gainesville: University Press of Florida.

Dowd, Gregory Evans (1992) *A Spirited Resistance: The North American Indian Struggle for Unity, 1745–1815*. Baltimore, MD: Johns Hopkins University Press.

Hickey, Donald R. (1995) *The War of 1812: A Short History*. Champaign: University of Illinois Press.

Owsely, Frank Lawrence, Jr. and Smith, Gene A. (1997) *Filibusters and Expansionists: Jeffersonian Manifest Destiny, 1800–1821*. Tuscaloosa: University of Alabama Press.

Remini, Robert (2001) *The Battle of New Orleans: Andrew Jackson and America's First Military Victory*. New York: Penguin Books.

Rothman, Adam (2005) *Slave Country: American Expansion and the Origins of the Deep South*. Cambridge, MA: Harvard University Press.

Sugden, John (1998) *Tecumseh: A Life*. New York: Henry Holt.

Part III: The Postwar Nation Looks Forward

Burin, Eric (2005) *Slavery and the Peculiar Solution: A History of the American Colonization Society*. Gainesville: University Press of Florida.

Forbes, Robert Pierce (2007) *The Missouri Compromise and Its Aftermath: Slavery and the Meaning of America*. Chapel Hill: University of North Carolina Press.

Friend, Craig Thompson (2005) *Along the Maysville Road: The Early American Republic in the Trans-Appalachian West*. Knoxville: University of Tennessee Press.

Hatch, Nathan O. (1989) *The Democratization of American Christianity*. New Haven, CT: Yale University Press.

Newman, Richard S. (2002) *The Transformation of American Abolitionism: Fighting Slavery in the Early Republic*. Chapel Hill: University of North Carolina Press.

Rothbard, Murray N. (2007) *The Panic of 1819: Reactions and Policies*. Auburn, AL: Ludwig von Mises Institute.

Part IV: The Work of a New Republic

Boydston, Jeanne (1990) *Home and Work: Housework, Wages, and the Ideology of Labor in the Early Republic*. New York: Oxford University Press.

Cohen, Patricia Cline York (1998) *The Murder of Helen Jewett: The Life and Death of a Prostitute in Nineteenth-Century New York*. New York: Alfred A. Knopf.

John, Richard R. (1998) *Spreading the News: The American Postal System from Franklin to Morse*. Cambridge, MA: Harvard University Press.

Johnson, Walter (1999) *Soul by Soul: Life inside the Antebellum Slave Market*. Cambridge, MA: Harvard University Press.

Larson, John Lauritz (2001) *Internal Improvement: National Public Works and the Promise of Popular Government in the Early United States*. Chapel Hill: University of North Carolina Press.

Meyer, David R. (2003) *The Roots of American Industrialization*. Baltimore, MD: Johns Hopkins University Press.

Schocket, Andrew M. (2007) *Founding Corporate Power in Early National Philadelphia*. DeKalb: Northern Illinois University Press.

Sheriff, Carol (1996) *The Artificial River: The Erie Canal and the Paradox of Progress, 1817–1862*. New York: Hill & Wang.

Stott, Richard B. (1990) *Workers in the Metropolis: Class, Ethnicity, and Youth in Antebellum New York City*. Ithaca, NY: Cornell University Press.

Tadman, Michael (1989) *Speculators and Slaves: Masters, Traders, and Slaves in the Old South*. Madison: University of Wisconsin Press.

Zonderman, David A. (1992) *Aspirations and Anxieties: New England Workers and the Mechanized Factory System, 1815–1850*. New York: Oxford University Press.

Part V: Renewal and Reform

Abzug, Robert H. (1994) *Cosmos Crumbling: American Reform and the Religious Imagination*. New York: Oxford University Press.

Dorsey, Bruce (2002) *Reforming Men and Women: Gender in the Antebellum City*. Ithaca, NY: Cornell University Press.

Ginzberg, Lori D. (1990) *Women and the Work of Benevolence: Morality, Politics, and Class in the Nineteenth-Century United States*. New Haven, CT: Yale University Press.

Heyrman, Christine Leigh (1997) *Southern Cross: The Beginnings of the Bible Belt*. Chapel Hill: University of North Carolina Press.

Jeffrey, Julie Roy (1998) *The Great Silent Army of Abolitionism: Ordinary Women in the Antislavery Movement*. Chapel Hill: University of North Carolina Press.

Johnson, Paul E. and Wilentz, Sean (1994) *The Kingdom of Matthias: A Story of Sex and Salvation in Nineteenth-Century America*. New York: Oxford University Press.

Masur, Louis P. (2001) *1831: The Year of Eclipse*. New York: Hill & Wang.

Mintz, Stephen (1995) *Moralists and Modernizers: America's Pre-Civil War Reformers*. Baltimore, MD: Johns Hopkins University Press.

Stewart, James Brewer (1996) *Holy Warriors: The Abolitionists and American Slavery*, rev. edn. New York: Hill & Wang.

Walters, Ronald G. (1997) *American Reformers, 1815–1860*, rev. edn. New York: Hill & Wang.

Part VI: Jackson's America

Altschuler, Glenn C. and Blumin, Stuart M. (2000) *Rude Republic: Americans and Their Politics in the Nineteenth Century*. Princeton, NJ: Princeton University Press.
Earle, Jonathan H. (2004) *Jacksonian Antislavery and the Politics of Free Soil, 1824–1854*. Chapel Hill: University of North Carolina Press.
Hinks, Peter P. (1997) *To Awaken My Afflicted Brethren: David Walker and the Problem of Antebellum Slave Resistance*. University Park: Pennsylvania State University Press.
Holt, Michael F. (1999) *The Rise and Fall of the American Whig Party: Jacksonian Politics and the Onset of the Civil War*. New York: Oxford University Press.
Huston, Reeve (2000) *Land and Freedom: Rural Society, Popular Protest, and Party Politics in Antebellum New York*. New York: Oxford University Press.
Marszalek, John F. (1997) *The Petticoat Affair: Manners, Mutiny, and Sex in Andrew Jackson's White House*. New York: Free Press.
Miles, Tiya (2005) *Ties That Bind: The Story of an Afro-Cherokee Family in Slavery and Freedom*. Berkeley: University of California Press.
Remini, Robert V. (2001) *Andrew Jackson and His Indian Wars*. New York: Viking.
Shade, William G. (1996) *Democratizing the Old Dominion: Virginia and the Second Party System, 1824–1861*. Charlottesville: University Press of Virginia.
Varon, Elizabeth R. (1998) *We Mean to Be Counted: White Women and Politics in Antebellum Virginia*. Chapel Hill: University of North Carolina Press.
Wallace, Anthony F. C. (1993) *The Long, Bitter Trail: Andrew Jackson and the Indians*. New York: Hill & Wang.
Watson, Harry L. (1990) *Liberty and Power: The Politics of Jacksonian America*. New York: Hill & Wang.
Wilentz, Sean (2005) *The Rise of American Democracy, Jefferson to Lincoln*. New York: W. W. Norton.

Part VII: The American Continent

Blackhawk, Ned (2006) *Violence over the Land: Indians and Empires in the Early American West*. Cambridge, MA: Harvard University Press.
Foos, Paul (2002) *A Short, Offhand Killing Affair: Soldiers and Social Conflict During the Mexican–American War*. Chapel Hill: University of North Carolina Press.
Haynes, Sam W. (2005) *James K. Polk and the Expansionist Impulse*, 3rd edn. New York: Longman.
Hurtado, Albert L. (1999) *Intimate Frontiers: Sex, Gender, and Culture in Old California*. Albuquerque: University of New Mexico Press.
Jeffrey, Julie Roy (1994) *Converting the West: A Biography of Narcissa Whitman*. Norman: University of Oklahoma Press.

Johnson, Susan Lee (2000) *Roaring Camp: The Social World of the California Gold Rush*. New York: W. W. Norton.

McCaffrey, James M. (1992) *Army of Manifest Destiny: The American Soldier in the Mexican War, 1846–1848*. New York: New York University Press.

Reséndez, Andrés (2004) *Changing National Identities at the Frontier, Texas and New Mexico, 1800–1850*. New York: Cambridge University Press.

Stephanson, Anders (1995) *Manifest Destiny: American Expansionism and the Empire of Right*. New York: Hill & Wang.

Warhus, Mark (1997) *Another America: Native American Maps and the History of Our Land*. New York: St. Martin's Press.

Winders, Richard Bruce (1997) *Mr. Polk's Army. The American Military Experience in the Mexican War*. College Station: Texas A&M University Press.

Index